the ultimate guide to Art Quilting

SURFACE DESIGN • PATCHWORK • APPLIQUÉ
QUILTING • EMBELLISHING • FINISHING

LINDA SEWARD
ILLUSTRATED BY THOMAS MESSENGER

sixth&springbooks
NEW YORK

sixth&spring books

161 Avenue of the Americas
New York, NY 10013

sixthandspringbooks.com

EDITORIAL DIRECTOR
Joy Aquilino

DEVELOPMENTAL EDITOR
Lisa Silverman

ART DIRECTOR
Diane Lamphron

DESIGNER
Jane Glennie

PROOFREADER
Beth Baumgartel

VICE PRESIDENT
Trisha Malcolm

PUBLISHER
Carrie Kilmer

PRODUCTION
MANAGER
David Joinnides

PRESIDENT
Art Joinnides

CHAIRMAN
Jay Stein

DEDICATION

To my finest artistic creations: Alysson, Emily and Keith.
And to the man who made them and this book possible, my husband, Robert.

This book features over 1000 full-color step-by-step illustrations that show how to do hundreds of art quilt techniques. Most of these methods can be combined in various ways, offering literally thousands of ideas. It is assumed that the reader already has a basic knowledge of sewing and quilt making.

This book provides decimal and Imperial measurements. When strict precision isn't required, an exact conversion has not been given, as quilters in the US will buy a yard of fabric or measure a quart of water, while European quilters will purchase a meter of fabric or use a liter of water, since these are the simplest measurements for them to use. However, when measurements are critical, precise conversions are always given.

Copyright © 2014 by Linda Seward.
All quilts are copyright of the maker.

Library of Congress Cataloging-in-Publication Data is available from the Library of Congress.

ISBN: 978-1-936096-71-8

Manufactured in China

1 3 5 7 9 10 8 6 4 2

First edition

CONTENTS

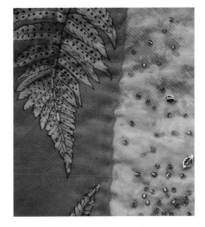

1 ART QUILTS

color abstract
fabric pictorial
paper innovation
metal design
texture cheesecloth
modern quilt wood
experimentation

1

1

INTRODUCTION

Art quilt. Is that a contradiction in terms? Can what was once considered a commonplace object now be deemed a work of art? Originally, quilts were regarded as women's work, of no particular value except as ordinary household items. A shift in attitude occurred in 1971, when the Whitney Museum of American Art hung Amish quilts on their walls. Suddenly, quilts could be viewed as valuable commodities in terms of ornament rather than function. This elevation of the quilt to a museum object, and the subsequent popularization of making quilts for America's Bicentennial in 1976, helped move quilting toward the thriving industry it is today, and turned it into an activity that continues to encourage creativity and enrich the lives of those who have embraced it.

🔽 Pink Dawn—© Kate Findlay, Reading, UK. Photo by Richard Sedgwick. Inspired by the word liminality, which means a "threshold," and the artist's conception of the threshold between night and day, dawn and dusk. The artist is interested in the way light might interact with a piece of work, so that the viewer has a different experience, depending on the amount of light on the work and the way colors change it. Dyed cotton covered with layers of sheer fabric, fiber optic cables lit with color-changing LED's. Machine appliquéd, machine quilted by Karen Florey. 36 x 24"/91 x 61cm. 2013.

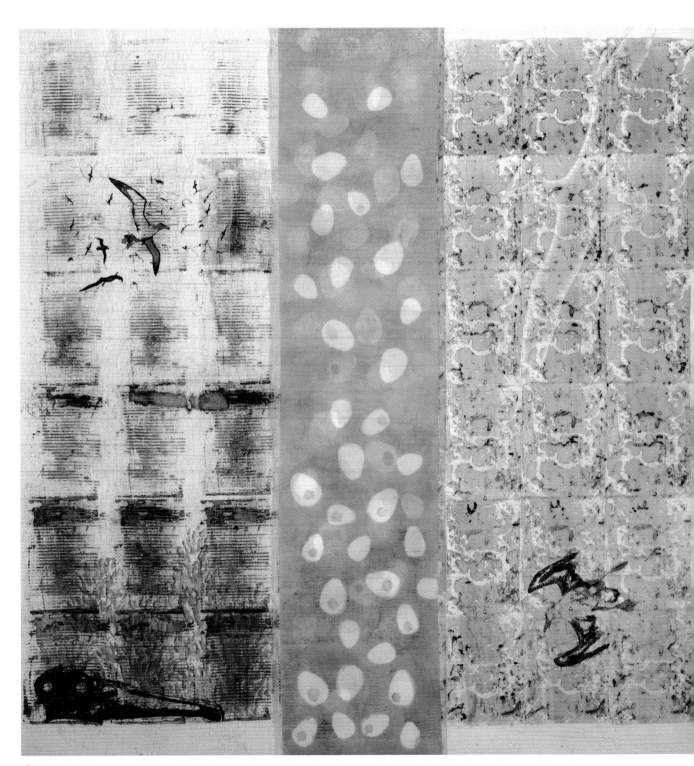

⬆ Life Cycle – Albatross—©Charlotte Yde, Copenhagen, Denmark. The quilt not only depicts the life cycle of the albatross but also addresses the issue of endangered species. Many albatrosses are found dead because they have swallowed huge quantities of plastic found floating on the open sea. Cotton and silk organza, reflective thread. Soy wax resist for egg design, deconstructed screen printing on side panels, details colored with paintstiks, digitally programmed stitched drawings, painted, machine quilted. 55 x 54"/140 x 138cm. 2012.

Afro-Kimono—©Odette Tolksdorf, Durban, South Africa. Photo by Jurgen Tolksdorf. The artist wanted to integrate an African and Japanese spirit in this work. The kimono theme was given an African twist through the use of Ugandan barkcloth and woven raffia for the background and African prints for the kimonos. Silk and cotton fabrics, woven raffia, barkcloth (made from tree bark; it has a fibrous texture, but is easy to stitch, paint or print), glass beads. Machine pieced, machine appliquéd using decorative stitches (on edge of kimonos), machine quilted, glass beads. 20 x 39"/52 x 98cm. 2011.

The popularity of quilting has continued to grow exponentially over the past 40 years and the availability of fabrics and tools to enhance the quilting process has expanded right along with it. In great contrast to the huge assortment of fabric styles and colors available today, quilters of a certain age will remember a time when there were no fabrics available that had been manufactured specifically for quilt making. During the subsequent period of growth and popularity, quilters have experimented with new and exciting techniques and materials—continually stretching the boundaries of that early conception of the quilt as a household object.

This artistic emancipation has taken some time to be accepted, and in fact remains a debated topic—but thanks to innovative artists, quilts made out of steel or paper have found a place in contemporary exhibitions, alongside quilts made of more conventional materials. As evidenced by the amazing pieces throughout this book, it is a great time to be a quilt artist.

This introductory chapter highlights artists who have taken risks with their work, creating cutting-edge art quilts that feature unusual materials and techniques—from cheesecloth to paper, painting to photography, wood to metal, and from upcycling to fiber optics. Instructions are not given for work exclusive to the artists featured in this chapter, but rather the pieces are presented as inspiration for original work that you can create yourself. Step-by-step instructions and illustrations for many art quilt techniques that will expand your knowledge and boost your confidence are included in the chapters that follow.

The Ultimate Guide to Art Quilting has taken over three years to write, and it represents a lifetime of study and experimentation. I've been stitching since I could hold a needle, and was taught to do needlework by my mother and grandmothers. My early career saw me working for magazines and book publishers, honing my skills as a technical writer and editor, specializing in needlework and crafts. It was a privilege to learn many new techniques as part of my job. But nothing prepared me for the thrill that I found when I discovered quilt making. Quilting encompasses everything that excites me—color, design, stitch and fabric—all in one lovely package.

My first step-by-step book covers the basics of quilt making. Over the years, quilters and students suggested that I write another book incorporating the techniques that have evolved since that first book was published 25 years ago. I was finally convinced that the time was right for a guide to art quilt techniques.

Working on this book has given me another wonderful opportunity to "learn on the job." Some of the techniques were new to me when I started, but with the help of excellent teachers I learned how to do each of those methods. Approaching and writing about techniques from a beginner's point of view enabled me to understand and describe the procedures more clearly.

This book does not attempt to teach every detail of complex processes such as computer-generated embroidery or printing photos on fabric. These sections are intended to expose you to new ideas and provide a general understanding of how each method is accomplished. Even if you are not tempted to try the techniques yourself, I hope that you will come away with a better understanding of the work behind the art quilts that you see displayed in exhibitions, magazines and books. If your interest is piqued and you do want to explore some of the procedures further, there are books written by top experts in the field listed in the bibliography. And don't forget—a great way to learn new techniques is to attend workshops—nothing beats a hands-on lesson with an experienced teacher.

Enjoy the journey.

⬇ Wing Chairs—©B J Adams, Washington, DC. Photo by PRS Association, Maryland. The artist enjoys putting unusual sizes of disparate images together, and considers a chair an eccentric stage for birds and insects. Inspired by the complicated still life paintings of the Dutch and Flemish 17th-18th century artists. Cotton fabric, thread, acrylic paint on canvas. Free-motion machine embroidery, dimensional appliqué, painting. 28 x 28"/71 x 71cm. 2011.

⬇ Taking Dictation—©Alma de la Melena Cox, San Rafael, California. This piece was inspired by the gods Viracocha, from the artist's Peruvian heritage, and Athena, goddess of wisdom, who influence her creativity and awareness. Acrylic paints, cotton and metallic fabrics and paper on wood. Made in the artist's own technique of Telamadera Fusion and wood burning. 18½ x 18½"/47 x 47cm. 2012.

Sizing Up—©Mary Pal, Ottawa, Canada. Photo by Ray Pilon. Collection of Jennifer Day. This piece was inspired by a photograph by Clint Colbert, Tennessee. Cheesecloth, buckram, acrylic paint. Cheesecloth sculpted with PVA adhesive, machine appliquéd with monofilament thread to an acrylic-painted background, machine quilted with cotton thread. 12 x 12"/30 x 30cm. 2012.

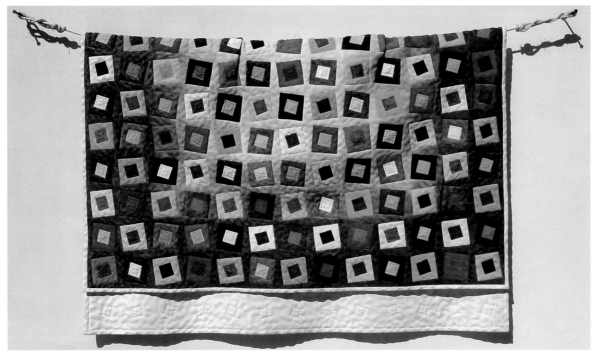

Square Dance 2—©Fraser Smith, St Pete Beach, Florida. An exercise in *trompe l'oeil*, this seemingly supple work is actually carved entirely of wood, down to the "hand stitches" that create the textured effect. It was inspired by contrast, and the visual energy of the shaded colored squares moving across the variously shaded backgrounds. Basswood, silk dyes. Hand carved, sanded and painted. 60 x 41 x 4"/152 x 104 x 10cm. 2005.

Broken—©Carol Wiebe, Kitchener, Ontario, Canada. Inspired by the fact that all people travel between states of frailty and strength. When the artist began this piece, a number of people she knew were experiencing health and emotional issues; this quilt was her response. It's made in two layers with rolled paper bead spacers in between. Paper, paint, printed collage papers of the artist's original digital designs, gesso, acrylic medium, thread, felt batting, rolled paper beads. Hand painted, hand stitched collage, freeform crochet, free-motion machine quilted, slashed. 34 x 35"/86 x 89cm. 2011.

Urban London Landscape—©Pam Holland, Aldgate, South Australia. Inspired by a visit to the Spitalfields Markets in London during a traumatic time. Photographic canvas, hand-dyed and commercial cotton fabrics, hand-dyed cheesecloth, organza. Photos transferred to canvas with high quality printer, appliqués illustrated with pigment ink using brush and pen, ghost images outlined with thread, free-motion machine quilted, hand quilted. 37 x 31"/95 x 79cm. 2011.

⊙ "Quilt"—©Kim Schoenberger, Queensland, Australia. Photo by Natalija Brunovs. Inspired by the connection between mother and daughter, grandmother and granddaughter—an unbroken chain of wisdom and knowledge shared across the generations and often celebrated with a cup of tea. Recycled tea bags, muslin/calico, tea leaves, linen thread. Muslin/calico hand-dyed with recycled tea leaves, sewn with a treadle Singer sewing machine. 67 x 77"/170 x 195cm. 2010.

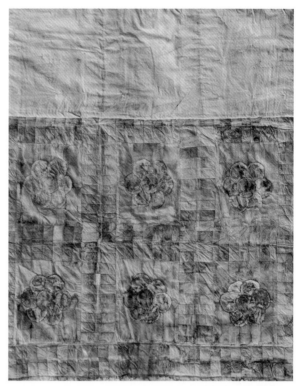

⊙ Red Mud II—©Eszter Bornemisza, Hungary. Photo by Tihanyi & Bakos. This quilt is part of a series made in response to the "red mud catastrophe" that happened in Hungary in 2010 when the dike of a reservoir holding bauxite refining waste broke, and villages were flooded by the alkali sludge. Cotton fabric, cotton netting, tissue paper, rice paper, silk yarn. Hand-dyed fabric, silk screened, painted with acrylics, appliquéd, free-motion machine quilted. 63 x 39"/160 x 100cm. 2012.

⬆ Kgale Hill Shadows—©Cindy Friedman, Merion Station, Pennsylvania. This "shadowscape" was inspired by the artist's love of the geometry in block pattern quilts and human body shapes and movement. She loves working with silks because they catch and reflect light and add transparency. Silk fabric, silk organza, fusible woven stabilizer. Machine pieced, fused organza appliqués, free-motion machine quilted, thread painted. 29 x 39"/74 x 99cm. 2012.

➔ Convergence—©Latifah Saafir, Los Angeles, California. Convergence is about coming together and meeting at a common point but it is also about approaching limits. This quilt embodies both of these concepts in a literal as well as symbolic sense. It was designed from a desire to create a bold modern quilt by simply appliquéing bias strips onto a background fabric, and was inspired by the artist's love of Scandinavian design. Cotton fabric. Machine appliquéd bias strips, machine quilted. 61 x 73"/155 x 185cm. 2012.

◄ Pink M 24 Chaffee—©Marianne Jorgensen, Denmark. Photo by Barbara Katzin. A combat tank that was used in World War II is the setting for this work of art. As a protest against Denmark's involvement in the Iraq war, the tank was covered from the cannon to the caterpillar tracks with more than 3500 patches of pink squares knitted and crocheted by people from many European countries and the USA. When a tank is covered in pink patchwork, it loses its authority and becomes unarmed. The process of covering the tank was documented in a video shown in the Nikolaj Copenhagen Contemporary Art Center in Denmark as part of the exhibition *Time* from April to June 2006. Pink yarn. Knitted, crocheted, hand pieced. 6"/15cm squares. 2006.

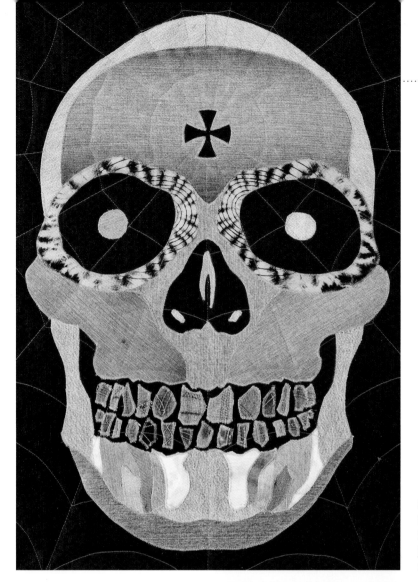

⬅ Iron Skull—©Ben Venom, San Francisco, California. Photo by Randy Dodson. Inspired by the denim quilts of Gees Bend. Used denim jeans, cotton fabrics. Machine appliquéd, machine quilted. 22 x 29"/56 x 74cm.

➡ Downshifting—©Gudrun Heinz, Karlsruhe, Germany. Inspired by the fact that people are beginning to recalibrate their lives so they have more time and happiness, but make less money—known as downshifting in Germany. Cotton and cotton blend fabrics, used shirts, wool vest/waistcoat, silk tie, synthetic leather, tulle, colored pen drawings printed on paper, polythene, paintstik rubbings, newsprint, seeds. Reverse appliquéd, hand and machine appliquéd, free-motion machine embroidered, free-motion machine quilted. 47 x 47"/120 x 120cm. 2012.

➔ Fire Equipment—©Arunas Oslapas, Bellingham, Washington. Inspired by an old wooden sign that was discarded in a junkyard and discovered while traveling through the state of Utah. Reclaimed metal strapping (formerly used in lumberyards to band lumber), pieces of old signs, old toy train, wooden yardstick, painted rivets, metal tape measure. The reclaimed metal strapping was painted, distressed, and left outside to rust. Once materials were ready, the strips were either riveted or adhered to a wooden surface with a high-strength adhesive. 42 x 42"/107 x 107. 2010.

⬆ Autumn Diptych—©David Paul Bacharach, Cockeysville, Maryland. Photo by Norman Watkins. The work was inspired by the landscape surrounding the artist's studio on a cold autumn evening, when frost had set in after an Indian summer day, and the leaves of the maples and beeches had stretched the last of summer's energy to achieve a rich, warm palette. Woven copper, steel, wood, patina, paint. Woven copper panels joined with copper wire and nails. Coloration is achieved with chemical and heat patinas. 48 x 28"/122 x 71cm. 2011.

⬇ The Power of Gold—©Lucinda Carlstrom, Atlanta, Georgia. Collection of Novartis Pharmaceutical, Atlanta, Georgia. Inspired by a box of chocolates received on Valentine's Day and a trip to Japan, where the artist purchased papers in a variety of textures and shades of gold. Paper—some decorated with gold leaf and metal leaf, Dupioni Indian silk, silk from upcycled thrift store dresses/kimonos, batting, cotton fabric back. Machine pieced papers, paper confetti; quilt was layered and tied with perle cotton, sewn to mat board and framed under glass. 29 x 54"/73 x 137cm. 2010.

⬆ Visions and Actions—©Alysn Midgelow-Marsden, Derbyshire, UK and New Zealand. Inspired by a combination of two linked ideas: a parent's desire that her children make the most of their talent and energy, and a quote from Nelson Mandela, "Vision without action is dreaming, action without vision is just passing time, but with vision and action we can change the world." Fabric woven from fine stainless steel wires and treated with heat to create the color, hand painted and heat distressed Lutradur, reverse appliquéd eyes and hands, free-motion machine and hand stitched details, quilted by knotting. 47 x 77"/120 x 195cm. 2010.

2 THE BASICS AND BEYOND

paper sewing machines
needle felting
exercises marking
spunbonded materials
wet felting
upcycling
enlarging sizing

2

THE BASICS & BEYOND

Most quilt makers practice their craft using medium-weight cotton fabric—it is easy to cut, sew and press, and is reliable in its performance and finished appearance. The variety of colors, finishes and prints that are available make cotton the quintessential fabric to choose when creating a quilt.

Ruffled Feathers—©Roxanne Nelson, Calgary, Alberta, Canada. This piece was inspired by a photo of Gayle Reeder's parrot, Jimmy Bob. Commercial cotton batiks and prints. Raw-edge machine appliquéd, free-motion machine stitched/quilted with monofilament thread. 29½ x 38"/75 x 96cm. 2010.

Many quilters feel little need to look further than this natural textile to create their art quilts, preferring instead to explore the many treatments that can alter the color and texture of cotton fabric (fully covered in Chapter 3).

But as shown in the previous chapter, art quilters are increasingly choosing materials other than cotton to express their creativity—with amazing and unexpected results. To give you a taste of working "outside the cotton box," this short chapter will provide some practical instructions for exploring a few of the unconventional mediums that can be used to construct or embellish an art quilt. Also included in this chapter are some basic guidelines to be referred to again and again when experimenting with the many other quilt art techniques covered in this book.

⬆ Personal Space—©Terry Jarrard-Dimond, Clemson, South Carolina. Photo by Tom Dimond. This is a visual representation of the personal space into which some people are allowed and others are not. Hand-dyed, hand painted, monoprinted and discharged cotton fabric. Machine pieced, hand appliquéd, machine quilted. 41¾ x 60"/106 x 152cm. 2012.

PAPER TEXTILES

Art quilters have been experimenting with "paper textiles" for some time, enjoying the textural results and the ease with which they can be stitched. While regular paper can be cut out and adhered or stitched to fabric (see Upcycling on page 31), you can also construct your own pliable yet strong textiles using craft tissue paper or silk fibers. Silk fibers are available with or without sericin, a gummy substance that acts as a glue; instructions for using both are given here.

Paper textiles can be dyed or painted at any stage of construction, or left in their natural colors. Inclusions such as glitter, snips of fabric and paper, dried flowers, etc. can be incorporated within the layers/fibers for added interest. Paper textiles can be used as a base material, or cut into any shape and appliquéd onto cloth or a quilt surface.

TEXTILE PAPER

1 You will need: plastic tablecloth or sheeting, craft tissue paper, thin base fabric such as scrim, cheesecloth or muslin, white fabric glue, plastic tray, foam roller, gloves, liquid dye or paint, paint brushes. Optional: decorative inclusions, metallic wax, paintstiks.

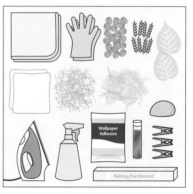

2 Cover work area with plastic. Pour white glue into plastic tray; thin with water to creamy consistency. Using foam roller, apply layer of glue to plastic to same size as base fabric. Smooth base fabric on top of glue. Roll thin layer of glue on top of fabric.

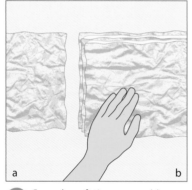

a   b

3 Crumple craft tissue paper (a); open and smooth evenly on fabric. Roll with gluey foam roller. Cover with another tissue layer; roll glue on top. Add final paper layer (b); glue. Optional: arrange scraps of paper or fabric, glitter, dried flowers etc. on glued surface.

4 Apply paint or dye, manipulating color to emphasize textured areas (or add color after textile paper is dry). Allow to dry undisturbed for 24 hours. When dry, peel paper textile off plastic. Rub with metallic wax or paintstiks if desired to highlight texture.

SILK PAPER

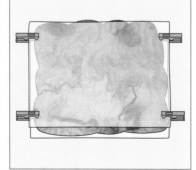

You will need: silk fibers with sericin, baking parchment, spray bottle, iron. For non-sericin fibers: plastic tablecloth or sheeting, 2 pieces nylon tulle, wallpaper paste, gloves, sponge, clothes pins. Inclusions for both: angelina, glitter, dried flowers, skeleton leaves, etc.

SERICIN SILK FIBERS

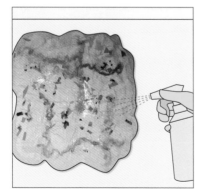

Gently tease out and arrange fibers in a thin layer on baking parchment. Decorate with angelina, glitter, thread, fabric snips, etc. Cover thinly with more silk fibers; spray with water. Cover with baking parchment. Press with iron to bond fibers together.

SILK FIBERS WITHOUT SERICIN

Silk paper with skeleton leaves constructed by the author.

1 Cover work area with plastic; place a layer of tulle on top. Arrange silk fibers and any decorative inclusions on tulle. Place second layer of tulle over the fibers/inclusions. Secure edges of layers together with clothespins to prevent shifting.

2 Mix wallpaper paste to creamy consistency; pour small amount on tulle. Use sponge to rub paste into fibers, wetting them thoroughly. Apply more paste if needed. Turn over and rub paste on other side in same way. Hang to dry. Peel off tulle.

SPUNBONDED SYNTHETIC MATERIALS

Spunbonded synthetics are non-woven materials that have captured the imaginations of adventurous art quilters. Made from polyester or nylon filaments that have been bonded into a random web, they range from almost transparent and light in weight to dense and sturdy, with many variations in between. Virtually all the surface design methods covered in Chapter 3 can be used on spunbonds and there are excellent books, DVD's and websites that fully explain how to work with these exciting materials; see the Bibliography (page 247).

The three most popular types of spunbonded synthetic materials are Lutradur, Evolon and Tyvek. Lutradur was devised for the automotive industry and can be used for everything from delicate appliqué work to robust 3D pieces. Evolon is a soft suede-like cloth from the same manufacturer; it quilts beautifully and can be intricately cut with a soldering iron for lacy effects. Both Lutradur and Evolon can be brilliantly colored with transfer dyes and inks, and display an almost luminous quality when colored with water-based paints and dyes.

Tyvek is used in the packaging and disposable uniform industries, and is a great favorite with upcyclers. It is available in a textured paper form or as a softer "fabric." Tyvek can be printed and colored in a variety of ways.

Spunbonded synthetics do not fray, and this quality can be fully exploited by art quilters: delicate appliqués and intricate edges can be cut or soldered without fear of unraveling. But the best attribute is that spunbonds can be heat distressed to great effect, creating wonderful textured surfaces; see pages 100–101. Each will impart a different result, so experimentation is essential.

HANDLING

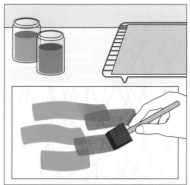

Apply water-based color to one or both sides of spunbonds; allow to dry. Next, stamp, print (using printer, screen or monoprinting) or do other surface design if desired. Then cut out shapes. Layer and stitch before heat distressing, as melted areas are not easy to sew.

CUTTING

Cut shapes with scissors, soldering iron or rotary cutter. Holding metal stencil or ruler firmly on material, run tip of soldering iron along edges to cut. Tip: Secure spunbonded material to fusible web first so cut shapes can be ironed straight onto a background.

⬆ Free as a Bird Dress—©Ineke Berlyn, Bromsgrove, UK. Photo by Tim Ayling. Inspired by red kite birds. Thermofax-printed hand-dyed vintage French linen, cotton, organza, scrim and painted Lutradur bonded on organza. Free-motion machine quilted, dress shape cut with soldering iron. 18 x 47"/45 x 120cm. 2012.

HEATING

Lutradur layered and stitched with organza, then distressed with a heat gun by the author.

Use a heat gun to distress spunbonds, creating texture with holes and bubbled areas. The lighter the weight, the quicker the material will react to heat; hold gun about 1"/2.5cm from surface. Lutradur and Evolon remain flexible after heating; Tyvek becomes rigid.

TRANSFER (DISPERSE) DYEING

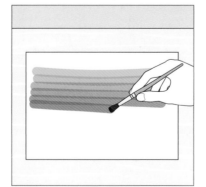

① Prepare transfer dye following manufacturer's instructions; see Health & Safety Rules on page 46. Paint thin glossy paper with dyes using sponge, brush or roller; allow to dry (colors will turn dull when dry). Place aluminum foil on ironing board.

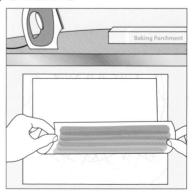

② Place parchment on foil. Lay Lutradur or Evolon on parchment, and the dry painted paper face down on top. Cover with more parchment. Press slowly and thoroughly with very hot iron, moving iron steadily. Lift paper to reveal transfer. Color will be permanent.

WET FELTING

Felt making is an ancient craft that has been practiced all over the world for generations. Felt is created when wool fibers are abraded while wet so they mat together. As the scales of the fibers tangle, they lock, creating a firm, strong fabric. Because of its wide-ranging qualities, felt is used to make shoes, rugs and clothing as well as musical instruments. Felt can be be sculpted into shapes to make hats, toys and jewelry. It is also used to great effect to make art quilts.

When wool is cleaned and carded (combed) in preparation for spinning, the result is called roving—the fiber of choice for felt making. Merino is the best option. Roving fibers are arranged on a surface and rubbed by hand using water and soap, creating pre-felt. Because the scales have not been fully interlocked, pre-felt has a soft hand and is capable of being felted further. It also can be cut into shapes or used as a base for needlefelting; see following pages. When pre-felt is fulled (shrunk through repeated rolling) it becomes conventional felt.

Used woven woolen clothing can be machine-felted and subsequently upcycled; see pages 30–31. Knitted sweaters can also be machine-felted, but will usually still have some "give."

Nuno felt combines roving with a sheer open-weave natural-fiber fabric such as cotton gauze or silk organza, creating a soft, textured result. Roving fibers are almagamated into the fabric by gentle rubbing and rolling with a foam roller, such as a swimming pool noodle. The work is then thrown repeatedly onto a hard surface, a process known as shock fulling. This causes uneven locking of the scales, creating unexpected and exciting distortions in the finished textile.

EQUIPMENT

Plastic sheet or tablecloth, bamboo placemat or sushi mat, bubble wrap (small bubbles), Merino wool roving (various colors), nylon tulle, plastic squeeze bottle with spout, hot water, liquid hand soap, apron, towels, elastic bands, foam pool noodle (nuno felt).

LAYERING FIBERS

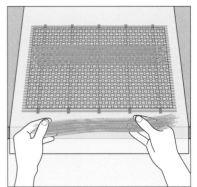

1. Spread plastic sheet on work surface with bamboo mat on top. Place bubble wrap (bubbles up) on mat. Untwist roving. Grasp one end; gently pull off lengths. Open out fibers width-wise; arrange on bubble wrap in desired shape, with fibers in same direction.

WETTING

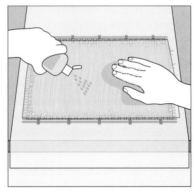

Mix hot water with liquid soap in plastic squeeze bottle (about 1 tablespoon liquid soap to 1½cups/350ml water). Gently sprinkle over tulle and fibers until wet, but not saturated. Press with flat hand to remove air bubbles and thoroughly wet the fibers.

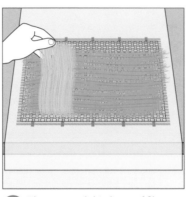

2. Place second thin layer of fibers perpendicular to first, using same color or mix of colors. Arrange third layer of fibers at a 90° angle to second layer. Continue in same way, making 3–4 layers depending on desired thickness. Cover with one layer of tulle.

PRE-FELTING

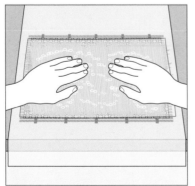

1. To interlock wet fibers together, massage tulle and fibers in a circular motion, working gently over entire piece. Gradually increase pressure and intensity. Fibers will enmesh, making a matted fabric. Carefully flip over; rub other side. Continue, alternating sides.

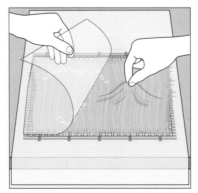

2. Periodically lift tulle to check degree of felting. Pinch with thumb and forefinger to see how fibers are meshing. If layers move apart or fibers lift away, replace tulle and continue rubbing. Stop when fibers are just holding together. Rinse and dry thoroughly.

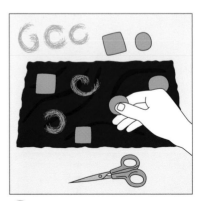

3. Cut pre-felt into shapes and place on wool roving or another piece of pre-felt. Secure pieces together by fulling; see next page. You can also add wisps of wool roving, silk fibers or wool yarn on top of pre-felt to create a complex design, then full to secure.

FULLING

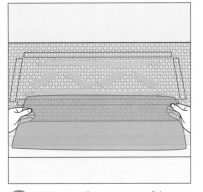

1 Gently slide pre-felt off bubble wrap and onto bamboo mat, which will provide added friction to lock and shrink wool when rolling. Press with towel to absorb excess water, then roll pre-felt tightly inside the mat. Secure ends of roll with elastic bands.

2 Place rolled mat on a towel to prevent roll from sliding. Roll mat back and forth firmly for a minute. Unroll mat and turn felt 90°; roll felt in mat in new direction. Continue rolling until you are happy with the result, changing direction of felt regularly as it fulls.

FINISHING

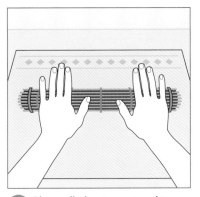

Felt will shrink 20–50% in size as it is fulled. When felt is desired thickness, rinse in tepid water. Soak in vinegar water (1 tsp vinegar to 4 cups/1 liter water) for 10–15 minutes. Rinse in cool water. Press out water with towels. Shape on flat surface. Allow to dry.

NUNO FELTING

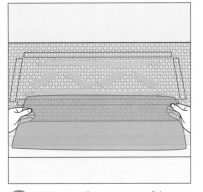

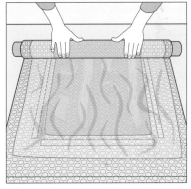

1 In nuno felt, wool fibers bond together through an open-weave fabric. As fibers shrink during felting, fabric is pulled and ruched, making a soft, supple textile. Fibers can be felted to one or both sides, or between two pieces of fabric. *Felt by Marina Shkolnik.*

2 Mark size of open-weave fabric on surface with tape; cover with bubble wrap. Arrange wisps of wool roving on bubble wrap within marked shape. Cover roving with fabric. Arrange wool wisps on top of fabric in chosen design. Cover with tulle when finished.

3 Sprinkle cool soapy water over work so it penetrates fibers. Press to encourage water to soak in. Stroke gently all over surface until matted. Roll onto foam noodle; secure with elastic. Roll for a few minutes, unroll, roll from other end. Shock full or finish as above.

SHOCK FULLING

Study felted fabric to see if fibers are migrating through surface, then immerse in very hot water. Scrunch into ball and throw repeatedly into sink. This action shrinks fibers randomly and increases crinkling of nuno felt. Wet felt can also be shock fulled. Finish as above.

WASHING MACHINE FELTING

1 Only felt garments of pure wool or natural hair fibers such as angora, cashmere, mohair. Do not use machine-washable clothes; these will not felt. Deconstruct garments, removing seams and pockets; soak 30 minutes in warm soapy water. Put in washing machine.

2 Agitate in hot water on cotton setting for approximately 30 minutes (add pair of jeans for friction if desired). Spin and drain. Check felting; if not satisfied, agitate again. Rinse in cold water. Tumble dry for additional felting.

NEEDLE FELTING

In needle felting, fibers are secured to a base by interlocking rather than stitching, creating an original material that cannot be made any other way. It is done using sharp, barbed felting needles that repeatedly penetrate the fibers, enmeshing them together. In the process, fibers are pushed through the surface and appear on the other side. While there is no right or wrong side to the finished material, the working side will have a crisper look than the other side, which will look softer and fuzzier.

Needle felting can be done by hand on a foam pad or felting brush mat using a single felting needle or a multi-needle tool. This can be time consuming and laborious, though good results can be achieved. Some sewing machines have special attachments and throat plates for needle felting; however, felting by machine produces many loose fibers that would need to be thoroughly cleaned away before using the machine again for sewing.

Alternatively, you can use an embellisher. Although it looks like a sewing machine, an embellisher does not use any thread. Barbed felting needles in a variety of sizes and numbers are attached to an arm that moves up and down; the needles quickly punch through the fibers to interlock them. Because there are no feed dogs, the material is moved under the needles in much the same way as free-motion quilting. However, the needles can break, and it is expensive and time consuming to replace them. To prevent breakages, don't move the fabric too quickly, especially thick fabric. You will notice that embellishers are much noisier than sewing machines. However, using an embellisher is an enjoyable experience, as creativity is unleashed and myriad special effects can be achieved with minimal effort.

For the base, use wool, pre-felt, acrylic or wool felt, batting (dyed or natural), a water-soluble stabilizer or any other material that isn't too dense. Then, layer and felt small pieces of natural or synthetic fibers, yarns or woven fabrics onto the base. This is an excellent way to use up the scraps that quilters usually have in abundance. Experimentation is the key to making the most of an embellisher.

Needle felted pieces can be embroidered or beaded and cut into shapes for appliqué. Existing articles of clothing such as sweaters or scarves can be needle felted to give them a brand new appearance. Finished work can be framed or stitched to a firm backing and hung. See page 32 for three different examples of needle felted textile art.

BY HAND

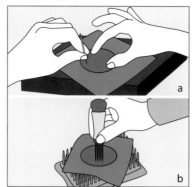

Hand needle felting can be done on a foam base (a) or bristle-brush mat (b), using a single needle or multiple-needle felting tool. To prevent breakage, the needle must be kept perpendicular to the foam or brush. Punch layers many times to firmly interlock fibres.

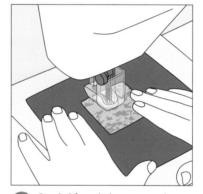

2. Gently lift and place area to be needle-felted under embellisher needles. Place hands on either side of area to be punched. The needle guard prevents fingers from getting near needles; it is essential that this guard is always down while needle felting.

4. Remove work from machine and turn over to see which areas need to be further punched—these areas will look fainter. Mark the faint area with your finger and return to the machine to needle punch that area again.

BY EMBELLISHER

1. Choose material for base (see main text). Cut a piece of thin stabilizing fabric for the back (such as muslin or cotton voile) that is larger than the base all around; center base on stabilizer. Cut a piece of fabric to needle felt onto base.

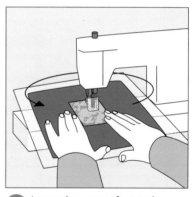

3. Lower the presser foot and turn wheel to lower needles into fabric to start. Press machine foot gently to begin; start slowly and pick up speed as you get used to the machine. Move fabric freely in circles or lines until fibers are enmeshed.

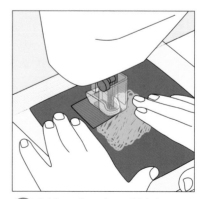

5. Add another piece of fabric to base, adjacent to or overlapping first piece. Needle punch as before. Because felting needles pull fibers into the base, original size and shape of new pieces will change dramatically depending on weave and weight.

ADDING OTHER FIBERS

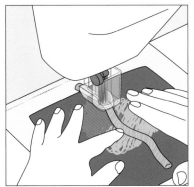

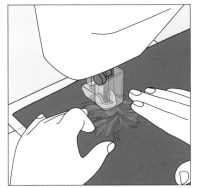

1 Lay yarn on the base to create a stem or outline, to accentuate a shape or add texture or color. Begin punching from the middle, holding yarn in place with a finger as shown. Then go back to the middle of the yarn and punch in the opposite direction.

2 Arrange wisps of wool roving or carded wool on base, holding edges down with your fingers to keep it from getting caught up in the needles. Begin punching fibers in place. If roving catches, stop machine, lift up needle guard and carefully remove fibers.

TUCKS

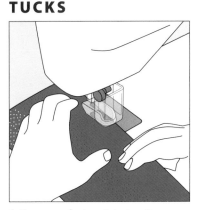

Follow manufacturer's instructions to attach a single needle and a single hole throat plate. Fold felted fabric and punch close to the fold to create a tuck. A single needle can also create fine lines for adding highlights.

WORKING FROM THE OTHER SIDE

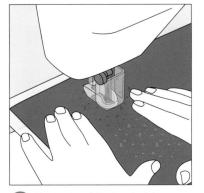

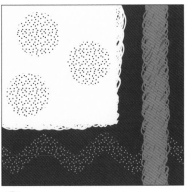

1 Try turning felted material over and working from the other side; small fiber dots or tiny loops will appear on the top side. If you wish, add a piece of fabric to contrast with the top side so the loops will be even more visible.

2 You can create ghostly shapes, outlines or letters on the top side by punching a shape or line over and over from the other side. The color of the fabric you are punching through will appear on the front.

FINISHING

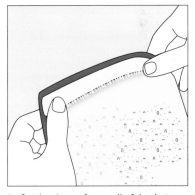

To finish edges of a needle felted piece, trim edges of stabilizing fabric so they extend ½"/12mm beyond base. Place under needles and punch edges of base to stabilizer all around. Then fold edges of the stabilizer behind base and punch again to secure.

TROUBLESHOOTING

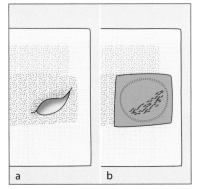

a   b

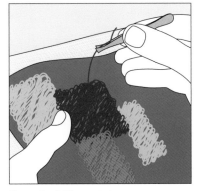

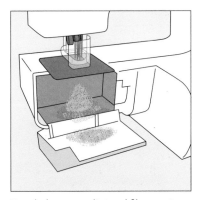

If one area is punched too much, a hole may form (a). Add a small piece of fabric to wrong side over the hole. Pinch and slightly overlap edges of hole on right side; punch until edges are secured to the fabric added on the back (b).

If you don't like a result, use tweezers to gently extract the fibers. Needle punched fibers can be pulled apart unless very firmly punched. However, the more the fibers are punched, the more firmly they become interlocked.

Regularly remove lint and fibers out of the embellisher and throw away as they cannot be recycled. Keeping the machine clean and lint-free will extend its life and enable it to run more efficiently.

UPCYCLING

Historically, quilt making embodied what we now call "upcycling"—making something of improved value without downgrading the original material or generating pollution in the process. Our quilting ancestors upcycled when they used fabric scraps or worn clothes to make patchwork, or when they used an old quilt as batting for a new one. This is opposed to "recycling" which changes items into a lesser form, often using energy and creating pollution in the process. For example, when fabrics are sent to specialist firms for shredding and fiber reclamation, they have been recycled. When the same fabrics are used to make a work of quilt art, they have been upcycled—a subtle, but important difference.

Our quilting predecessors didn't even realize they were upcycling when they constructed their patchwork quilts as the concept had not yet been born. As the years passed and textiles gradually became less scarce and valuable, quilters began purchasing fabric specifically for making quilts—a perplexing concept for non-quilters, who could never understand why people would buy perfectly good fabric only to cut it up and sew it together again. However, history has come full circle and now it is not only fashionable, but also desirable to create quilt art from found or waste materials. Art quilters upcycle discarded textiles of all kinds, as well as paper, plastics and even metal—literally whatever can be incorporated into a piece of textile art.

Using things destined for the trash is creatively liberating because quilters can be experimental without the risk of cutting into expensive or pristine materials. In addition, utilizing materials with a history or personal significance can give added meaning to an art quilt.

CUTTING AND RIPPING

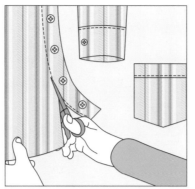

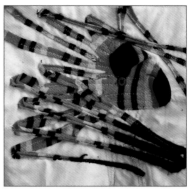

1 Take apart old clothes using a seam ripper, scissors or a rotary cutter. When deconstructing shirts or trousers, keep interesting parts such as button plackets, flat-fell seams, collars and pockets for later use.

2 Rather than cutting garments into unrecognizable pieces, retain the basic structure, but cut into only one edge such as the sock shown here. Rearrange on another fabric and stitch in place. Embellish with buttons or beads. *Sock Monster by Jane Glennie.*

LAYERING

Layer fabrics on a foundation to create textile art. When layering distressed or torn areas, pay attention to the fabrics underneath as they will show through and highlight the distressed areas. Mat and frame when finished.

EMBEDDING

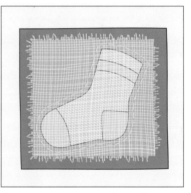

Showcase precious textiles such as baby clothes or a memorable outfit by placing them on a colorful background beneath sheers or cheesecloth; outline-stitch or embroider layers together, or use an embellisher to needle felt the layers; see pages 28–29.

WEAVING

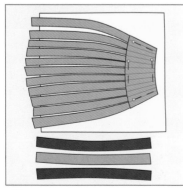

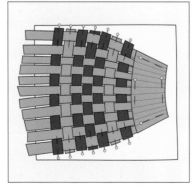

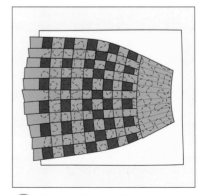

1 Use scissors to cut strips of regular or random widths from fabric or from a felted woollen garment, such as the sweater sleeve shown here. Pin to a foundation of fabric, cork or foam. Cut or rip strips from other fabrics to interweave.

2 Weave first strip through cut fabric, going over and under alternate strips; pin each end to base fabric. Weave next strip through cut fabric, going over and under opposite strips as shown. Continue until finished, pinning new strips to foundation at end of each row.

3 Free-motion machine stitch woven fabric to hold all pieces in place, or stitch with perpendicular lines using walking foot. Alternatively, use an embellisher to mesh the fabrics together, or fuse the layers to a background using fusible web.

ANTIQUE TEXTILES

① Give new life to family heirlooms or antique treasures by featuring them on a quilt or in a collage. Invisibly hand or machine stitch crocheted, knitted, embroidered or tatted doilies to a quilted background. Embellish with buttons or beads if appropriate.

② Collect vintage embroidered doilies, tablecloths, dresser scarves and handkerchiefs. Cut out embroidered or printed motifs using sharp scissors; use as appliqués, embellishments or in a collage. Alternatively, quilt, embellish and frame undamaged pieces.

LACE

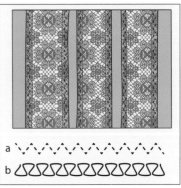

Appliqué scraps of lace on top of fabric or use as inserts between other fabrics as shown here. To finish off fabric edges and keep lace from fraying, use the three-step zigzag (a) or an overlock stitch (b) to apply or insert lace to fabric.

KNITS

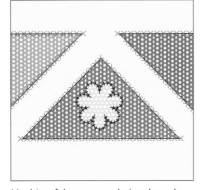

Machine-felt woven or knitted wool garments in a washing machine; see page 27. Cut felted textiles into appliqué shapes; secure to base fabric with embroidery. For patchwork, pieces will be thick so butt edges together; machine zigzag or embroider seam.

TIES

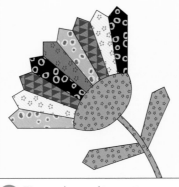

① Ties can be used to create a design; just cut off excess tie and appliqué to a fabric base as shown here. Alternatively, deconstruct ties using a seam ripper, saving lining and labels which can also be upcycled. Press bias-cut tie fabric carefully as it will stretch.

② Cut foundation from muslin or interfacing; mark placement lines. Rotary-cut ties into strips and sew to foundation using the stitch-and-flip method; see page 158. Designs with straight seams are best. *Detail from The Ted Dexter Cricket Quilt by the author.*

DENIM

① Collect old jeans in different colors. Cut into simple shapes using different parts of the jeans to feature faded areas and attain different colors. Use the seams as design elements. Stitch together and embroider or needlefelt using an embellisher.

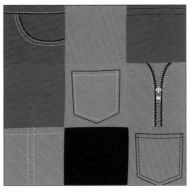

② When cutting jeans into geometric shapes for patchwork, make a feature of the pockets, seams and zippers. Utilize many different denim colors for an interesting arrangement. Piece together with ¼"/6mm seams or sew with flat fell seams; see page 139.

PAPER

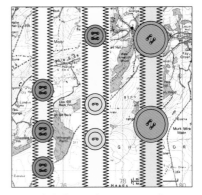

Crumple lightweight paper; stitch to fabric as an embellishment. Use colorful candy wrappers or cut paper into shapes and stitch to a fabric base. Or, machine stitch fabrics to sturdy paper such as a map to create a collage; add buttons and other embellishments.

⊗ Remnants 7—©Janice Gunner, London, UK. Private collection. Inspired by dressmaking remnants, taking the artist back to where she started and why she got into textile art. Hand-dyed linen and cotton on indigo-dyed cotton batting, silk and cotton thread. Machine needle felted, hand and machine quilted, embroidered. 16 x 15"/41 x 38cm. 2010.

⊗ Isolation—©Anne Jolly, Hamilton, New Zealand. Photo by Bård Haerland. Nature is a constant source of inspiration for this quilt artist, whose aim is to create texture in whatever she makes. Merino wool roving, felted pieces, cotton fabric, thread, tulle. Wet felted, needle felted, hand and machine embroidered. 38 x 36"/97 x 92 cm. 2009.

⊗ Lifepath: Time and Emotion—©Jane Glennie, Berkshire, UK. This piece represents the path the artist takes through life: round and round, up and down, two steps forward and one step back. The vertical wires of the electric blanket mark the passage of time and significant dates; the space-dyed fibers represent emotion. Recycled electric blanket, space-dyed bamboo fiber, wool fiber. Handspun yarn, machine needle felted, hand and machine stitched. 47 x 12"/120cm x 30cm. 2008.

⬆ Fantasy Forest—©Averil Stuart-Head, Introdacqua, Italy. The image in this textural collage is a native New Zealand beech tree, seen on a scenic drive through the ancient beech forests of the South Island. Commercial and hand-dyed cotton fabric, cotton canvas, cheesecloth, painted and dyed antique crocheted doilies. Raw edge collage, image printed with inkjet printer onto textured, painted fabric using archival ink, appliquéd, free-motion machine quilted, embellished with gold leaf. 27 x 29"/68 x 74cm. 2012.

SIZING & MARKING DESIGNS

Some art quilts are created spontaneously, others are carefully planned. But at some point, most art quilters will need to resize a design and mark it on a fabric. This spread covers some of the ways to do this.

First, the percentage of enlargement or reduction of the design must be determined; see *Resizing,* right. The simplest way to resize a design is to take it to a copy center and tell them how big or small you wish it to be. If you want to do it yourself, the manual way to resize a pattern is by the grid method, which requires nothing more than paper, a ruler and a pencil. Or, you can use a home computer, printer or scanner—many will have the software for changing the size of a design, allowing you to print it out to a new size on however many pages it takes (usually up to 25). All you have to do is match up the lines and tape the sheets of paper together to get a full-size pattern. Be sure to read the manual for your machine to find out how to do this, as instructions will vary from one manufacturer to another. An overhead projector (if you have access to one) is useful for drawing very large patterns.

There are a number of websites that will resize designs for you. Some will make a line drawing from a photograph, size it to your specification and allow you to print out the full-size pattern. Each website has its own way of doing this, so take advantage of the free trials to see which one you prefer.

Once the pattern is the correct size, it must be labeled, copied (keep a master for reference) and marked on the fabric; see opposite page for some of the ways this can be done. Always test markers on scrap fabric as many a project has been spoiled by "disappearing" markers that refuse to cooperate!

RESIZING

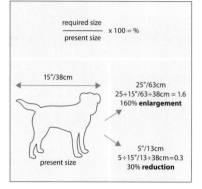

$$\frac{\text{required size}}{\text{present size}} \times 100 = \%$$

15"/38cm — present size

25"/63cm
$25 \div 15" / 63 \div 38\text{cm} = 1.6$
160% enlargement

5"/13cm
$5 \div 15" / 13 \div 38\text{cm} = 0.3$
30% reduction

Take one measurement (length or width) of the pattern to be resized: present size. Determine the size you wish the new pattern to be: required size. Divide required size by present size and multiply it by 100 to get the percentage of enlargement or reduction.

HOME PRINTING

1 Read instruction manual for your printer/scanner or directions for your software to see if it has a resizing facility. Determine resizing percentage (see above) and program into machine or software. Print out test pattern on scrap paper.

2 Some machines will allow tiling (an enlarged pattern is printed on several sheets of paper). Print out tiled pattern if your machine or software can do this. Trim off extra paper and tape sheets together, matching lines carefully.

USING A GRID

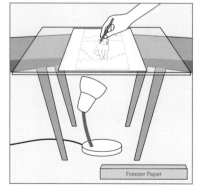

Make a line drawing of the design. Using a different color pencil, draw a grid on top. Draw a second grid with same number of squares to size of enlargement or reduction required. Working one square at a time, draw lines of design on new grid.

PROJECTOR

Draw or trace design on acetate; place on glass of overhead projector. Project image on paper taped to a wall. Adjust machine until image is desired size. Trace lines onto paper to create master pattern.

MAKING PATTERNS

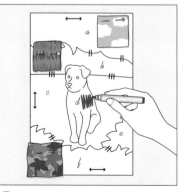

1 You will need a master pattern for reference and a working pattern for use. Label every piece of each pattern. Draw grainlines and marks for matching pieces if required. Indicate colors with fabric scraps or colored markers on master pattern.

2 Trace master pattern for working pattern in one of the ways shown on the opposite page. Label all pieces. Cut apart and use for marking/cutting fabric. If making a working pattern from freezer paper (see pages 130–131), trace design in reverse (on the dull side).

TRACING TECHNIQUES

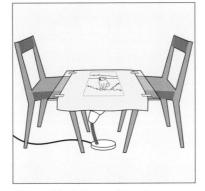

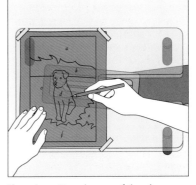

Tape pattern to a well-lit window. Tape fabric securely over pattern. Trace all lines with hard-lead pencil, quilters' pencil (white, yellow or silver), water- or air-soluble fabric markers, chalk marker or soapstone marker. Always test markers before using on final fabric.

Arrange Plexiglas or safety glass securely on a pile of books or between two chairs. Place light source beneath, shining up through glass. Tape master pattern to surface. Tape fabric over pattern. Trace lines with pencil or markers, listed left.

If you have it, make use of the clear acrylic surround (or table) available for many sewing machines (used to expand the size of the sewing area). Place light source under the surround and use as a light box.

TRANSFER MARKING METHODS

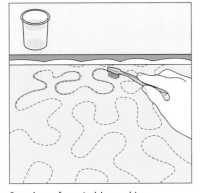

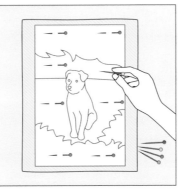

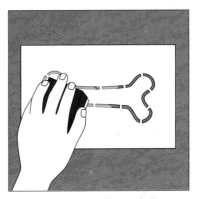

See above for suitable marking tools. Trace pattern onto right side of fabric. Some marks will become permanently set with warm water or a hot iron. If using water-soluble markers, remove marks with cool water and soft toothbrush.

Trace quilting (or embroidery) designs onto water-soluble or tear-away stabilizer; see *Stabilizers* on page 220. Pin or baste to fabric; free-motion machine stitch or embroider, following lines. Remove stabilizer as directed by manufacturer after stitching is complete.

Use chalk pounce pad to mark designs on fabric with stencils. To charge pad, bang it once on work surface before removing it from case. Remove pad and rub over stencil to transfer design. To make a stencil, see pages 66 and 131.

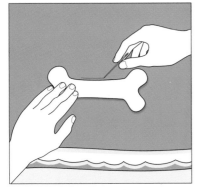

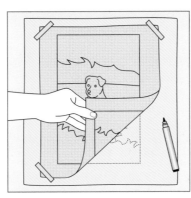

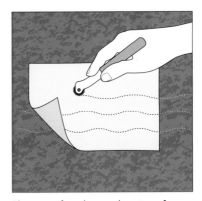

Needle-mark temporary lines onto an already sandwiched quilt. Place template in position on quilt and firmly trace around edges with blunt tip of needlepoint/tapestry needle to make indented guidelines on fabric that will disappear after quilting over them.

Use netting to transfer simple outlines to fabric. Place netting over pattern; trace lines with marker. Tape marked netting on fabric; trace over lines with chalk pencil or fabric marker to transfer dotted lines to fabric.

Place wax-free dressmakers transfer paper, colored side down, on fabric. Use dressmakers tracing wheel to transfer simple long lines or shapes. For intricate designs, place pattern on top and trace lines with a stylus.

SEWING MACHINE TIPS

While most readers of this book will already have an intimate familiarity with their sewing machine, here are some tips on how to care for your most indispensable piece of equipment. A beautifully running machine will enable you to expand your artistic skills without worrying about the glitches that can occur with one that's improperly maintained. Listen to your smoothly humming machine, particularly after it's been serviced or cleaned. When the sound becomes loud or harsh, you'll know it's time to clean it again.

Because there are hundreds of different types of sewing machines, the tips given here are quite general. Sewing machine manufacturers are constantly updating their products, adding new features and improving old ones. If you have an old machine, it may not have some of the features discussed here. However, most of these tips will be useful for working with any age and type of sewing machine.

While the latest sewing machines are made with many different options, imaginative quilt artists can achieve great results with a basic machine. Top of the line machines can stitch just about anything, but you have to factor in whether you will actually make use of all the extra stitches and features. If you are in the market for a new sewing machine, "test drive" a number of different ones; bring fabrics and quilt sandwich samples to help you assess and compare each machine's capabilities. Invest in a table with a recessed area for the machine so the sewing area is level with your table top. This will enable you to maintain a correct posture while sewing. See pages 38–39 for exercises to do when sewing for long periods of time.

PERUSE

While this may seem obvious, read the instruction manual that comes with your machine. Even if you've been using the machine for a while, there is always more to learn by studying the manual. You may discover a feature you didn't know you had.

CLEAN

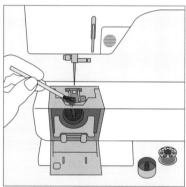

Clean your machine regularly, especially after completing a project. Remove the entire bobbin assembly and throat plate; use a soft brush and lint-free cloth to eliminate the lint that has accumulated. Have your machine professionally serviced once a year.

PROTECT

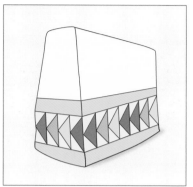

Keep your sewing machine covered when not in use to prevent dust from settling in the machine, which can cause a variety of problems. Dust can lodge in the working parts of the machine, increasing resistance and restricting thread flow.

OIL

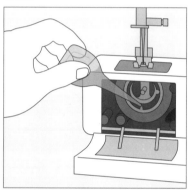

Oiling your machine with white sewing machine oil will prevent wear and rust, and will lubricate the moving parts. Refer to the manual for the exact spots to oil; some new machines may not need oiling. After oiling, stitch on scrap fabric for a while to get rid of any excess oil.

NEEDLE

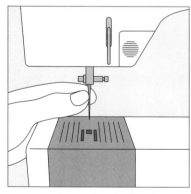

If your machine is skipping stitches change the sewing machine needle. This is almost always the root of the problem. A blunt needle can be caused by sewing over pins, so always remove pins before stitching over them.

FEET

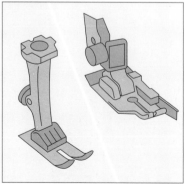

1 Invest in an accurate quarter-inch/ 6mm foot made specially for your machine; it is also called a patchwork foot. This will prove invaluable for sewing all your patchwork.

2 Many modern machines offer a stitch regulator foot. A sensor beneath the foot follows the movement of the fabric and adjusts the stitch length accordingly. This results in stitches of equal length, and is useful for free-motion work.

THROAT PLATE

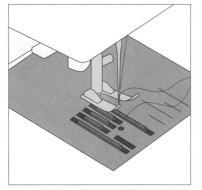

Use a straight stitch throat plate for intricate patchwork and free-motion quilting. It has a small round hole for the needle to pass through, preventing fabric from puckering or being sucked into machine. Change to the regular throat plate for decorative stitches.

THREAD TENSION

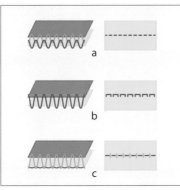

1. Thread tension is perfect when stitches look even on both sides (a). If tension on top thread is too tight, bobbin thread will show on upper fabric (b). If tension on top thread is too loose, top thread will show on bottom fabric (c).

2. If top tension is too tight, as in b on the previous illustration, loosen top tension on thread tension wheel by decreasing the number. If top tension is too loose, as in c, tighten top tension by increasing the number.

BOBBIN

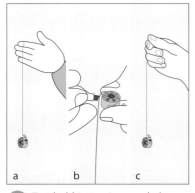

1. Test bobbin tension regularly. With full bobbin in case, draw out length of thread (a). Mark thread near case (b). Drop your hand abruptly and raise again; case should drop 1–1½"/ 2.5–4cm (c). If not, adjust screw on bobbin case, making minute adjustments.

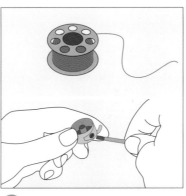

2. To adjust bobbin tension, turn screw in tiny increments: left to loosen, right to tighten. Test by sewing on scrap fabric until perfect. Damage to metal bobbins can distort tension; if dropped on a hard floor, discard bobbin even if it looks intact.

3. Use a Teflon washer in bobbin case to reduce static electricity, allowing bobbin to spin smoothly. The result is perfect tension on the back, particularly when quilting. Put drop of oil in bobbin case, insert washer, then insert bobbin normally.

USEFUL FEATURES

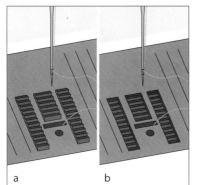

Feed dogs help move fabric when sewing (a). Sewing machine must be able to drop the feed dogs (b) to do free-motion quilting, embroidery or thread painting. With the feed dogs dropped, you can easily slide the fabric beneath the presser foot to stitch.

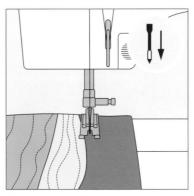

A "needle down" function is very useful as it prevents the work from slipping when you stop stitching. Use this feature especially when free-motion quilting, and when sewing circles or turning corners.

Some machines have a knee lift bar that allows you to lift the presser foot to adjust the direction of stitching while keeping your hands and eyes on your work. Get accustomed to using this as it is an invaluable tool.

EXERCISES FOR QUILT MAKERS

Quilters often become so engrossed in their work that hours pass as if they were mere seconds. While this means that much work gets accomplished, it's important for all quilters to take breaks while quilting. A prolonged static posture will inhibit blood circulation and eventually take a toll on your body, while a supple body will enable you to work longer and with enjoyment. These exercises are easy to do and will make you feel better immediately after doing them.

Exercise throughout the day or whenever your muscles tighten up. Take a short break or change tasks every hour. In particular, look after your hands and wrists to avoid repetitive strain injury. Periodically rest your hands, and always keep wrists in a neutral (straight) position. Try to maintain a correct upright posture when working.

HEAD

Gently lower ear to shoulder and hold for 10 seconds. Repeat on the other side. Do this several times in a smooth motion, without jerking your neck.

Turn head slowly to look over left shoulder and hold for 5 seconds. Repeat on the other side. Do this several times, especially if you have been bending over hand sewing.

NECK

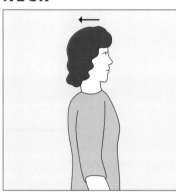

Raise your head to straighten your neck. Tuck your chin in and backwards creating a double chin (do this in private!). Hold for 5 seconds and repeat severai times.

Rotate your head to stretch your neck. Bend your head forward, then gently move it to one shoulder, bend head back, then bend to other shoulder. Return to original position. Repeat 5 times clockwise, and 5 times counterclockwise.

EYES

To avoid eye fatigue, rest and refocus your eyes periodically. Look away from your sewing toward something in the distance. Gaze out the window or at a favorite quilt hanging on the wall for a few minutes before returning to your work.

SHOULDERS

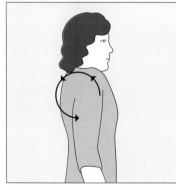

Take a break from stitching to loosely roll your shoulders forward in a circle several times, then repeat, rolling shoulders in a backward direction. Repeat 3–5 times.

To massage a painful knot in your shoulder blade, put a tennis ball in a sock. Sling sock over your shoulder until ball is over the exact spot; lean against a wall and rub ball up and down to release knot.

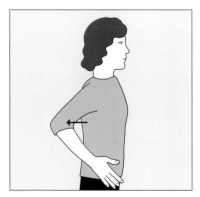

Just before sitting down to sew, stretch your shoulders and upper back by bending your elbows back behind your body at chest height while standing up straight; hold for 5 seconds. Repeat 5 times.

HANDS

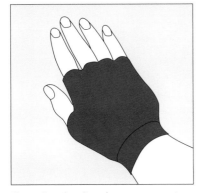

If your hands ache when rotary cutting or sewing, invest in stress relief gloves that help support hand muscles and alleviate pain. These are fingerless so they don't restrict movement or fine finger control.

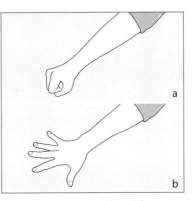

Release tension in your hands by making a tight fist for 5 seconds (a), then slowly open your hands to spread your fingers wide (b). Hold for 5 seconds. Repeat 5–10 times.

Stretch your thumb out to the side, gently pulling on it with your opposite hand. Hold in the stretched position for 5 seconds, then release. Do the same with your other hand. Repeat 5 times each.

WRISTS

A hand exerciser is available in different weights and can be kept by the side of your sewing machine. Squeeze it every now and then to strengthen your hands, particularly your main sewing hand.

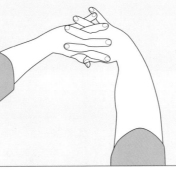

Interlace fingers, then turn palms outwards and straighten arms in front, feeling a stretch in your wrists and shoulders. Hold for 10 seconds and repeat several times.

Stretch both hands out to the sides with your hands clenched into tight fists. Make small circles with both fists 10 times in a clockwise and 10 times in a counterclockwise direction. Repeat, making big circles with your fists.

BACK

Support your lower back by strengthening your abdominal muscles. Stop sewing periodically and sit upright in your chair. Suck in your abdominal muscles and hold for 5 seconds, then release.

To stretch your mid-back, bend your elbows with one arm over your head and one arm behind you; hold for 5 seconds. Switch to do same stretch on the other side. Repeat 5 times.

Stand straight up with palms on lower back for support. Gently bend backwards as far as you can without straining. Bounce minutely a few times, then return to normal standing position. Repeat.

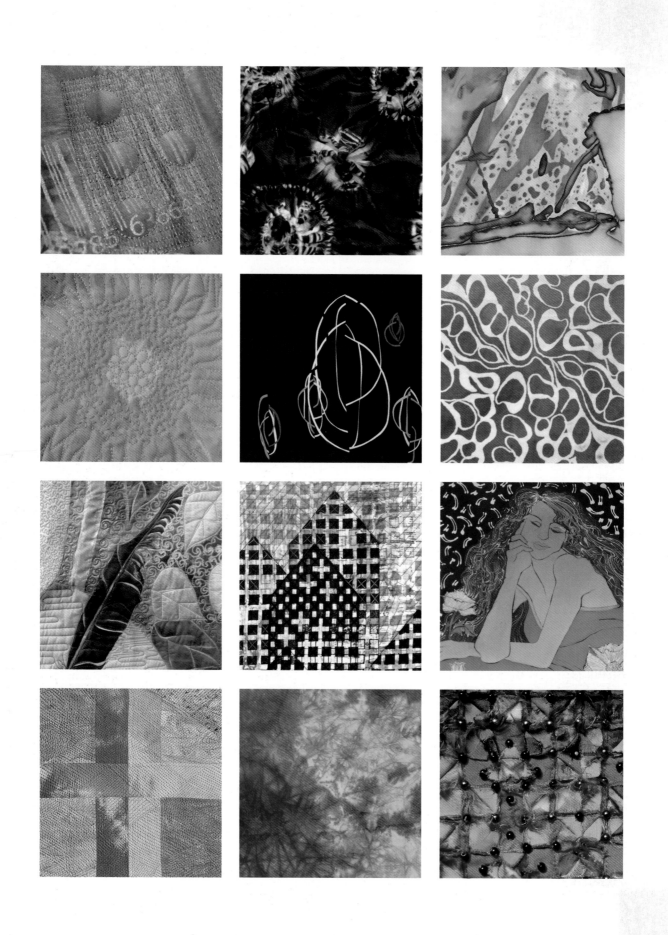

3 SURFACE DESIGN

dyeing painting
marbling foiling rusting
discharge texture
resists cyanotype
screen printing slashing
monoprinting
image transfer

3

3

SURFACE DESIGN

Contemporary quilters are expressing their artistic talents in ways never before contemplated for textiles. The acceptance and employment of surface design has transformed quilt makers into quilt artists, and they are creating fabrics that are imaginative, quirky and unique.

⬆ Confidante—© Linda Kemshall, Wolverhampton, Staffordshire, UK. Crows are known for their intelligence. These wise birds tell the secrets of men and their doings to their solemn faced confidante who listens intently before recording them in the ledger. Cotton poplin. Hand painted, free-motion machine quilted, more pastel and paint applied after quilting. 57 x 55½"/145 x 141cm. 2008.

Hand-dyeing was probably the first surface design technique to be embraced whole-heartedly by quilters. But dyeing is only the beginning of the surface design adventure. Adding color with paints or thickened dyes, inks and markers has opened up another world for textile artists when combined with the many methods of application that are available. Stamps can be used to make repeated designs or add texture to fabric. Stenciled and painted surfaces have moved from walls and furniture onto quilts and textiles. In addition, artists are screen printing fabric, using all kinds of media and resists. Monoprinting has brought quilters back to childhood days when dabbling in paint and making a mess was acceptable and encouraged. And once dye is put on a fabric, why not take it off? Discharging is a fascinating diversion for many surface designers, who enjoy the excitement and unpredictability of the results. Resists such as stitching, tying with string, wax, soya wax and even flour can be used in combination with many of these techniques to block out color, imparting further texture to textiles.

Products used for different crafts, such as paintstiks, metallic foils, glitter, crayons and other artists' materials, can also be used to mark and highlight fabric. Marbling looks just as amazing on fabric as it does on paper. Snow-dyeing, rusting and cyanotype are further ways to create distinctive outcomes.

⬆ Winter Garden—©Margaret Applin, Lowell, Massachusetts.
A personal design was drawn on paper, then manipulated in Photoshop Elements to create a Thermofax screen. The artist randomly printed the same image over a large piece of fabric using acrylic paint colors that worked well together; sometimes there was not enough paint, which produced the slightly distressed areas. Cotton fabric, silk embroidery floss. Computer manipulated image, Thermofax screen printed, free-motion embroidered and quilted, hand embroidered edges. 13 x 24"/33 x 61cm. 2012.

Photos and other images can be printed on fabric, opening up endless possibilities for stunning textile compositions. For adding even more impact to a quilt, texture can be imparted by slashing, ruching, pleating, melting and burning. Best of all, any or all of these techniques can be combined with one another to generate even more special effects.

⬇ *Fleurs de Corail*—©Anne Woringer, Paris, France. Photo by Bruno Jarret. An experiment in combining shibori and discharge. After discharging the fabric and removing the stitches, the artist was disappointed to find little contrast. Two months later, she realized she could see some patterns, so decided to highlight each one with embroidery. Antique indigo cotton fabric. Shibori-dyed, discharged, hand embroidered. 40 x 69"/101 x 175cm. 2010.

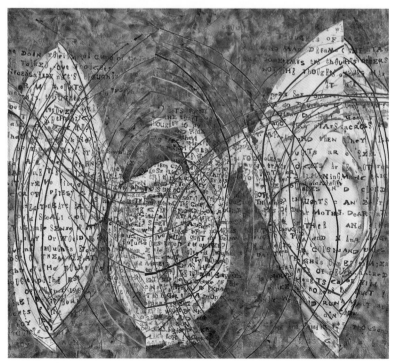

⬅ Thoughts—©Jayne Willoughby, Edmonton, Alberta, Canada. Photo by Gregory Case. This piece was inspired by a series of personal losses and the thoughtful ruminations in dealing with the grief of those losses. Cotton fabric, fabric paint. Machine pieced, machine quilted, hand painted, text stamped with fabric paint. 73 x 114"/185 x 290cm. 2010.

⬅ My Gentle Giant – Ben— ©Patt Blair, Mt. Baldy, California. This piece was inspired by an article on the plight of the mountain gorilla and was 3 years in the making. It was painted in 2008 and stayed on the artist's design wall until it was quilted in 2011. Ben represents the Silverback, the large male leader of a mountain gorilla family. There may be 700 mountain gorillas left, mostly in Congo national parks, where rangers attempt to protect them. White cotton fabric, clear monofilament, variegated and black metallic threads. Painted with pigment ink, free-motion machine quilted. 31 x 41"/79 x 104cm. 2011.

Experimentation is essential and failure is not a consideration because unhappy results can always be overprinted or disguised. For any quilter who finds the exploration of these techniques a bit intimidating, this chapter will demystify all of these processes and show how simple they really are.

⬆ A Natural Landscape—©Angela Daymond, Boston, Lincolnshire, UK. Photo by David Cawkwell. Inspired by the vast skies and flat rural fenland landscape surrounding the artist's home. Mordanted cotton fabric. Hand-dyed with natural plant materials: red cabbage, cutch, weld and woad. Machine pieced, raw edge appliquéd, free-motion machine quilted, hand quilted. 83 x 27"/ 210 x 70cm. 2012.

DYEING: ESSENTIAL STEPS

Fabric dyeing was one of the first surface design techniques to be embraced by art quilters. Yet there are still some quilt makers who resist dyeing their own fabrics because they feel it is too complicated, time consuming or messy. While dyeing isn't the tidiest technique, it is easy to do, as well as being exciting and addictive. But more importantly, a basic understanding of the dye process is essential for many of the surface design techniques covered in this chapter, so study these pages carefully to gain a good understanding of the basics of dyeing.

This section will cover Procion MX dyes, which produce bright, intense colors by chemically bonding with natural cellulose fibers; in effect, the dye becomes part of the fabric itself. This bonding requires the use of a soda ash fixative (or activator) to become permanent. Other chemical solutions (known as auxiliaries) can also be used to enhance the dyeing process; see the recipes for these on the facing page.

There are almost as many ways of dyeing as there are dyers. Numerous books are available that go into great detail about different dyeing recipes and methods; refer to the Bibliography for a selection of the best ones.

Health & Safety Rules

- Always wear an apron, gloves, goggles and a dust mask or respirator when working with dye powders and soda ash.
- Work in a well-ventilated area that is free from drafts.
- If possible, work in a box or tray lined with damp newspaper to catch any stray powder. Mop up spills immediately.
- Use only tools and containers dedicated to dyeing—do not reuse for food preparation.
- Procion MX dyes will react with copper and aluminum so use plastic, glass, or silicone supplies.
- Do not use stainless steel—soda ash will corrode it.
- Measure powders quickly and carefully; wear full safety equipment; work away from children and pets; recap containers immediately. Once mixed, Procion MX dyes pose no health hazard and will remain viable for up to one week.
- If handled improperly, soda ash and Hydros (see page 57) could burn skin and eyes.
- Wipe work area with a damp cloth to catch loose dye particles.
- Unused Procion MX dye solutions can be poured down the sink.

SCOUR FABRIC

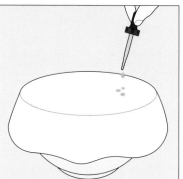

Fabric must be prepared for dyeing (pfd) in advance to remove any dirt, oil or finishes. Machine-wash fabric on hottest setting using fabric detergent. Test dry fabric with water drops; if drops absorb, fabric is ready to dye. If drops bead up and roll around, wash again.

MIX DYE

Make urea solution as directed opposite (optional). Place container for dye in plastic tray lined with damp newspaper. Measure and dissolve dye powder in small amount of warm water or urea solution; mix to a paste, then add remainder of water and stir carefully.

BATCH (CURE)

Soak fabric in dye for time specified for method and dye colors. To batch or cure, remove fabric from dye, squeeze out excess liquid and wrap in plastic. If dyeing in container, pour out excess dye; cover with plastic wrap. Leave fabric in warm place for several hours.

SODA ASH

Make soda ash solution as directed opposite. Soak pfd fabric in solution for at least 20 minutes, stirring to totally immerse. Hang fabric to air dry; do not put in clothes dryer. Or, add solution to dye bath according to dyeing recipe and method.

APPLY DYE

Soak fabric in warm water for 20 mins; wring out. Pour dye in bucket, cup or bag and immerse fabric. Or arrange fabric in a container and spray or squirt with dye solutions decanted into plastic bottles. For application techniques, see dyeing methods on following pages.

RINSE & WASH

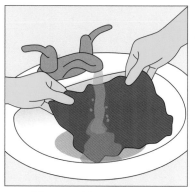

Rinse fabric in cold water to remove soda ash. Hot-rinse several times; then steep in hot water with Synthrapol (or its equivalent) for 10 minutes. Hot-rinse until water runs clear. Finally, machine-wash on hottest setting with detergent suitable for colored fabrics.

FABRIC

For the best results, choose fabrics made of 100% cellulose (plant) fibers such as cotton, linen, viscose rayon, hemp, bamboo or Tencel. Silk can also be Procion MX dyed.

Fabric weight will influence the amount of dye required: heavy-weight fabric will need more dye powder to achieve a rich color than light fabric. The amount of fabric in the dye bath will also affect the color: the more yardage being dyed, the more dye is needed.

DYE

Dyes are sold in powder form. For best results when using Procion MX dyes, mix dye powder in urea and work at room temperature (70°F/21°C). The MX number is the manufacturer's code for a specific color; dyes without an MX code have been mixed by the distributor. Individual pigments will vary in weight and balance: stronger, heavier dyes such as fuchsia will overwhelm others and/or strike (fix to fabric) at different times, which can create interesting effects. Test colors on a paper towel, which dries quickly. **Recipe:** Use 2 tsp/10g dye per 1 cup/250ml water or urea solution.

SODA ASH

Soda ash (or sodium carbonate) makes an alkaline solution that enables dye to fix permanently to cellulose fibers. It can be purchased from dye manufacturers or swimming pool companies (only use pure forms with no additives). Do not use baking soda. Soda ash solution will last indefinitely at room temperature, but when added directly to a dye bath will exhaust dye quickly so must be used immediately.

Recipe: Wear gloves and goggles. Using funnel, measure ½ cup/8tbl soda ash into clean, labeled 4 pint/2 liter plastic bottle. Half-fill with hot water; cap and shake well. Fill to top with hot water; cap and shake to mix.

UREA

Urea is an optional chemical that helps dye dissolve quickly and easily in water, producing strong colors. It also serves as a wetting agent, keeping fabric damp for longer so that the dye has more time to react.

Recipe: Dissolve 9 tbl/100g urea into 4 pints/2 liters warm water (110°F/44°C). Cool and decant into clean, labeled plastic bottle using a funnel. Make enough solution for every color; use the same quantity of urea solution as water when mixing dyes. Solution will last indefinitely at room temperature.

SALT

Salt breaks down an electrical charge in fabric that resists dye. Salt then pushes dye out of the water and onto the fibers. It is required for techniques where a lot of water is used. Salt can also speed up the time it takes dye to fix.

Recipe: Dissolve 1lb/450g plain salt into 4 pints/2 liters boiling water. Cool and decant into clean, labeled plastic bottle using a funnel. Solution will last indefinitely at room temperature. Shake before using.

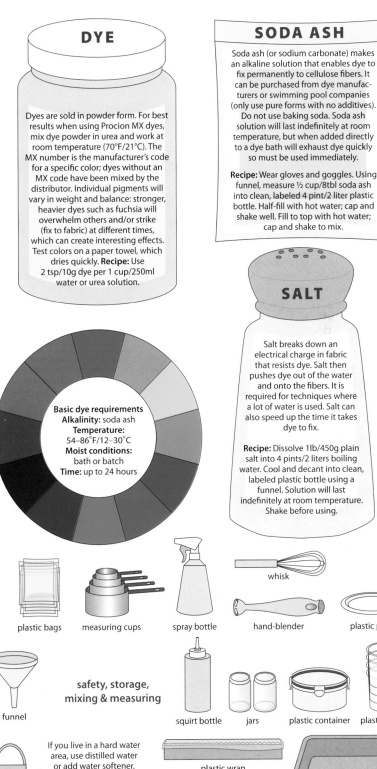

Basic dye requirements
Alkalinity: soda ash
Temperature: 54–86°F/12–30°C
Moist conditions: bath or batch
Time: up to 24 hours

SYNTHRAPOL

Synthrapol (Metapex and similar products by other manufacturers) is a pH-neutral fabric detergent specially formulated for dyers; follow manufacturer's instructions for quantity needed. Use Synthrapol after dyeing to remove excess dye particles that have not bonded to the fabric. Synthrapol will keep these loose dye particles suspended in the water so they don't stain or contaminate other fabrics.

measuring jug   plastic bags   measuring cups   spray bottle   hand-blender   whisk   plastic plate

safety, storage, mixing & measuring

plastic spoons   funnel   squirt bottle   jars   plastic container   plastic cups

If you live in a hard water area, use distilled water or add water softener.

plastic wrap

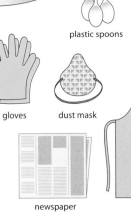

goggles   gloves   dust mask   apron   stirring rods   deep plastic tray

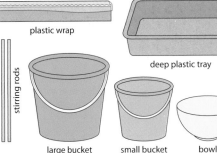

plastic tablecloth   newspaper   apron   4 pint/2 liter bottles   large bucket   small bucket   bowl

DYEING: IMMERSION

Immersion dyeing, where soda ash solution is added to the dye bath, gives a wide range of results. When dyeing was first embraced by the quilt community, the smooth, even color that was created on the fabric through solid shade immersion dyeing was preferred. Imperfections such as lines or spots were frowned upon and rejected. But as quilt artists began to experiment with dye methods, these ostensible flaws became desirable. Dyers developed ways to create textured or crackled effects by crushing fabrics into small trays, cups or plastic bags and using less water—low water immersion dyeing. The results of these dye methods create beautiful one-of-a-kind fabrics that work very well in art quilts.

The basic recipes given here will produce good results using Procion MX dyes, but it's always best to read the manufacturer's instructions and adapt the recipes for the weight and type of fabric you are dyeing. While dyeing is naturally imprecise, you can replicate colors by keeping careful records of quantities and proportions. If dyeing more or less fabric than specified in the recipes, increase or decrease the amount of dye, water and auxiliary solutions proportionally. To create lighter colors, reduce only the amount of dye, not the auxiliary solutions.

Procion MX dyes are particularly good for dyeing batik (pages 80–81) and water-soluble resisted fabrics (page 84), because the tepid water temperature will not melt the wax, resulting in precise separations between the waxed and dyed areas.

A benefit of dyeing is that you can create fabrics in color gradations just by varying the amount of dye used in each bath. The resulting fabrics will appear to blend seamlessly into one another.

SOLID SHADE IMMERSION DYEING

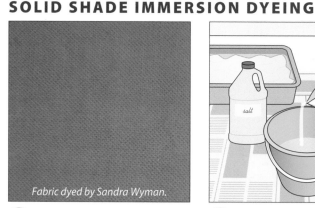

Fabric dyed by Sandra Wyman.

1 **Recipe:** 1 gal/4 liters hot water, 1 yd/m prepared for dyeing (pfd) cellulose fabric, 2 tsp Procion MX or other cold-water fiber reactive dye, 1 cup/250ml water/urea solution, 1 quart/liter salt solution, 1 quart/liter soda ash solution, Synthrapol (optional).

2 Pre-soak fabric in warm water for 20 minutes while preparing dye bath. To prepare dye, fill bucket with 1 gal/4 liters hot water or enough to cover fabric and allow for stirring without spilling. Pour in salt solution.

3 Mix dye powder separately in water/urea solution to make paste; add warm water/urea to make 1 cup/250ml; pour into bucket and stir. Wring out soaked fabric; add to dye bath. Stir for 10 minutes, then allow fabric to soak in dye for 20 minutes, stirring regularly.

4 Remove fabric from dye bath; carefully stir in soda ash solution. Return fabric to dye bath. Use stick to swirl fabric; allow it to soak for at least an hour, stirring every 10 mins so dye penetrates fibers thoroughly. For deep color, leave fabric in dye for 4–24 hours.

AFTER DYEING

Remove fabric from dye bath and rinse immediately in cold water to remove soda ash. Pour exhausted dye solution down the drain. Wash and rinse as directed on page 46. Dark and red colors may need an additional hot wash; check that water runs clear.

DYEING WAX-RESIST FABRICS

1 To dye fabric with wax or soy resists, follow recipe above for dye; dye bath must be tepid. Pour dye into large flat tray if you wish to prevent wax from cracking. Refrigerate batiked fabric (pages 80–81) just before dyeing to harden wax.

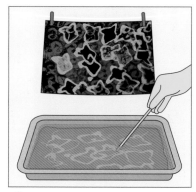

2 Soak waxed fabric in dye bath for an hour, occasionally moving it gently in the bath with a stick. Batch (page 46) 4 hours or overnight, then rinse, hang to dry and remove wax (page 81). If dyeing more colors, wax in different areas, dye, batch and rinse.

GRADATION DYEING

1 **Recipe:** 1½ yds/m pfd cellulose fabric cut into 6 fat quarters, each 18 x 22"/46 x 56cm, Procion MX dye, warm water or urea solution, 6 large plastic freezer bags, soda ash solution, salt solution (recipes on page 47). *Fabric dyed by Sandra Wyman.*

2 Presoak fat quarters in warm water. Measure and mark line to indicate 1 cup/250ml on a clean glass jar. In jar, make a paste with 1 tsp dye in warm water/urea solution (page 47). Top up with warm water/urea to marked line. Pour half the dye into first bag.

3 Top up solution in jar to marked line with warm water/urea. Pour half the dye into 2nd plastic bag. Top up again; pour half the contents into 3rd bag. Continue to fill remaining bags in same way. Dyes will become progressively weaker, making paler colors.

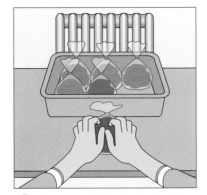

4 Pour ½ cup/100ml each of soda ash and salt solutions into each bag of dye. Wring out fabrics; add one fat quarter to each bag. Knead bags well, squeeze out air and knot or zip closed. Leave in warm place overnight; remove fabrics. Rinse; see page 46.

VARIATION

For textured effect, do not knead the fabrics in bags; let them batch without agitation. Another variation: pre-soak fabric in soda ash; dry. Crush fabric in bag; pour one color dye on one side, and a different color on the other; dyes will blend with unexpected results.

LOW WATER

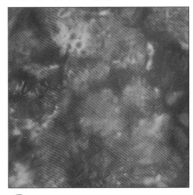

1 **Recipe:** 1½ yds/m pfd cellulose fabric, salt solution, plastic tray, 2 tsp Procion MX dye, 1 cup/250ml warm water or urea solution, 1 cup/250ml soda ash solution (recipes on page 47). *Fabric dyed by Sandra Wyman.*

2 Pre-soak fabric in bucket of salt water solution. Wring out fabric, then arrange in plastic tray, pleating and crinkling to get good textured effects.

3 In measuring jug, make a paste with 2 tsp dye in warm water/urea solution (a); top up with rest of warm water/urea solution. Add soda ash to dye solution. Pour dye/soda ash solution evenly over fabric arranged in plastic tray (b).

4 For textured result, allow fabric to soak in solution for about 2 hours without agitating fabric in any way. For less texture, mash fabric into dye to eliminate any undyed areas. When done, remove fabric from tray, batch and rinse as directed on page 46.

DYEING: DIRECT APPLICATION

Dyeing fabric is an art form in itself, and quilters revel in using the gorgeous results. Applying dye directly to fabric opens up many options for combining and blending colors. The techniques take advantage of the fact that dyes will fix (strike) to the fibers at different times depending on the colors used and the temperature and humidity of the room, with unpredictable effects.

Read Dyeing: Essential Steps on pages 46–47. Make up dye solutions in a variety of colors—after mixing dyes, test colors on paper towels before using on fabric. Dyes must always be used in conjunction with soda ash, so either pre-soak fabric that has been prepared for dyeing (pfd) in soda ash for 20 minutes or add soda ash to pure dye solution immediately before using. Decant dye solutions into jars, or squirt or spray bottles for easy use.

DIRECT APPLICATION DYE RECIPE

1 For medium color, mix 2tsp dye (4tsp for black) with 1 cup/250ml warm water/urea solution. First mix dye into paste, then top up with the water/urea. (Optional: Add 1 cup/ 250ml soda ash solution to pure dye.) Decant solution into labeled squirt/spray bottle or jar.

2 Cover work area with plastic. If using pure dye, pre-soak pfd fabric in soda ash solution for 20 mins; wring out or hang to dry. For rich color, squirt liberal amount of dye on fabric; blot any dye that hasn't soaked in with a paper towel. Batch and rinse.

TIE DYEING

Tie, pleat or twist pfd fabric (wearing gloves if fabric has been pre-soaked in soda ash); see following steps for some ideas. Using squirt bottle, apply dye to different areas of fabric, pushing tip of bottle into folds. Batch and rinse as directed on page 46.

STRIPES

Loosely roll or twist fabric into a long log shape. Tie string tightly at intervals along length of log to create a striped pattern on fabric. Place on plastic-covered work area and squirt one or several different color dyes on fabric in between each tie.

PLEATS

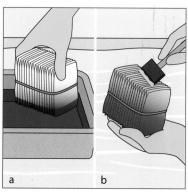

Starting with short edge, fold long length of fabric into even concertina pleats. For more pattern, fold again in opposite direction. Secure with string or elastic. Paint or dip edges into dye (a). For variation, dip or paint opposite edges with different colors (b).

DONUT

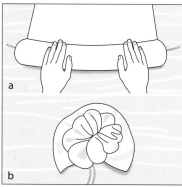

Roll fabric around a length of string (a); tie string in a knot, scrunching fabric as tightly as possible on string (b). After dyeing and batching, untie string and roll open to reveal a honeycomb effect. Interior area will be lighter and can be dyed again if desired.

SPIRAL

1 Lay fabric on plastic-covered work area; pinch small pleat for center of spiral. Twist fabric. Lift fingers and pinch again, smoothly twisting fabric and straightening edges as you go. Folds should be about ½"/12mm high; split large folds into smaller ones.

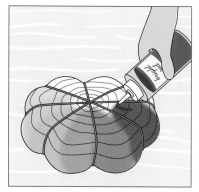

2 Once fabric has been fully spiraled, wind string firmly around bundle; knot to secure. Squirt or spoon dye solutions onto different quarters of bundle so color will spiral around center, but don't allow dye to mix in middle or effect will be muddy.

SPACE DYEING

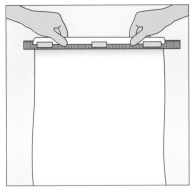

1 Use deep plastic tray and a ruler wider than tray. Cut long length of pfd fabric to width of tray. If using pure dye, pre-soak in soda ash solution for 20 minutes; hang to dry. Tape one short end of fabric to ruler. Wind fabric on ruler, leaving end to fill base of tray.

2 Squirt or pour dye on fabric in tray to depth of 1"/2.5cm; soak fabric in dye for 30 minutes. Unroll more fabric from ruler on top of first layer; soak 30 minutes. Continue until entire piece is dyed. Batch and rinse. Fabric will shade from dark to light.

3 To make fabric multi-colored, soak space-dyed fabric in soda ash (if using pure dye); hang to dry. Tape dark end to ruler; wind fabric on ruler, leaving pale end in tray. Squirt different color dye on fabric in tray; continue in same way as for step 2.

TEXTURED SPACE DYEING

1 Prepare several dye colors, mixing with soda ash solution in a 1:1 ratio; dyes mixed with soda ash must be used immediately. Scrunch pfd fabric loosely in deep plastic tray; squirt or spoon dye on fabric. Do not overlap colors—dyes will blend as they spread.

2 Pour off any residual dye, cover and batch for 4 hours (or overnight for richer color).
Fabric dyed by Sandra Wyman using Yellow, Bright Red (Red GN), Red-Brown 5BR, and Dark Green mixed from Yellow 8G and Blue 2G (Navy) Procion MX dyes.

CRUSH DYEING

Mix dye and soda ash solution in equal amounts. Crumple pfd fabric tightly in small plastic cup or bag. Squirt dye into cup; allow to soak in. Then squirt different color on top; batch for 1–4 hours. Result will be gradations of crackled color.

SPRAY DYEING

Use a funnel to pour dye/soda ash solution into spray bottle; if using many colors, label each bottle. Place pfd fabric on plastic-covered work area. Lightly spray with one or more dyes in a random pattern. Or arrange objects artistically on fabric; spray.

DYE PAINT

Use a sponge or bristle brush to paint liquid dye on pfd fabric that was pre-soaked in soda ash (or use dye/soda ash solution). Different effects can be achieved by painting wet or dry fabric. See pages 61–65 for dye paint recipe and more ideas.

THICKENED DYES

See page 61 for print paste recipe used to thicken dyes for printing, stenciling and stamping. Blend print paste with liquid dye to create a creamy yogurt-like mixture. If combined with soda ash, print paste must be used immediately.

⬆ Lair of the Amethyst Deva—©Sheila Frampton-Cooper, Van Nuys, California. This quilt was designed intuitively and pieced spontaneously to celebrate the Amethyst Deva: "In a realm, undetectable to most humans, lives a powerful and loving being. Her violet glow shines brightly throughout the universe as she guides us home." Cotton fabric hand-dyed by the artist. Machine pieced, free-motion machine quilted. 27 x 32"/68 x 81cm. 2012.

My Two TV's—©Kate Stiassni, Salisbury, Connecticut. Photo by Avery Danziger. Hand-dyed fabric by Lisa Reber. Quilting by Julia Graziano from pattern designed by the artist. This piece was inspired by the artist's memory of getting the family's first color TV for her 10th birthday. Hand-dyed cotton fabric, commercial fabric. Freehand rotary-cut, machine pieced, free-motion machine quilted. 76 x 42"/193 x 107cm. 2012.

Codes and Secrets— ©Hilary Gooding, Corfe Mullen, Dorset, UK. Inspired by the secrecy of codes and bringing them up to date with our modern world. An invented barcode and the artist's own Quick Response code were screen printed onto hand-dyed fabric. The quilting forms Braille letters and the "secret" message reads: "All humans are born free and equal in dignity and rights." (Article 1 of the Universal Declaration of Human Rights.) Cotton fabric, hand-dyed by Frieda Anderson. Screen printed, Braille letters digitized and machine quilted, trapunto. 36 x 34"/91 x 87cm. 2012.

NATURAL DYEING

Once you begin dyeing with natural ingredients, a walk in the garden or a trip to the supermarket will never be the same again. Flowers, roots, bark, leaves, vegetables—even spices—can be used to create gorgeous organic colors. The process is a bit more complicated than working with chemical dyes, but the purity and subtle complexity of the colors that can be achieved is worth the effort. Some plant dyestuffs will even emit a lovely aroma as they simmer, which adds to the pleasure of this technique. Only use dyestuffs you have grown yourself or bought for this purpose. While it's fine to scavenge the forest floor for leaves, pine cones and nuts, do not gather wild living plants or bark which can take a long time to regenerate.

Success in natural dyeing depends on a number of variables, but perhaps the most important is preparing the fabric for dyeing by scouring: this will remove any finishes that might inhibit the dyes from attaching to the fibers.

Some natural dyestuffs, called adjective dyes, will require a mordant —a chemical agent that adheres to both fibers and dye, binding them together; the term is derived from the Latin *mordere*, which means "to bite." Fabric must be mordanted before dyeing can begin, and can be done while the dyestuffs are being prepared.

Other dyestuffs, known as substantive dyes, do not require a mordant; these include onion skins, tea, turmeric, indigo, walnut husks and weld. Substantive dyes often prefer an acidic environment, so adding 1 cup/250ml of white vinegar to the dye bath will improve the color. A richer color can also be achieved by adding 1 table-spoon of salt to the dye bath.

If you wish to pursue this technique in depth, check the internet or buy a book on natural dyes that will provide recipes and the required mordants; see the Bibliography. While most natural fiber fabrics will have good results, this section only covers dyeing cotton fabric.

Once you become familiar with the process of natural dyeing, experiment to improve your skills as a dyer and produce different effects. Alter the amount of time the fibers are kept in solution, or test how the addition of salt or vinegar affects the color. For texture, wrap the fabric around the dyestuffs and steam it. Rusting naturally-dyed fabrics (see page 90) will change their colors because iron oxide is a mordant. Natural dyes are impacted by many elements, but that is part of their appeal—serendipity will often dictate the final outcome. See Dyeing on pages 46–47, especially the *Health & Safety Rules*, before beginning.

DYESTUFFS

Yellow: onion skins, daffodils, weld, marigolds, dandelions, carrot tops, turmeric, rape seed flowers
Blue/purple: woad, indigo, red cabbage, berries, logwood
Green: nettles, peppermint, artichokes, sunflower leaves, spinach
Red: madder, brazilwood, beets, rose hips, avocado skins (dusky pink)
Orange: pomegranate, onion skins, carrot roots, eucalyptus
Brown: walnut husks, tea, bark, cutch, red maple leaves, pine cones

Listed are some of the many substances you can use to dye fabric naturally. The more exotic dyestuffs can be bought from natural dye distributors or the internet. They will usually come with directions for how to prepare and mordant them.

SCOUR

Even fabric that is prepared for dyeing (pfd) must be scoured before using natural dyes. Machine-wash fabric in hot water on long cycle with pH-neutral fabric detergent and no fabric softener, or hand-soak 15 minutes with 1tsp/5ml Synthrapol added; rinse in warm water.

2 Turn off heat and leave fabric to cool in mordant solution for 8 hours or overnight. Remove from solution, wring and rinse well to remove any unfixed mordant. Pour mordant solution safely down a foul drain or lavatory (not garden or septic tank).

EQUIPMENT

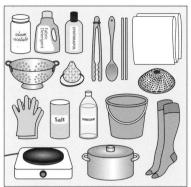

Gloves, mask, large (2½gal/10 liter) stainless steel pot, heat source, strainer or colander, steamer, plastic bucket, tongs, steel spoon, stirring sticks, nylon stockings, cotton fabric, pH-neutral fabric detergent or Synthrapol, alum acetate, salt, vinegar.

MORDANT

1 Pre-soak 3½oz/100g scoured fabric in warm water. Use boiling water to dissolve 1tsp/5g alum acetate in small container. Half-fill dye pot with water; pour alum solution into pot; stir. Wring out fabric, add to pot; bring to simmer. Simmer for 1 hour, stirring often.

PREPARE DYE

1 Collect large amount of the dye-stuffs you wish to use in a quantity equal to or up to twice the weight of fabric being dyed. Dry all flowers and petals before use. If using roots, bark or vegetables, chop with a knife or use a food processor; soak overnight.

IMMERSION DYE

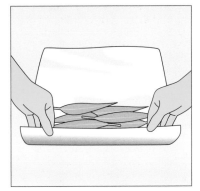

STEAM DYE

2 Add dyestuffs to pot. Cover with water; bring to boil. Quickly lower heat; simmer 1 hour. Cool solution overnight. Pour through colander or strainer to extract dyestuffs. Discard dyestuffs, or place in nylon stocking; put back in solution for deeper color.

Pour strained dye back into dye pot. Pre-soak scoured and/or mordanted fabric in warm water. Wring fabric, immerse in dye solution; heat to a simmer. Simmer fabric in dye until desired color is achieved, stirring often. Allow fabric to cool in dye pot.

For textured result, roll dyestuffs in mordanted fabric; secure with string or elastic. Fill base of pot with water, place rolled fabric in colander, and colander in pot. Steam with lid on for 1–2 hours, topping up water in pot so it does not boil dry. Unroll fabric when cool.

RINSE

TEA & COFFEE

SPICES

When dye solution has cooled, remove fabric from pot with tongs (a). Rinse until water runs clear. Soak in pH-neutral fabric detergent (b), then rinse. Hang to dry; color will be paler when dry. Safely discard dye solution or use to dye more fabric (color will be lighter).

The tannins in non-herbal tea or coffee will stain and darken fabric to a beige/brown; some fruit teas will impart a red/pink color. Make tea or coffee with boiling water; steep for strong color. Place damp pfd fabric in bucket. Pour solution on fabric; steep overnight.

Measure 4tbl ground spice (mustard, turmeric, ginger, paprika) into a nylon stocking and knot to secure; place in 4 cups/1 liter water; simmer 1 hour. Pour in 1 cup/250ml white vinegar. Add fabric, stir; simmer 30 minutes or until desired color is achieved. Do not boil.

ONION SKINS

VEGETABLES/FRUIT

FLOWERS/LEAVES

No mordant is required, but pre-soak fabric in a vinegar solution for better color. Place onion skins and 1 tbl salt in dye pot, bring to boil; simmer for 1 hour. Cool; strain. Place damp pfd fabric in dye. Bring to boil, then simmer for 1 hour. Cool fabric in dye bath overnight.

Use berries, plum and red grape skins or chopped vegetables such as red cabbage and beetroot. Place in dye pot and cover with water; simmer 1 hour. Cool. Strain out dyestuffs; put in nylon stocking, then put back in dye. Immerse damp mordanted fabric; simmer 1 hour.

Gather and dry large amount of flower heads, petals or leaves; place in dye pot. Cover with water, bring to boil and simmer for 1 hour. Strain dye; discard dyestuffs. Return liquid to pot. Place damp mordanted fabric in dye; simmer for 2 hours Cool overnight in dye bath.

INDIGO-DYED SHIBORI

It's difficult to choose the most magical aspect of indigo-dyed shibori. First there is the amazing transformation of the shimmering green fabric that emerges from the dyebath into a deep blue as oxidation takes place. Then there's the anticipation before the stitches are removed, and finally the marvel when the pattern is fully revealed. The only slightly negative aspect to this technique is the strong smell of the dye, so it is best to work outside or in a well-ventilated area.

Shibori is a Japanese term that means "wring, squeeze or press," and the procedure has been honed to a fine art over the centuries throughout Japan, primarily in Arimatsu and Kyoto. Fabrics are shaped and manipulated through stitching, folding, pleating, wrapping and compressing before immersion in a dye bath. The stitched and manipulated areas act to resist the dye, and so remain the original fabric color. Because the fabrics are pulled and gathered after stitching, the resulting patterns have an almost three-dimensional quality. Although many shibori designs can be reproduced, there is always a serendipitous element to the outcome, which makes this procedure so thrilling.

While natural indigo dye has traditionally been used for Shibori, synthetic indigo has been formulated to give more uniform results; it is available in a granular form. Indigo dye is different from fiber reactive dye as it sits on the surface of the fabric, so the more times it is dipped, the darker the fabric will become. The same cloth can be dyed several times using a different resist method each time. Shibori can also be done using fiber reactive dyes. Read the *Health & Safety Rules* for dyeing on page 46 before beginning.

EQUIPMENT

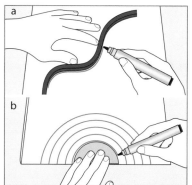

Water-soluble marker, rulers (curved and straight), poles or PVC piping, string, rubber bands, prepared for dyeing (pfd) white or previously dyed fabric in cotton, silk or rayon, sewing needles, strong thread, scissors, thimble, large bucket of warm water.

STITCH RESISTS

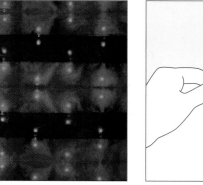

1 Insert strong thread in needle; stitch with doubled thread to prevent breakage and for better resist. Knot end, leaving long tail. Work running stitches along marked lines; large stitches make more interesting patterns. Parallel lines produce a wood grain effect.

FOLDING

Fold fabric in quarters and stitch through all the layers to create a repeated design. Alternatively, just clamp the fabric at regular intervals to achieve the design shown here. *Fabric Procion MX dyed yellow, folded, clamped and overdyed in indigo by the author.*

MARK FABRIC

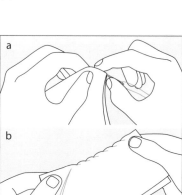

Using water-soluble marker, draw straight or curvy stitching lines on pfd fabric with ruler or templates (a). Or use templates to draw other shapes such as leaves or hearts. For squares or circles, fold fabric in half; mark half the shape (b) and stitch the doubled fabric.

2 To make chevron-shaped marks, fold fabric and oversew the fold (a), making a whip-stitch as shown here (b). Or, you can make a row of running stitches parallel to the fold to produce a double row of marks that are thought to resemble little teeth.

CROSSING SEAMS

3 When beginning a line of stitching along a fold, first stitch through a scrap of fabric to hold the knot and prevent it from making an unsightly mark in the middle of the design. Do this at the beginning and end of every stitching line along a fold.

If design lines cross, do not make a double fold when stitching across the seams. Instead, push needle through fold that has already been sewn to the other side and continue stitching.

CAPPING

Covering an area with plastic (capping) will enable that area to resist the dye. The area can be dyed later or left the original background color. Wrap plastic over area and secure with overhand knots (similar to casting on for knitting) or wrap tightly with string.

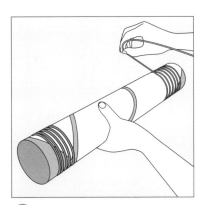

② For diagonal lines, place fabric on table. Roll fabric diagonally on pipe; do not allow edges to overlap. Secure bottom with rubber bands. Wrap with string or other cord. Compress fabric tightly on pipe as in previous step. Pleats and string will act as resists.

③ Lift off plastic wrap, removing surface scum with it. Wearing gloves, gently immerse prepared fabric (pre-soaked in warm water). Submerge fully. Remove after 5 minutes; don't allow dye to drip back into solution. Fabric will be greenish-yellow.

DRAWING UP

When all stitching is done, pull threads firmly and steadily to draw up fabric, gathering fabric evenly along threads as you pull. Ensure threads are drawn as tightly as possible, then knot leaving a tail. Soak in a bucket of warm water for a few minutes. Dye as described below.

INDIGO DYEING

① Apron, face mask, goggles, gloves, newspaper, wooden stirring sticks, 2 gallon plastic bucket, measuring jug, plastic wrap, 10 pints/5 liters water, 2tbl/ 30g soda ash (or 4tbl/60g washing soda), 2tsp/10g Hydrotherm DD (Hydros), 2tbl/ 30g Indigo Vat 60% grains (see page 245).

④ Hang on clothes line or arrange on grass. Allow dye to oxidize—it will turn blue. If darker color is desired, return to solution after oxidation. When finished, squeeze out excess dye; allow to dry overnight. Rinse in cold water, then wash in non-biological detergent.

POLE WRAPPING

① For parallel lines, measure circumference of a pipe. Cut full width of fabric to circumference measurement plus seam allowances. Stitch long edges together to make a tube. Insert pipe in tube; secure end with rubber bands. Compress fabric.

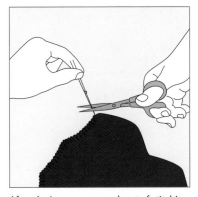

② Wear face mask, goggles and gloves. Pour 4 pints/2 liters hot water in bucket; add 6 pints/3 liters warm water. Add soda ash; stir. Add Hydros; stir. Add indigo slowly; gently stir until dissolved. Cover with plastic wrap to exclude air. Leave for 1 hour.

REMOVE STITCHES

After dyeing, remove each set of stitching lines and fabric scraps, if using. Pull tail of thread until knot is clear of fabric; snip off knot, being careful not to cut through fabric. Pull out threads to reveal design. Or, remove string from pole wrapped fabric; remove fabric from pole.

⬆ After Glow—©Janice Gunner, London, UK. One of the artist's many pieces of stitched resist indigo-dyed shibori designs. Hand-dyed cotton, rayon, cotton and phosphorescent thread, plastic cord. Stitched resist shibori, indigo-dyed, machine quilted, couched cord. 22 x 34"/55 x 86cm. 2012.

⬅ Indigo-dyed shibori samples—©Lynne Gefre and Linda Seward, London, UK. Made during a workshop with Janice Gunner. From top: hand-dyed yellow fabric oversewn in parallel lines, parallel curved lines folded then sewn with running stitch, pole wrapped shibori, hand-dyed turquoise fabric sewn with running stitch in a cross-hatch design. Cotton fabrics, some hand-dyed before being indigo-dyed. Shibori resist techniques. 2012.

Red Licorice Swirl—©Aryana B. Londir, New River, Arizona. The artist loves the movement created by the Arashi Shibori (pole wrapping) technique, as the colors and lines swirl around and around in much the same way as thoughts and emotions. Hand-dyed and commercial cotton fabrics. Arashi Shibori, machine pieced, machine quilted. 50 x 62"/127 x 157cm. 2012.

Once you start applying color to fabric, manufactured prints will never have the same appeal. Being able to control the most essential element of an art quilt is an empowering feeling, and surface designers who apply color to create their own designs can be assured that their work is utterly unique.

Many of the surface design methods in this chapter rely on the use of paints, dyes and inks—referred to in this book generically as "color." The main types of color used on fabric are featured here—consult these pages when selecting the best type of color to use for stamping, painting, stencilling, printing and marbling. Each brand of paint, dye or ink will have its own characteristics, and as you become familiar with them, you'll discover which products you like best. You may find that you favor one brand for brush painting, another for stenciling and a third for stamping or screen printing. Experimention is the best way to clarify your preferences.

A popular option is to use water-based acrylic textile colors/paints. These colors do not bind with the fibers, but adhere to the fabric's surface, so can be used on any fiber or weave (although natural fibers work best with water-based colors). Acrylic textile colors are permanent once fixed, either by heat setting or curing—follow the manufacturer's instructions for the color you are using. Textile colors are interchangeable and can be mixed to create a limitless palette. Keep in mind basic color theory—too much blending will create a muddy result. Textile colors can be thinned with water, augmented with extender and lightened with white. Some colors can be used with stencils for sun printing. Non-textile acrylic paints can also be used on fabrics when mixed with a textile medium such as Liquitex.

Procion MX dyes bind permanently to natural fibers, producing a transparent glowing color and leaving the fabric with a soft hand. Dyes can be used in a free-flowing liquid form or thickened to prevent them from spreading and to make crisp marks on fabric through stamping, stencilling, screen and mono-printing. Dyes can be painted on natural fibers only and must be used in conjunction with soda ash. Read Dyeing: Essential Steps on pages 46–47.

Fabric inks are another alternative to paints and dyes; these will leave the fabric with a soft hand and don't bleed, so are useful for wholecloth painting or adding fine details. Fabric paint pens are handy for coloring small areas and adding highlights. Expandable paint creates a raised texture. Fabric color can also be sprayed either with an airbrush or straight from a bottle or can.

TEXTILE COLORS/PAINT

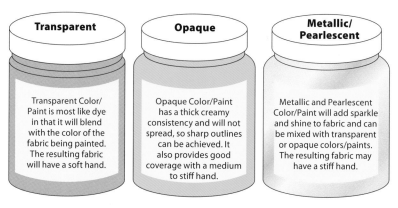

Transparent

Transparent Color/Paint is most like dye in that it will blend with the color of the fabric being painted. The resulting fabric will have a soft hand.

Opaque

Opaque Color/Paint has a thick creamy consistency and will not spread, so sharp outlines can be achieved. It also provides good coverage with a medium to stiff hand.

Metallic/Pearlescent

Metallic and Pearlescent Color/Paint will add sparkle and shine to fabric and can be mixed with transparent or opaque colors/paints. The resulting fabric may have a stiff hand.

- acrylic paint specially formulated for fabric
- use to paint, stencil, print, stamp or airbrush
- contains an adhesive binder that "glues" color to fabric
- thin with water for more fluidity and transparency
- mix with transparent extender to increase quantity without thinning
- add white to lighten color to pastel
- follow manufacturer's instructions for fixing by air drying or heating

FABRIC INKS

alternative to dye paint

use straight from bottle

will not bleed on dry fabric

pearlescent inks will add shine

- dilute with water for translucent wash of color
- use for painting, marbling, airbrushing
- thicken with extender (such as Versatex) to stencil, print or stamp
- heat set with hot iron and press cloth
- will not change texture of fabric

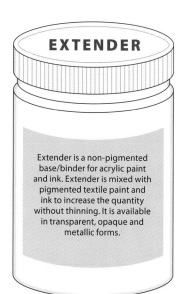

EXTENDER

Extender is a non-pigmented base/binder for acrylic paint and ink. Extender is mixed with pigmented textile paint and ink to increase the quantity without thinning. It is available in transparent, opaque and metallic forms.

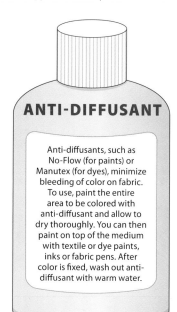

ANTI-DIFFUSANT

Anti-diffusants, such as No-Flow (for paints) or Manutex (for dyes), minimize bleeding of color on fabric. To use, paint the entire area to be colored with anti-diffusant and allow to dry thoroughly. You can then paint on top of the medium with textile or dye paints, inks or fabric pens. After color is fixed, wash out anti-diffusant with warm water.

APPLYING COLOR: DYES & ALTERNATIVES

DYE PAINT

Recipe for medium color:
2tsp/5g Procion MX dye powder, 1cup/250ml warm urea solution. Add dye powder to measuring jug; mix into paste with ¼ cup/60ml urea solution. Top up with urea solution to make 1 cup/250ml. Mix thoroughly to use as fabric paint.

THICKENER

Purchase ready-made thickener such as Superclear or Manutex. Thin with water or urea solution to desired consistency. Add liquid Procion MX dye solutions to thickener for painting, screen printing, monoprinting and stamping.

DYE THICKENER/PRINT PASTE

Recipe: 4 tsp/20g sodium alginate, 1 qt/1 liter urea solution, 1 tsp/5g Calgon. Pour 1 cup/250ml urea solution into bowl or blender; add 1 tsp/5g sodium alginate and the Calgon. Whisk or blend until smooth. Add same amount alginate and urea solution 3 more times, and blend until alginate is fully amalgamated into urea solution. Pour into plastic container; allow to thicken in cool place overnight. Divide thickener into 4 small, lidded containers. Add 2 tsp/10ml strong liquid dye solution (double amount for black) to each 1 cup/250ml of thickener; mix thoroughly. Thickener should be consistency of thick yogurt, but can be thinned gradually with water if necessary. **Note:** Store plain thickener (without dye or soda ash) in labeled lidded container in refrigerator for up to 6 months.

Refer to Dyeing: Essential Steps on pages 46–47 for soda ash and urea recipes, and for directions on batching and rinsing dyes.

PAINTSTIKS

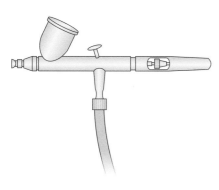

- sticks of oil paint solidified with wax
- available in matte or metallic
- rub directly on fabric
- colors are easily blended
- permanent when dry

PENS/MARKERS

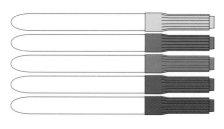

- add accents or outlines
- nibs vary in thickness
- will not stiffen fabric
- great for using with children
- fix by ironing with press cloth

EXPANDABLE PAINT

- creates raised design
- apply thin layer
- use brush, spatula, brayer or squeegee
- allow to dry at least 6 hours
- heat to expand and puff up

AIRBRUSH

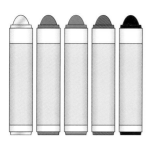

- air-operated tool that applies paint through diffusion
- use airbrushing ink, textile ink, textile color/paint or dye paint
- make sharp designs using stencils
- spray from distance for misty effect

FABRIC SPRAY PAINT

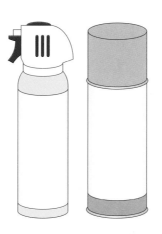

- make sharp designs using stencils
- spray from distance for misty effect
- fabric remains soft
- follow manufacturer's instructions for fixing

TEXTILE MEDIUM

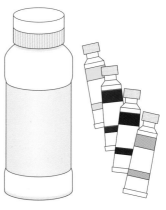

- blend medium such as Liquitex with artists' acrylic paints
- medium helps fabric absorb paint
- prevents fabric from becoming too stiff after application of paint
- heat set with iron and press cloth when dry

APPLYING COLOR: ESSENTIAL STEPS

The previous spread gave an overview of the different colors that can be applied to fabric. The following pages explain how to use the colors in a variety of ways—from stenciling and painting to stamping and printing. This page gives basic practices that apply to all the color application techniques in this chapter. The equipment step lists the essentials—addditonal equipment is listed with each method.

Keep in mind that many of the techniques covered here can be used in combination with one another, creating multi-layered designs. Allow dyes, inks or paints to dry before adding another layer. Have fun while you experiment and don't expect perfection. If you're not happy with the results, you can always overprint the fabric or cut it up—large splodges of color look quite different when viewed in small pieces.

BASIC EQUIPMENT

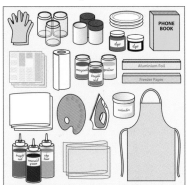

Apron, rubber gloves, newspaper or plastic to protect work area, paper towels, plastic plates or palettes, freezer paper, prepared-for-dyeing (pfd) fabric, jars, plastic containers, appropriate colors/mediums, old telephone book, iron, aluminum foil (optional).

WORK AREA

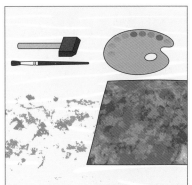

Cover work area with plastic or newspaper. Press freezer paper to wrong side of fabric to stabilize it and prevent leaking. Or work directly on paper or plastic surface, moving work often so color doesn't pool beneath fabric or dry and stick to the surface.

FABRIC

Best results are achieved by using high-quality, tightly-woven prepared-for-dyeing (pfd) fabric in natural fibers. See page 46 for instructions on scouring fabric to prepare it for dyeing. Before beginning, always test color on a scrap of the same fabric you are using.

CONSISTENCY

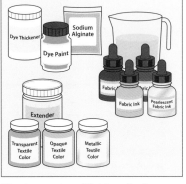

Check texture and fluidity of color. Adjust color to desired consistency with extender (for textile colors/paints and inks), dye thickener/print paste (for Procion MX dyes) or water (for inks); see pages 60–61. Test airbrush, sprays or expandable paint on scraps.

APPLY COLOR

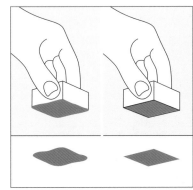

① Ensure that color is well mixed before using by shaking or stirring it; remove any lumps. Apply paint, dye or ink judiciously, using much less than you think you'll need. Too much color on a stamp, brush, roller or brayer can create a messy result with little definition.

Damp fabric painted with textile colors by the author and then scrunched before being allowed to dry.

② You can achieve different effects by coloring wet, damp or dry fabric. Dry fabric will impart crisp lines/edges. Damp fabric will soak up more color. Wet fabric will cause color to spread, imitating the effect of a watercolor painting, as shown here.

CLEAN EQUIPMENT

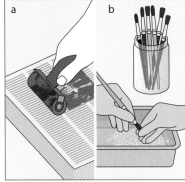

Use an old phone book as a place to wipe off excess color from stamps, brushes, brayers and rollers (a). Then rinse all equipment immediately in lukewarm water with mild detergent, rubbing gently to remove all traces of color (b). Allow to thoroughly air dry.

FIX

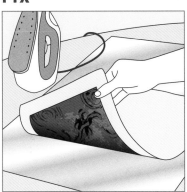

Follow manufacturer's instructions for fixing color. If heat fixing, place aluminum foil, shiny side up, on ironing board. Place fabric, color side down, on foil. Use pressing cloth to press with dry iron at hottest setting for fabric. Move iron to prevent scorching.

APPLYING COLOR: STAMPING

Stamping is a quick and easy way to decorate fabric, whether carried out as a technique in its own right or in conjunction with other surface design methods. Choose from the many commercially-made stamps available, or, to avoid copyright issues, use textured everyday items or make your own stamps. Any of the colors featured on pages 60–61 will work for stamping; experiment to find your preferred medium. Detailed designs and crisp lines are best attained using inks or ink pads. Reload stamp with color each time, or make a second print without reloading for a subtle look. When designing letters or numbers remember that a stamp will produce its mirror image on fabric. Always test a stamp on scrap fabric to prime it and establish how much pressure to apply. Clean stamps with a soft toothbrush.

EQUIPMENT

Stamp-carving media: erasers, rubber, styrofoam tray/plate, craft foam. For base: cardboard, plastic or wood. Soft-lead pencil, tracing paper, brayer, cutting mat & tools, craft knife, non water-soluble glue, sponge, ink pad, spoon, Plexiglas plate, heat gun.

TRANSFER DESIGN

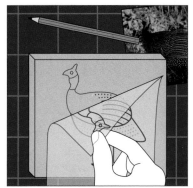

Draw design on tracing paper with soft-lead pencil. Place tracing, pencil side down, on the stamp-carving media you have chosen to use (rubber or erasers work best). Burnish back of paper to transfer pencil lines onto stamp media. Or cut out design and trace around it.

CARVE A STAMP

Use utility knife and carving tool to incise image on rubber or foam. Start carving delicate inner details with fine blade; switch to larger blade to cut away bigger pieces to depth of 1/8"/3mm. Move block rather than the blade, pushing tool away from you.

GLUE A STAMP

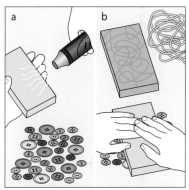

Cut shapes from cardboard, rubber, craft foam or polystyrene. Or use string, trim, bubble wrap, keys, buttons, steel wool, beads or other textured household items. Glue shapes to cardboard, plastic or wooden base using glue that is not water-soluble.

PRESS A STAMP

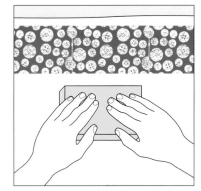

Use moldable craft foam to press stamps. Arrange dimensional object(s) on work area. Cut foam to size; heat one side with a heat gun until surface is shiny (a). Press heated surface firmly on dimensional object(s) for 30 seconds to make reusable stamp (b).

APPLY COLOR TO STAMP

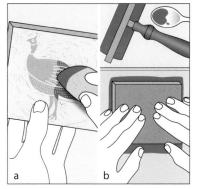

Spoon color on Plexiglas plate. For small stamp, dip sponge in color and lightly pounce an even coating on raised areas of stamp (a). For large stamp, roll brayer on plate to spread color smoothly out to size of stamp. Press stamp firmly on color (b).

If using an inkpad, pounce stamp lightly onto inkpad rather than pressing it down heavily. Repeat until all raised areas are evenly coated with ink but without getting color into the incised details of the design. Reload with ink for each stamp.

STAMP

For best results, work on foam or a padded surface; see page 68. To stamp, bring loaded stamp straight down on fabric without shifting it. Press firmly and evenly with your hands, then smoothly lift stamp straight up off the fabric without rotating it.

APPLYING COLOR: PAINTING

Painting fabric gives the art quilter ultimate control over the finished piece. There are countless ways to paint fabric and a few of these are covered on these pages. Even if your drawing capabilites are somewhat limited, you can still pick up a brush and try some of the techniques that rely on serendipity rather than sketching skills.

If you find it difficult facing a blank canvas, pencil in some outlines to fill with color. Or use a photo as the basis for a design. Simplify the main image, tracing the outlines on a sheet of paper before transferring them to fabric.

Alternatively, use a fine brush to paint highlights or subtle details on a printed or appliquéd design. Allow your imagination free rein—the sky doesn't have to be blue, or the grass green. Study colors and essential steps on pages 60–62 before beginning.

EQUIPMENT

Bristle and sponge brushes in different sizes, foam rollers, brayers, palette knife, sponge, old rolling pin or thick dowel, syringes, pipettes, droppers, bottles with nozzles, white and dark mechanical pencils, palette or plate for paint, textured items, string, cardboard.

WET PAINTING

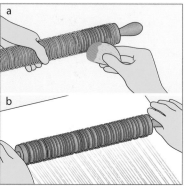

1 Painting wet or damp fabric will encourage color to bleed and spread, creating a homogenous appearance. Dampen fabric or spread on work area and spritz with water. Use large brush to apply color with sweeping strokes, blending edges together.

PAINTED TEXTURE

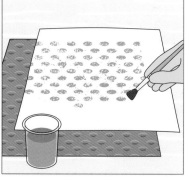

Place dry fabric over textured surface. Dip brush in thickened color; tap to remove excess. Brush color across fabric to transfer texture. Color of background fabric will show through, so try using dyed or printed fabric to introduce other color if desired.

ROLLED TEXTURE

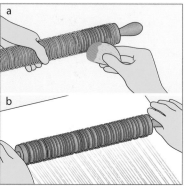

Glue thick string around old rolling pin or dowel. Dab on color with sponge (a). Roll, pressing firmly, on fabric pinned to padded surface (see page 68) so it doesn't move. Design will repeat, then fade as color runs out (b). Dab on new color; roll from light end.

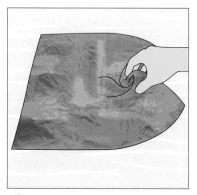

2 Or, use foam brush to spread 2–3 colors across damp fabric, blending edges as little as possible. Scrunch fabric and leave to dry. Colors will mingle and the wrinkles that form will create lines that will add a textured look to fabric; see result on page 62.

SHIBORI

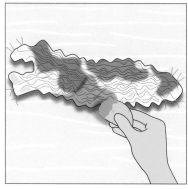

See Indigo-Dyed Shibori on pages 56–57 for stitched resist methods. Work with small pieces of fabric as textile colors/inks won't soak through many layers. Brush and dab colors on fabric that has been stitched or scrunched. Dry overnight, then remove resists.

SUN PRINTING

Some textile colors are suitable for sun printing. Tape fabric to plastic-covered cardboard; paint with one or more colors following manufacturer's instructions. Arrange flat objects or stencils on wet paint. Place in the sun or under a sun lamp until dry. Iron reverse side to fix.

EXPANDABLE PAINT

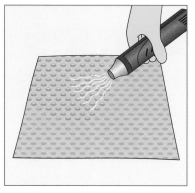

Mix expandable paint with color or use in white or black. Apply thin layer onto fabric with brush, spatula or foam roller; allow to dry for 6 hours. Gently iron face down on towel for 3 minutes without pressure, or heat with hair dryer or heat tool to expand medium.

FUSIBLE WEB

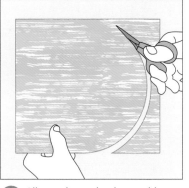

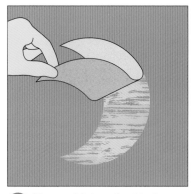

1 Painting a fine fusible web will create an "appliqué" that requires no stitching. Place Misty Fuse (a lightweight paper-less web) or the textured side of regular fusible web on plastic surface. Apply thin coat of diluted color.

2 Allow color to dry thoroughly; wetness of color may cause paper backing (if using) to buckle. This will not affect finished work but will add the impression of texture to the appliqué. When fully dry, cut out painted web into desired shape.

3 Place on fabric, paint side down, cover with baking parchment and press for a minute with a hot dry iron. Remove parchment. If using paper backing, carefully peel it off the fused web when cool, leaving only the painted web on the fabric.

WHOLECLOTH PAINTINGS

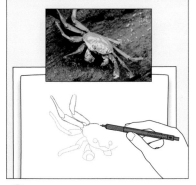

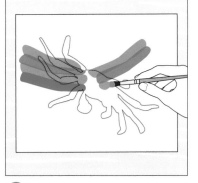

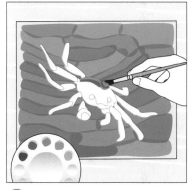

1 Many quilt artists enjoy painting on fabric, then layering and quilting it. Refer to Sizing & Marking Designs on pages 34–35 to transfer a design to fabric. Use fabric inks to paint dry fabric, using extender rather than water. Mix with white for pale color.

2 If painting a background, make freezer paper stencil(s) of main image(s). Iron on fabric in correct position. Paint background from middle of stencil outward so edges of freezer paper do not lift. Allow to dry thoroughly before removing stencil(s).

3 Add highlights or create texture on background using transparent colors: paint with diluted color, let dry; overlap with new layer of color. Then remove stencil when background is dry. Paint main design with fine brush, mixing colors to create a graded sequence.

SHADING COLOR

MISTAKES

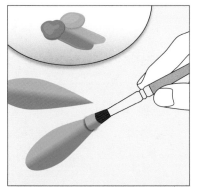

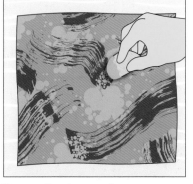

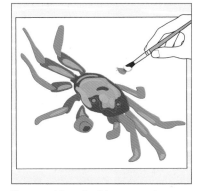

For blended 2-color stroke, place both colors next to each other on flat surface. Load brush with both colors at same time; tap off excess. Brush on fabric in smooth even stroke. Twist brush slightly at the end while lifting to make a point—good for leaves and petals.

You can disguise an unfortunate splodge of color due to a drip or having too much paint on the brush. Dip sponge in contrasting color. Dab splodge lightly with sponge to break it up and add some textural interest.

If you accidentally drip some color in the wrong place, carefully paint over it with a color that matches the background fabric. If the mistake can't be covered in this way, make a feature of it.

APPLYING COLOR: STENCILING

Stenciling is an excellent way to transfer crisp graphic designs to fabric. Because you can place a stencil exactly where you want it, this technique is very effective for adding details and highlights, as well as text and images.

You can buy ready-made stencils from a variety of sources, or find copyright-free stencil designs in books or on the internet. Or use plastic items with open spaces—see *Found Stencils*, right. Art quilters may prefer to make their own stencils; instructions for doing this are given here. When designing a stencil, keep it simple and remember to connect the internal elements (islands) with bridges so that the central areas don't fall out.

Use well-pressed natural fiber fabric with a smooth surface for the best results. Tape fabric to a non-slip surface that is easy to clean. Load a stencil brush or sponge with color, using as little color as possible, and pounce the brush or sponge on the fabric to transfer the color. It's better to apply another layer than to have too much color that may saturate the fabric or bleed under the stencil. Work with dry brushes and use a different one for each color. Experiment with sponges, steel wool pads, etc. for a textured look.

Refer to pages 60–61 for the colors that can be used when stenciling. Use thickened color to prevent it from seeping beneath the stencil. If reusing the same stencil elsewhere, clean the back to ensure that you don't transfer unwanted color to the new area. Clean brushes and reusable stencils directly after use; allow to dry thoroughly. Store stencils flat in a protective envelope.

You can also use stencils to screen print (pages 68–71), discharge (pages 76–77) and apply foil to fabric (pages 78–79).

EQUIPMENT

Freezer paper or sticky-back contact paper, template plastic or Mylar, craft knife or heat tool. Flat-topped stiff stencil brushes, foam brushes, sea or cosmetic sponges, mini foam roller with handle, tape, spray adhesive, flat plastic plates, paper towels, soft toothbrush.

MAKING STENCILS

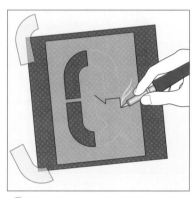

1 Draw design on sticky-back contact paper or freezer paper. Cut out using a craft knife as shown on page 69. Internal design details must connect to main stencil with bridges, or unattached central areas will fall out. Leave at least 1½"/4cm margin around the edges.

2 If making stencil in Mylar or other plastic, use a heat tool for cutting. Clearly mark outlines of design on plastic. Working on a heatproof surface, lightly guide tip of heat tool on plastic following marked lines. For straight line, use heat tool with metal-edge ruler.

FOUND STENCILS

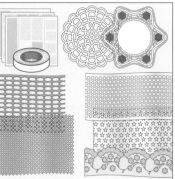

For reusable stencils, find plastic items with open areas such as sequin waste, mesh and fencing in various sizes and weights, lacy mats and doilies, etc. For one-off stencils, use masking tape and paper, cut or ripped into shapes. Use wide tape for straight lines.

NEGATIVE IMAGE

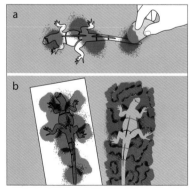

Cut-out parts of a stencil can be used as stencils in their own right to print a negative image. Carefully cut out shape and secure to fabric. Apply color around shape (a); it will remain background color. Also try flipping stencils over to get a reversed image (b).

SECURE

Stencil must be attached securely to fabric to prevent color from leaking underneath it. Spray back of stencil lightly with fabric adhesive and press in place on fabric. Alternatively, use double-sided tape or, if using freezer paper stencil, iron it onto fabric.

LOAD COLOR

If using liquid color, pour a small amount on plastic plate. Ensure that color is thick and not runny. Lightly dip tip of brush or sponge into paint, then tap on plate several times to work paint into bristles or sponge. Then dab on paper towel to remove excess color.

TECHNIQUE

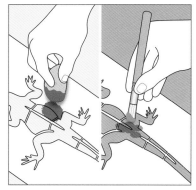

1 Holding loaded sponge or brush vertically, pounce evenly up and down over stencil openings to fill with color. Test pressure to ensure color does not leak beneath stencil but gives good coverage. Reload sponge or brush; tap several times. Dab off excess. Repeat.

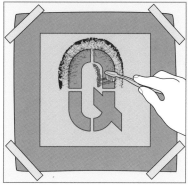

2 Alternatively, apply color with a foam roller. Pour color on plate and roll out with foam roller until color is fully absorbed. Roll on paper towel to remove excess color, then roll over open areas of stencil several times to transfer color.

PAINTSTIKS

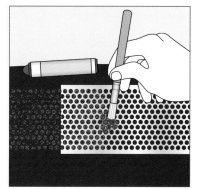

Prepare paintstik for use as directed on page 79. Rub paintstik on plate, then load brush or sponge from plate. Using circular or scrubbing motion and exerting some pressure, apply color through stencil openings. Color from paintstiks will not leak under stencil.

AIR BRUSH

Read and follow the manufacturer's instructions for using air brush; use scrap fabric to test that all equipment is working properly. Hold airbrush like a pen. Spray color in light coats through stencil openings; do not saturate fabric. Clean equipment carefully when done.

BLENDING

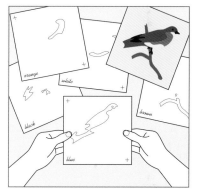

To create a blended, shaded effect, use a soft clean toothbrush to drag color from edges of stencil toward middle of open area. Apply color on edge of stencil opening; gently drag color off the edge of the stencil and onto the fabric. Rub color lightly into fabric.

MULTIPLE COLORS

Cut a different stencil for each color of design, being sure to draw registration marks on each stencil so design matches up. Write color to be used on each stencil to prevent confusion. Use each stencil in turn; allow color to dry thoroughly before adding new color.

MASKING

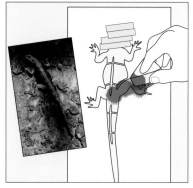

To make a multicolored stencil design without cutting more than one stencil, block off the parts of the design you do not wish to color by covering those openings with masking tape. Or, slip paper or plastic beneath stencil to mask off certain areas.

MULTIPLE LAYERS

Make same stencil design in different sizes and overlap to create an impression of depth. Always allow stenciled design to dry (or use a hair dryer) before applying new colors. Create multi-layered design using a variety of different stencils.

REMOVE STENCIL

When color is dry, carefully lift stencil to check design. If you missed a spot, replace stencil and redo. If using contact or freezer paper, gently pull fabric on bias so edges lift, then remove. Clean off any color on back of stencil before using it again.

APPLYING COLOR: SCREEN PRINTING

Screen printing enables art quilters and textile designers to create patterned fabrics that are exciting and unique. While this technique may seem daunting, it is actually quite simple. A resist such as a stencil mask or screen filler is applied to a fine fabric screen held taut in a frame. A color medium is then "pulled" across the screen with a squeegee. The pressure from this action forces the color through the screen and onto the fabric beneath. Then the frame is carefully lifted and moved to another spot where the process is repeated. While the procedure is straightforward, the potential for creativity and innovation is unlimited.

Depending on how you apply a resist to the screen, you can make a series of images that are virtually the same or that change slightly with each print. Crisp reproductions or fractured impressions can result. Screen printing can also be used to discharge images on fabric, to reproduce photos or scans with a Thermofax (page 71), to conceal unloved fabric, or to create a complex multi-printed textile. The possibilities are as endless as they are exhilarating.

Purchase a framed screen with a 110xx/43T multifilament mesh from an art supply store or the internet; choose a size larger than the designs you wish to print. Buy squeegees that feel good in your hand and that fit nicely inside the frame. The amount of pressure on the squeegee is important, so always test the pressure required to make effective pulls on scrap fabrics before you actually begin printing.

Study page 61 for information on the different color media that can be used for screen printing. Most popular are fabric inks/pigments specially created for this method, followed by acrylic-based textile colors/paints. Use a transparent extender to make textile colors go further and to slow down their drying time on the screen. Alternatively, use thickened Procion MX dyes; recipe is on page 61. Fabrics printed with dyes must be treated with soda ash, batched and rinsed as for other dyed fabrics; see Dyeing: Essential Steps on pages 46–47.

While thickened dyes can be left on the screen (see *Deconstructed Screen Printing* on page 70), do not allow acrylic media to dry on the screen or the screen will be ruined. Wash the screen gently between printing sessions and allow to dry before using it again.

Unless you have a space dedicated to printing, it's best to make a portable padded surface that is easy to store when not in use, and which can also be used for other surface design techniques. Use fabric drop cloths to protect the printing surface and wash them after each session.

EQUIPMENT

Padded printing surface, drop cloths, fine pins, pfd fabric for printing, framed screen, duct tape, squeegee, color, transparent print paste and/or extender, plastic gloves, plastic spoons, plastic waste pot for unwanted color, plastic lidded containers to store leftover color.

PREPARE FRAME

Cover all wooden parts of frame with duct tape to protect it from moisture. Overlap screen with tape by ½"/12mm on 3 sides of frame, and 1"/2.5cm along top edge to form a well for placing the color. Allow tape to bond to frame for 24 hours before using.

COLOR

See text (left) and study page 61 for description of color media that can be used for screen printing. Color should have a creamy consistency that will vary depending on fabric you are using and desired finished effect. Always test color on scrap fabric before beginning.

PADDED SURFACE

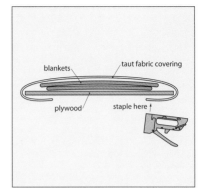

A padded surface is useful for many surface design techniques. Cover desired size piece of plywood with padding such as old blankets. Stretch muslin/calico taut over padding; staple to underside of plywood. Smooth away wrinkles (which would transfer to prints).

PREPARE FABRIC

Scour all fabrics to be printed, including pfd (prepared for dyeing) fabrics, to remove any dirt, oil or finishes; see page 46. Press carefully. If printing with thickened dyes, pre-soak fabric in soda ash solution; see pages 46–47. Hang treated fabric to dry before using.

PRINT PASTE

Use clear dye thickener/print paste (or Superclear or Manutex) for Procion MX dyes; see page 61. Print paste is also used for deconstructed screen printing and to wet water-soluble crayons, pencils and Aqua Briques for multicolor prints; see page 70.

MAKING STENCILS

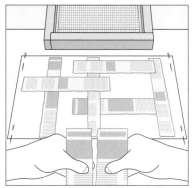

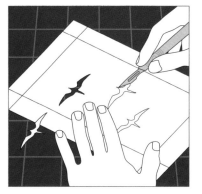

You can make paper stencils from ripped newspaper, scrap paper or shredded paper. Arrange paper design on fabric that has been pinned to padded surface; place screen on top. Pull color across screen. Paper will stick to back of screen for a number of prints.

Use masking tape as a stencil. Rip tape to make edges irregular; adhere to back of screen. Make several prints; remove tape. Clean screen. Allow fabric to dry. Tape different arrangement on screen; print again. *Screen printed with masking tape and other stencils by Marlene Cohen.*

Draw design on sticky-back contact paper or freezer paper. Place on cutting mat; cut out areas you wish to print with craft knife—solid areas will block color. Adhere sticky side of contact paper to back of screen or press freezer paper in place with iron.

SCREEN PRINTING

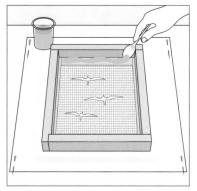

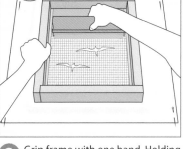

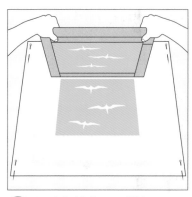

1 Smooth fabric to be printed on drop cloth placed over padded printing surface; pin so fabric won't move when screen is lifted. Position screen over area to be printed. Pour, squirt or spoon line of color in the well (created by duct tape) inside top edge of screen.

2 Grip frame with one hand. Holding squeegee in other hand, pull color firmly across screen in smooth steady movement, pushing color through screen onto fabric beneath. Scoop up excess color at end of pull; deposit back in well. Repeat pull if necessary.

3 Carefully lift frame off fabric so you do not smear print. Reposition in another area; make second print. Do not place frame over wet color or it may transfer to fabric. Allow color to dry completely. Scrape any leftover color into plastic waste pot for later use.

SCREEN FILLER

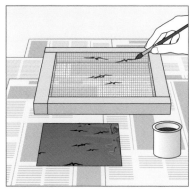

Use screen filler to paint a permanent stencil design on screen; painted areas will not print. Work from back of screen so surface is elevated. Use paintbrush or roller to apply screen filler in desired design. When screen filler is dry, screen is ready to print.

WASH SCREEN

When printing is done, quickly rinse off any color/media from screen. Fabric paint/printing ink or other acrylic media left in screen will become permanent or will ruin screen. Gently wash screen and squeegees in warm soapy water with soft sponge. Allow to dry thoroughly.

FIX COLOR

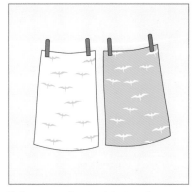

Follow manufacturer's instructions to permanently fix color. For textile colors or screen printing inks, hang to dry for 24 hours; press with dry iron between layers of parchment. For dyes, batch; see page 46. Wash in pH-neutral fabric detergent or Synthrapol after fixing.

Screen printing will replicate the same image over and over again, but that is usually not what art quilters want to do. Once the basics of screen printing have been mastered, it doesn't take long for designers to experiment, creating different results each time they make a print. Changing the type of color medium, varying the textures over which it is printed, and printing again over the finished piece are just some of the ways this can be accomplished.

There is another way to create unplanned effects that is not only great fun but highly effective. The process, invented by Kerr Grabowski, is called deconstructed screen printing. With this method, thickened Procion MX dye is applied to the screen and allowed to dry—it can be painted in a design or squeegeed on the screen over textured household objects to create an overall pattern. The screen with the dried dye medium is then placed on fabric. When print paste is pulled across the screen, the dried dye will randomly dissolve and release onto the fabric beneath. With each print, the design will degenerate. The same image can never be replicated, but will gradually change and develop, making designs that are completely individual yet related to one another.

Alternatively, you can make the same crystal-clear prints using a Thermofax machine (a type of mimeograph copier). A high-contrast photocopy of a photograph, scan or line drawing (made using carbon toner in a laser printer) is burned onto Thermofax film when passed through the machine, making a stencil. You can buy a Thermofax machine or send your designs to companies that will make the screens for you.

DECONSTRUCTED SCREEN PRINTING

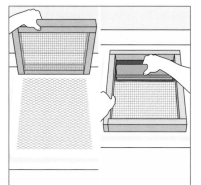

1 This is a two-step process. Place screen over a textured surface such as the mesh fruit bag shown here. Add thickened Procion MX dye to the screen's well; pull firmly several times to transfer textured pattern to screen. Lift screen; allow dye medium to dry fully.

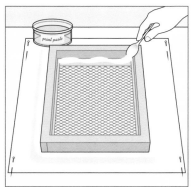

2 When screen has completely dried, place on fabric to be printed. Add clear print paste to well and pull squeegee over screen a few times to wet the dye medium and release it onto fabric beneath. Lift screen to reveal image. First print may be disappointing.

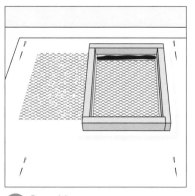

3 Reposition screen on new area. Add more print paste to well; pull squeegee several times over screen. After each pull, dye on screen will disintegrate and transfer unpredictably to fabric below. Add color to print paste as shown here to introduce a new element.

OTHER IDEAS

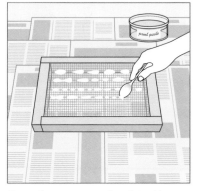

Use syringe, spoon or brush to drip, doodle, write or sketch a design on screen with clear print paste. Allow paste to dry; squeegee with thickened dye to create series of prints. Or color print paste with dye, apply to screen, dry, then release with clear print paste.

MULTICOLOR PRINTING

Try using water-soluble crayons and pencils or Aqua Briques for color. Draw a design on screen or place screen over uneven surface; rub firmly with colors to create texture. Lay colors thickly on screen for best results. Squeegee with clear print paste.

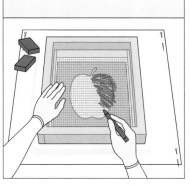

To make multicolor print with sharp edges, place stencil beneath screen; apply color thickly over stencil openings. Squeegee with clear print paste to release color. Continue to print until color has been released from screen. Wash screen.

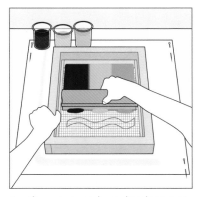

Another way to make multicolor prints is to add several different blobs of color to the well. Pull color across screen, which will print a blend of different colors at the same time. Do not make too many pulls or colors will mix and turn muddy.

WATER-SOLUBLE GLUE

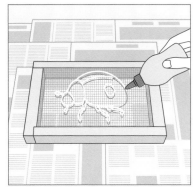

Draw design on raised screen using blue (or white) school gel or other water-soluble glue. Leave to dry. Place on fabric, add color to well; pull color across screen with squeegee. As glue gets wet, it will dissolve, resulting in decomposing effects.

SOY WAX

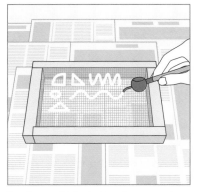

Read page 84 for instructions on using soy wax. Paint or drip wax onto back of screen; allow to harden. Screen print—waxed areas will resist the color. Wash screen carefully immediately after printing to remove wax and any color media left in screen.

EXPANDABLE PAINT

Read manufacturer's instructions for using expandable paint. Place stencil behind screen; squeegee paint through stencil openings onto fabric. Remove screen; wash immediately. Let paint dry for time specified; use iron, heat gun or hair dryer to puff paint.

DISCHARGE

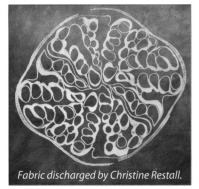

Fabric discharged by Christine Restall.

See Discharging on pages 76–77. You can discharge fabrics dyed or printed with Procion MX dyes using a screen. Add thickened bleach, deColourant or other discharge paste to screen's well; squeegee. Clean screen immediately. Rinse and neutralize fabric.

THERMOFAX PRINTING

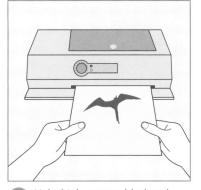

1 Make high contrast black and white carbon-toner photocopy of an image on a laser printer. Cut a piece of Thermofax film larger than image. Center film, shiny side down, over photocopy. Run both layers carefully through the Thermofax machine.

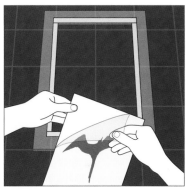

2 Adhere double-sided tape around inner edges of a plastic Thermofax frame. Gently separate Thermofax film from photocopy—it will make a ripping sound as image pulls away from film. Stretch and mount film smoothly on taped frame, shiny side up.

ADDING DETAILS

3 Place framed image, shiny side down, on flat surface. Wrap edges of frame with duct tape on both sides, overlapping textured side of film along top edge by 1"/2.5cm to make a well for the color.

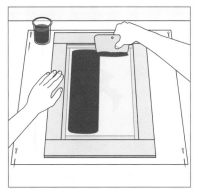

4 Place framed image, shiny side down on fabric. Apply color to well; use lightweight squeegee to pull color across screen. Do not push too hard on screen or you may damage it. Lift frame carefully. When finished, clean screen; allow to dry before reusing.

After prints are dry and set, add more detail and complexity to design using fabric paints, foils, pens, etc. Or use a screen to overprint on top of previous designs with more color or with discharge paste to remove color from dyed areas. *Screen print by the author.*

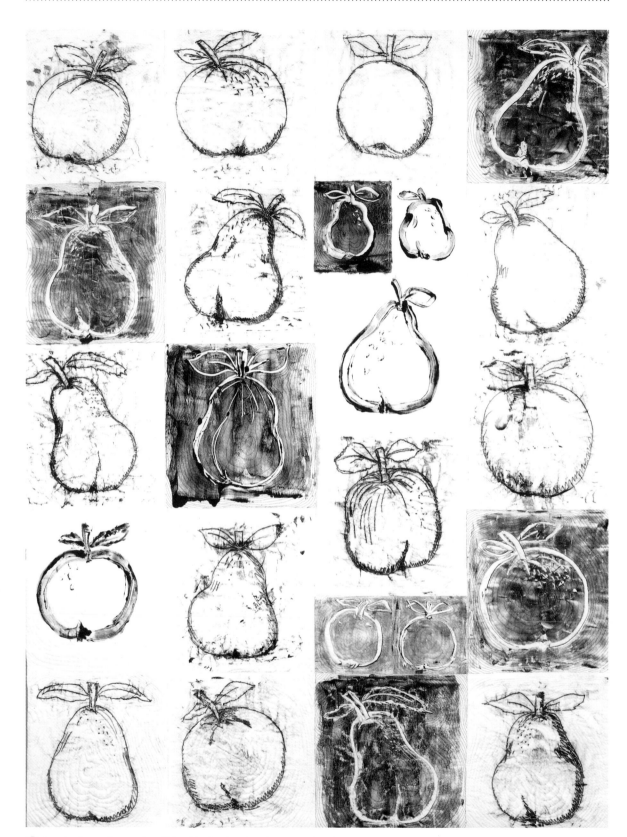

⬆ Pear, Apple—©Christine Restall, Hamble, UK. Photo by Mike Watson. One of a series using apples and pears to express human emotion. White cotton fabric, black acrylic paint. Three different monoprinting methods: direct print of a drawing, print of drawing scratched on black paint, drawing on fabric laid on top of black paint. Free-motion machine quilted. 51 x 67"/129 x 170cm. 2012.

⬇ Many Moons 1—©Leslie Morgan, Crawley, West Sussex, UK. This piece is a response to the passage of time and the wisdom of hindsight. Cotton fabrics: hand-dyed, shibori (clamp) resist, screen printed, hand painted; commercial prints by Nancy Crow and Loni Rossi. Machine pieced, free-motion machine quilted. 68 x 42"/172 x 106cm. 2013.

◀ Indian Summer—©Margaret Applin, Lowell, Massachusetts. The artist started with a paper monoprint of a real leaf and stem. She scanned that image into Photoshop Elements, then layered and blended it with additional imagery. The final image was printed onto a silk inkjet printer sheet and secured to a collaged background of coffee-stained white cotton batting. Silk fabric, cotton batting, collage background, copper beads and wire. Free-motion machine quilted, painted, embellished with beads and copper wire pounded to flatten the ends. 16 x 17"/41 x 43cm. 2011.

APPLYING COLOR: MONOPRINTING

A monoprint is an individual, one-off design printed on fabric. There are two ways to make a monoprint. You can add color to a printing plate and manipulate it to create a design (the additive method), or roll a light coating of color on the plate and then remove some of it to produce an image (the subtractive method). Both methods can be done by drawing with a finger or stylus, pressing or rubbing on textured items, or using surface design techniques such as painting, stamping and stenciling. Because almost all of the color transfers to the fabric, it is possible to make only one satisfactory print. However, there is usually enough color left on the plate to make a second print, known as a ghost print because it is much lighter and more subtle than the first one.

In this book, "print plate" refers to a dedicated printing surface that can be made of Plexiglas, glass, freezer paper, home-made gelatin or a purchased reusable Gelli plate. If using glass or plastic, make sure the edges are smooth or protected with tape. Using freezer paper makes it easy to clean up.

You can make a gelatin print plate using the recipe given on page 75. Gelatin has a malleable, responsive surface that feels good beneath the hands, but will slowly break down over time. This deterioration creates new textures and patterns that can be exploited. Or, purchase a reusable Gelli plate; it is slightly harder than gelatin but will last a long time if cared for properly.

Read Applying Color on pages 60–62 for the types of color that can be used and basic practices. Thickened liquid color/paint, inks or dyes are the best choices for this technique. Texture is an important element, so collect found objects to enhance your prints; see *For Texture* (above right) for some ideas.

EQUIPMENT

For print plate, use Plexiglas, glass, freezer paper, gelatine powder & tray or Gelli Arts Gel Plate. Liquid color, pfd fabric, gloves, foam brushes, brayers, palette knife, spoon, masking tape, styrofoam or foamcore, pen or stylus, 3D objects for printing (see page 75).

FOR TEXTURE

Fingers, stamps, combs, cord, string, wooden sticks, cotton swabs, crumpled paper or foil, lace, paper clips, thick trim or yarn, netting, elastic bands, bubble wrap, foam shapes, corks, coins, leaves, feathers, buttons, textured plastic items, bath mats, doilies, fencing, etc.

BASIC MONOPRINTING TECHNIQUE

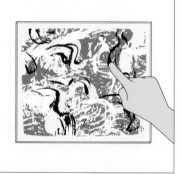

1a For the print plate, use Plexiglas or glass, or tape freezer paper shiny side up on protected work area. For an additive monoprint, squirt one or more thickened colors on paper or plate. Manipulate color(s) with brush, brayer or gloved fingers to make a design.

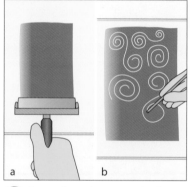

1b For a subtractive monoprint, brayer color(s) smoothly on print plate (a). Incise a design (b) or press a textured object into color on plate to remove the color. (Or brayer color on plate, lay fabric lightly on top and draw design with a stick or brush handle through the cloth.)

STAMP

You can also "stamp" a monoprint. Apply color to plate or freezer paper as in step 1a or 1b. Carefully pick up plate/paper by the edges; invert on fabric taped to work surface. Press plate or paper firmly and evenly on fabric. Lift or peel up without shifting.

2 When satisfied with design, carefully lay fabric face down on colored print plate, taking care not to shift it. Using your hands or brayer, gently and evenly press fabric into the color, running hands or brayer smoothly over fabric until it absorbs the color.

3 Carefully peel fabric off colored print plate and hang to dry. Make a second (ghost) print with new fabric or add more color to print plate and make an entirely new print in same manner. Immediately after finishing, clean print plate and tools thoroughly.

RESISTS

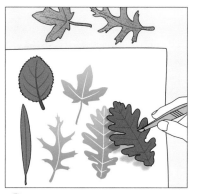

1 Use leaves, feathers, toothpicks, cut shapes, masking tape, etc. to act as resists. Brayer print plate with color(s), then place resists on top. Place fabric over plate; make a monoprint. Lift off fabric. Make ghost print if desired. Remove painted resists from plate.

2 Don't waste the painted resists! Use tweezers to place painted items, color side down, on new fabric. Cover with freezer paper or scrap fabric and brayer or rub with your hands to transfer the color. Ensure that painted item does not shift or it will blur.

STENCIL

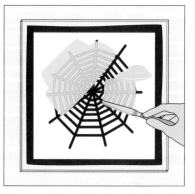

Place stencil on print plate. Apply color to edge of stencil; use palette knife to spread color through stencil openings. Carefully peel off stencil. Lay fabric on plate; make monoprint. You can also brayer color on print plate first (as shown here) then stencil color on top.

GELATIN PRINTING

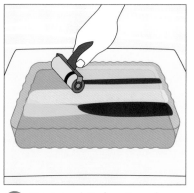

1 Pour water into foil or metal tray to ¾"/2cm depth; measure amount. For each 1 cup/250ml water, add 2tbl/30g powdered gelatine. Stir gelatine into half the water; boil rest of water, then stir back in until dissolved with no bubbles. Cover; refrigerate until firm.

2 Remove gelatin from tray; place on freezer paper. Apply 1–3 colors; brayer and blend slightly. Add a resist or incise a design, being careful not to cut gelatin. Monoprint. Gelatin will eventually break down; try using broken bits to monoprint for added texture.

GELLI PLATE

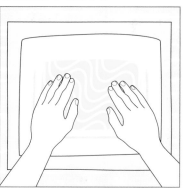

Peel off protective film; place on covered work area. Brayer thin layer of color on plate. Gently incise designs with tools or fingers or press objects on plate to remove color. Monoprint. Clean plate gently with water and cover with protective film when finished.

PRINTING TEXT ON GEL PLATES

1 Use styrofoam food packaging trays/plates or foamcore (available in most hobby stores—peel off paper on one side to expose foam). Cut to size. Use stylus or ballpoint pen to incise words or a design into foam. Apply liquid color; brayer color evenly on foam.

2 Make monoprint to remove surface color from foam, leaving color in incised areas only. Invert foam on gel plate. Brayer back of foam to transfer color in grooves onto gel. Lift up foam. Monoprint design with fresh fabric. Print will not be reversed so is good for text.

3D OBJECTS

Use paint brush or brayer to coat dimensional objects with color, such as keys, plastic animals or other flattish toys, seashells, fish, etc. Drape fabric over colored object. Gently rub with fingers to transfer color and texture to fabric. Lift off carefully.

DISCHARGING

Discharging is the process of selectively removing color from dyed fabrics with chemicals. There are two ways to do this: through an oxidative process with chlorine bleach or through a reductive process with discharge paste (Jacquard, deColourant), Formusol, Thiourea dioxide (Thiox) or Rongalit. There are books and websites devoted to the different methods and effects of using these chemicals. This section covers the two most popular ways for discharging cellulose fibers: chlorine bleach and discharge paste For further reading refer to the Bibliography.

How fabrics discharge their dye depends on many factors: the time the solution is on the fabric, the type of dye, fabric thickness and weight, humidity, temperature, sunlight, etc. Not all fabrics will discharge their dyes. Some dyes will not go white, but become a lighter shade or even a different color. Discharging is not predictable, and it shouldn't be undertaken lightly—see Health & Safety Rules. However, it can be an exciting and astonishing technique, making all the preparation and time worthwhile.

Pre-wash and iron the dyed cellulose fabrics you wish to discharge, choosing dark or very bright colors for the best results. Bleaching works quickly and directly on the fibers to remove color, but it can also damage them if it is not removed completely using sodium metabisulfite (Anti-Chlor). Reductive solutions such as discharge paste need to be activated with steam and heat, but will not damage the fabric as they affect only the dye molecules. Once the discharged fabrics have been neutralized and rinsed, they can be overdyed or subjected to many other surface design treatments.

Health & Safety Rules

- Always wear an apron, rubber gloves, goggles and a respirator with an acid gas cartridge.
- Always work outside or in a well-ventilated area as the chemicals have a strong odor.
- Use only tools and containers dedicated to discharging—do not re-use for food preparation.
- Make test samples.
- Never use bleach on silk or wool.
- Always neutralize bleached fabric.
- Measure powders and solutions quickly and carefully, wearing full safety equipment; recap containers immediately.
- Work away from children/pets.
- Leftover discharge solutions can be poured down a foul drain or lavatory (not in the garden or in a septic tank).

EQUIPMENT

Discharge chemicals, Anti-Chlor, pre-washed dyed cellulose fabric, respirator with acid gas cartridge, goggles, gloves, apron, plastic buckets, newspaper, flat plate, spoons, spray bottle, foam brush and roller, stamps, stencils, string, thread, freezer paper, masking tape.

Immersion discharge: Make an immersion bath using one part household bleach to five parts warm water. Prepare fabric with resists (page 77). Immerse in bath for up to 10 minutes; check color continually. Remove fabric, rinse and neutralize (below right).

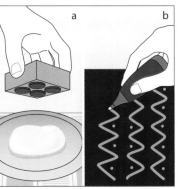

Discharge with thickened bleach: Use thickened chlorine bleach found in household cleaning/dishwashing gels (a) or bleach pens (b) for stamping, stenciling, monoprinting, screen printing and drawing. These must be rinsed and neutralized (next step).

CHLORINE BLEACH

Fabric immersion discharged in bleach by Lisa Reber.

Basic preparations: Read Health & Safety Rules. Protect work area with newspaper. If outside, work with your back to the wind. Apply bleach as below; allow to discharge for up to 10 minutes or until fabric is desired color. Rinse and neutralize fabric (below).

Spray discharge: Make bleach solution as for immersion discharge; pour into spray bottle. Prepare fabric with resists or place flat on newspaper; spray with bleach solution. Allow bleach to work for up to 10 minutes or until fabric is desired color. Rinse & neutralize (below).

RINSE & NEUTRALIZE

Fill one bucket with water and another with enough Anti-Chlor solution to just cover fabric. After discharging with bleach, immediately open out fabric (wearing gloves) and rinse in water, then place in Anti-Chlor for 5 minutes, agitating often. Rinse; air dry.

DISCHARGE PASTE

① Discharge paste (such as Jacquard or deColourant) removes color with heat and steam without changing the fabric's hand. Read Health & Safety Rules before beginning. Apply paste to dyed fabric using a brush, stamp, stencil, syringe or squeeze bottle with fine nib.

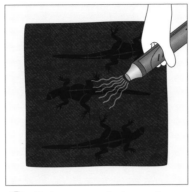

② Discharge paste is clear and not easy to see, so don't apply too much—fabric will just darken from the paste. Allow discharge paste to dry about 10 minutes or dry with heat gun until slightly damp. Do not iron paste right away or design may smear.

③ Protect ironing board and use steam iron devoted to discharge. Set iron to highest heat for fabric. Hover steaming iron over fabric until paste is dry, then press fabric until pattern appears. Continually move iron to prevent marking from sole plate holes.

④ Remove paste after it has fully dried: place fabric on protected ironing surface; cover with old newspaper. Spray newspaper lightly with water. Press, checking fabric frequently. When finished, rinse and wash fabric to remove any remaining paste.

⑤ To discharge a fabric and put a new color in its place all in one step, add textile color to plain discharge paste or use deColourant Plus, which already has pigment in it. Add textile color to plain discharge paste drop by drop until desired shade is achieved.

STITCHED RESISTS

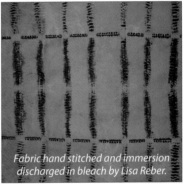

Fabric hand stitched and immersion discharged in bleach by Lisa Reber.

Hand-stitch resists on dark/bright fabric as directed on page 56, or machine baste fabric with carpet thread in bobbin (adjust tension) and quilting thread in needle. Brush on discharge paste or immerse in bleach. Rinse, neutralize; rip out stitches when done.

FOLDED RESISTS

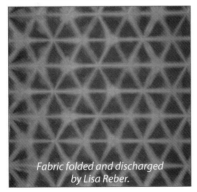

Fabric folded and discharged by Lisa Reber.

Press fabric to be discharged. Fold or pleat; design shown here was fan-folded and clamped with binder clips. Secure with string or elastic bands. Immerse in bleach or paint edges of pleats or folds with discharge paste.

DISCHARGE OVER QUILTING

Quilt discharged by Laura Kemshall.

① Discharging a quilted area creates an uneven result, with stitched areas retaining color and raised areas losing it. Use cotton or wool batting to prevent compression from heat and steam. Quilt so stitching lines are no more than ½"/12mm apart.

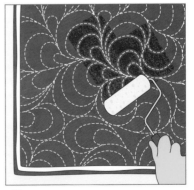

② Load foam roller with discharge paste and roll lightly over quilted areas. Allow paste to dry. Hold steaming iron over paste to initiate color change or use heat gun. If more discharge is desired, press lightly with steam iron.

FOILING, RUBBING & MARKING FABRIC

Any fabric can be enhanced by foiling, rubbing or marking. Adding accents or highlights with these methods and materials will not adversely affect the hand of the fabric, but will impart an exciting sparkle and hint of magic and mystery to an art quilt.

Textile foils are made from shiny plastic attached to cellophane. After the foil is secured to the fabric with an adhesive, the cellophane carrier is gently pulled away, leaving a permanent shiny design on the fabric in the exact shape of the adhesive. Other small, light items such as glitter, sequins, threads or yarns can be adhered to fabric in the same way. Add any decorative elements judiciously and work in layers to ensure that all the additions bond securely.

Color can be rubbed on fabric using paintstiks, oil sticks, oil pastels, fabric crayons and Inktense Blocks. These crayon-like markers are solidified sticks of pigment and wax (many are available in metallic or glitter forms) and are excellent for adding a subtle gleam of color. The attraction of rubbing color on fabric is the texture it adds, as the rubbings will pick up whatever is beneath the fabric. Some art quilters carry fabric and sticks with them to capture the texture of items they encounter every day, such as tree bark, manhole covers, or even the gritty surface of a road or sidewalk.

Fabric can also be marked with paint pens, Inktense pencils and fabric pens or markers. These are good for writing text, outlining images and highlighting.

All of these techniques can also be accomplished on quilted work if applied carefully; see pages 202–203. Before beginning, always read the manufacturer's instructions for the specific product you are using.

EQUIPMENT

Gloves, baking parchment, iron, paper towels, textured items, markers (see text left). For foiling: foil, foil adhesive or fabric glue, fusible web or thread, powder adhesive, foam brush, stylus. For rubbing: paintstiks/oil sticks/oil pastels/fabric crayons, non-slip grip mat.

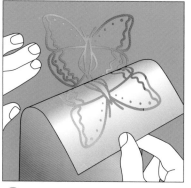

② Place foil colored/shiny side up on top of glued design. Use fingertip or back of spoon to rub foil, transferring foil to glue. Carefully peel off cellophane to expose design. If adhesive still shows or foil is lifting, use more pressure to burnish foil.

COLD FOILING

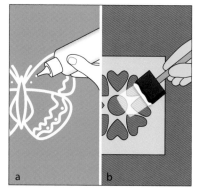

① Apply foil or fabric glue to right side of fabric: use nozzle of bottle to draw design, lines or dots (a); paint glue with brush freehand or use a stencil (b); squeegee glue for screen printing; brayer glue on a stamp. Allow glue to dry 3 hours or until transparent.

HOT FOILING

Apply fusible web, thread or adhesive powder to fabric. Place foil, colored/shiny side up, over design. Using side of iron near tip, apply heat to foil. Push iron away from you, pressing firmly on foil for 3–4 seconds. When foil is cool, carefully peel off cellophane.

FUSIBLE WEB

Use lightweight fusible web as an adhesive. Cut web in desired shape or rip to create rough edges. Press firmly on fabric with hot iron using baking parchment. When cool, peel off backing paper (if using). Adhere foil over fused design, pressing firmly with tip of iron.

FUSIBLE THREAD

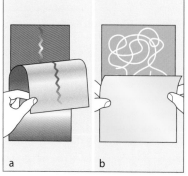

Wind fusible thread in bobbin. Stitch a design on wrong side of fabric, making stitches straight or decorative (a). Fusible thread will be on right side of fabric. Alternatively, arrange fusible thread on right side of fabric in random design (b). Press foil over fusible thread.

ADHESIVE POWDER

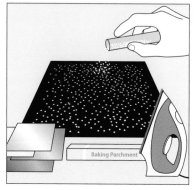

Use adhesive powder for a stippled effect. Sprinkle powder lightly on fabric, spreading it with a stylus or your finger to prevent clumps that will melt together. Cover powder carefully with foil without disturbing its position; press for 3–4 seconds using tip of iron.

MULTICOLORED EFFECTS

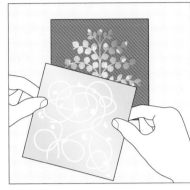

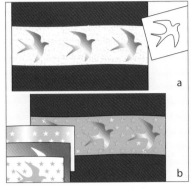

Any foil remaining on cellophane can be transferred to fabric—use leftover bits to add unexpected accents or highlights. For example, if foil has not completely covered adhesive, foil again using new color. If using several colors, foil added last will be dominant.

Use fusible web with stencils for multicolored effects. Adhere fusible web to fabric. Place stencil on top; adhere foil through opening (a); background areas will remain unfoiled. Apply new color foils using different stencils until all areas are covered (b).

GLITTER ETC

Apply adhesive of choice to fabric. Sprinkle with fine glitter, sequins, threads, delicate yarns, fibers, etc. Work in layers, using stylus to arrange pieces attractively. Cover with baking parchment; press with iron to secure. Remove parchment when cool.

RUBBING

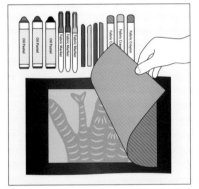

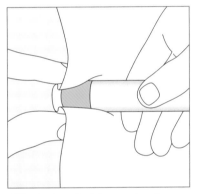

1 Use fabric crayons, oil pastels, oil or paintstiks or Inktense Blocks to rub textured color onto well pressed fabric. Place textured item or rubbing plate under fabric. To prevent fabric from moving, tape securely to work surface or place on a rubber grip mat.

2 If using oil sticks or paintstiks, remove self-sealing film by covering tip with paper towel and twisting gently. Or pare off film with knife. As you work, wipe tip occasionally with paper towel to remove any excess film that forms. Throw away all films/parings carefully.

3 Test color on scrap fabric to determine correct pressure. Holding down edge of fabric, gently glide side of crayon or stick lightly and evenly on fabric over textured item. Work in one direction to prevent fabric from moving and blurring design.

4 You can use stamps as rubbing plates: stretch fabric over stamp and rub gently with side of stick. Move fabric as necessary to make additional rubbings. Allow color to dry for 48 hours, then set following manufacturer's instructions.

DECORATIVE MARKING

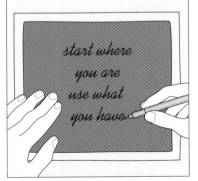

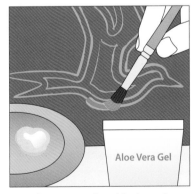

Use fabric markers or paint pens to write text, mark outlines or color specific areas. When writing text, stabilize fabric on freezer paper. Use marker or pen with wide tip for coloring large areas. Follow manufacturer's instructions for permanent color setting.

Use Inktense pencils or blocks to draw or rub a design on fabric. Instead of water, paint plain aloe vera gel or textile medium on marks to intensify color and inhibit bleeding. For speckled effect, grate color from blocks on fabric; spray lightly with water.

BATIK

The ancient art of batik, practiced for centuries by East Asian and African cultures, is experiencing a resurgence in popularity with textile artists all over the world. This method of resist dyeing produces intricate results through the controlled application of hot wax onto fabric. Hot batik wax (a combination of paraffin and beeswax) is brushed, dripped, drawn or stamped onto fabric that is stretched in a frame. When the fabric is dyed or painted, the unwaxed areas absorb the dye while the waxed areas retain the original color. Repeated waxing and dyeing will create a complex rainbow of colors as the dyes overdye and react with one another. It's important to work from light to dark when using multiple colors, keeping in mind how the colors will change each other. The wax is ultimately removed by melting it into soft paper towels and newspaper with a hot dry iron. Residual wax can be removed through dry cleaning or boiling. For a softer hand, immerse the fabric in hot water with some pH-neutral fabric detergent after the wax has been removed.

Methods of applying the wax are many and varied. Natural bristle brushes will paint wax onto fabric. A tjanting (canting) tool is dipped into hot wax which pours out of one or more spouts to create drawn or dotted designs. A traditional tjap (cap), a device made of patterned copper, is used to stamp wax on fabric. Metal household items can also be used.

Use lightweight 100% cotton or silk fabrics for best results. Fabrics must be prepared for dyeing (pfd) before use; see page 46. Heavier fabrics can be used, but wax will need to be applied to the back as any unwaxed areas will allow the dye to penetrate the fibers.

Stretch a small piece of fabric in an embroidery hoop so you can test your tools and become familiar with how the wax soaks into the fabric. If you make accidental drips, turn them into a design feature.

Safety precautions

- Only work in a well-ventilated area; fumes from hot wax are hazardous.
- Heat wax in a batik pot or electric frying pan, never near an open flame, which may cause it to ignite.
- Keep hot wax away from water, which may cause it to splatter.
- Do not leave hot wax unattended.
- Keep a fire extinguisher handy.

EQUIPMENT

Apron, gloves, old newspapers, batik wax pot or electric frying pan, pencil, pfd fabric, stretcher frame, thumbtacks, embroidery hoop, batik wax, Procion MX dyes, tray or bucket for dye, sponge, iron, paper towels, fabric detergent, wash bucket.

TECHNIQUE

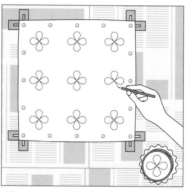

1 Attach pfd fabric to stretcher frame with thumbtacks or pins so that it is taut. Use pencil to sketch simple outlines of design on fabric. Stretch small piece of same fabric in embroidery hoop for testing wax. Place stretched fabrics on old newspapers.

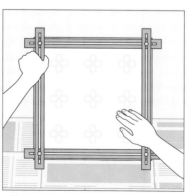

3 Assemble tools and stamps. Apply wax to fabric in one of the following methods. Wax should look clear when first applied. Check back of fabric to see if wax has fully penetrated as shown in illustration; if not, apply more wax to back of fabric.

TOOLS

Specialized batik implements such as tjanting tools and tjaps; natural bristle paint brushes; items for stamping such as corrugated cardboard, cardboard rolls, thread spools; metal kitchen equipment such as a fork, strainer, pastry cutter, potato masher, etc.

2 Ensure work area has proper ventilation. Heat wax in batik pot or electric frying pan to 240°F/115°C, or lowest temperature at which it melts; do not allow wax to overheat or smoke. However, if too cool, wax will just sit on surface of fabric and will not resist dye.

PAINTING WAX

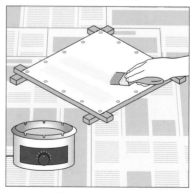

Use natural bristle brushes as synthetic brushes will melt in hot wax. Dip brush in wax and stroke on fabric to create lines that will resist dye; ensure wax has penetrated to the back. Wax cools quickly on brushes, so will require frequent dipping.

TJANTING (CANTING) TOOLS

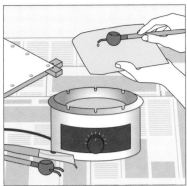

1. Tjanting tools are used to draw wax lines or dots. Nozzles and bowls come in different sizes. Size of spout and heat of wax determine width of waxed line. Dip tjanting tool in hot wax; keep there until bowl heats up. Hold paper towel beneath wax to catch drips.

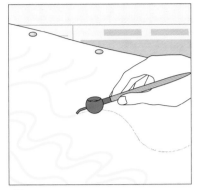

2. Work quickly, following drawn lines. Float spout just above fabric so it just touches the surface, enabling wax to flow smoothly onto the cloth. When wax cools, dip and hold tjanting in hot wax again; proceed as before. If spout clogs, clean with fine wire.

STAMPING

1. A tjap (cap) is a copper stamping tool used to create intricate batik designs. Place fabric on padded surface. Dip tjap in hot wax; hold until tool heats up. Quickly tap off excess wax then swiftly move tjap to stamp fabric. Lift carefully, reload with wax; continue.

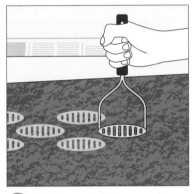

2. Metal household items can be used effectively for stamping wax on fabric. Stretch fabric on padded surface so it absorbs pressure from the stamp. Hold item in the hot wax to heat up, tap off excess, then stamp firmly on fabric. Reload and continue in same way.

CRACKING

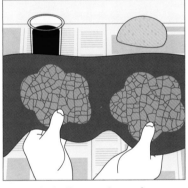

For cracked effect, apply parafin wax to fabric; allow to set. Scrunch waxed fabric so it cracks. Flatten on work surface. Dip sponge in dark dye; rub gently over wax so it penetrates cracks. Allow dye to set. Remove wax to reveal dark cracks.

PAINTED DYE

You can paint dye into areas outlined with wax. Or, paint dye on fabric, then wax over some areas and paint again to create multiple colors as shown here. See pages 64–65 for instructions on how to paint with dye. *Batik painted with dye by students of Jane Brunning.*

IMMERSION DYEING

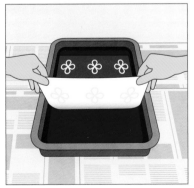

1. Refer to *Dyeing Wax-Resist Fabrics* on page 48. Remove waxed fabric from frame; dye in bucket or in a flat tray (to prevent wax from cracking). Gently roll in plastic wrap and batch 4–24 hours. Rinse and hand-wash in lukewarm water and fabric detergent; hang to dry.

Antique batik from the author's collection.

2. Waxing and dyeing must be repeated for each color used. Make first dye bath lightest color, working to darkest. Each new dye color will mix with previous ones unless covered with wax, so wax precisely and choose color combinations carefully.

REMOVE WAX

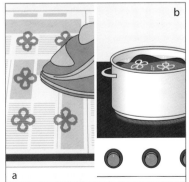

Place fabric between layers of old newspapers and paper towels; press with hot, dry iron to melt wax into the paper (a). Replace paper often. To remove residual wax, dry clean or place fabric in pot of water; boil for 15 minutes (b).

⬆ Winter Solstice—©Katalin Ehling, Carefree, Arizona. Photo by Helmut Ehling. Inspired by the aspen trees in Flagstaff, Arizona. The 7,000 ft/2,000 m elevation is perfect for these, the artist's favorite trees. Primissima cotton from Indonesia. Traditional batik waxing and dyeing, one color at a time. 14 x 15"/36 x 38cm. 2012.

⬆ *Sementes do Brasil: Cupuaçu*—©Maria Lúcia Ázara, Petrópolis, Rio de Janeiro, Brazil. Photo by Érica Marci Photo Studio. This piece is part of a series celebrating the diversity and richness of Brazilian fruits; the title means "Seeds of Brazil." *Cupuaçu* is a popular fruit found in the Amazon forest and is used for making juice and desserts. Hand-dyed and commercial cotton fabrics, felt, wool, colored threads, textile inks. Image of face computer edited and transferred to fabric, hand and machine appliquéd, details marked with textile inks, free-motion machine quilted and embroidered. 39 x 27"/100 x 70cm. 2010.

← Bluebell—©Cas Holmes, Maidstone, Kent, UK. Collection of The Embroiderers' Guild of the British Isles. Inspired by long-remembered childhood walks taken by the artist with her father, and picking bluebells, before she was conscious of the issues of environment and sustainability. Cotton fabrics, found materials, paper, old letter. Paint, print, dye, mixed-media collage, free-motion machine quilted, stitched, edges turned over and stitched to finish. 41 x 41"/105 x 105cm. 2011–2012.

↓ Beth Chatto's Bamboo II—©Annette Morgan, Thetford, Norfolk, UK. Photo by Kevin Mead. Inspired by the huge stands of bamboo in the Beth Chatto Gardens in Suffolk. Cotton fabric, black batting. Stitched, then burned with a soldering iron, to create lines, cut and rearranged with quilted sections, appliquéd. 43 x 63"/110 x 160cm. 2010.

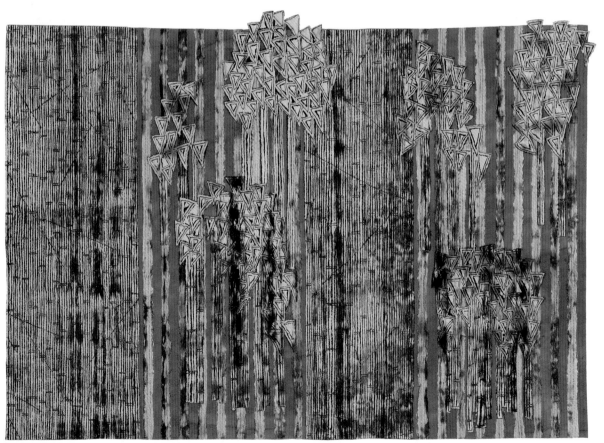

WATER-SOLUBLE RESISTS

Sooner or later, every surface designer will use a resist, whether it is a leaf, an elastic band, ripped paper, tape, string, thread, wax… and the list goes on. A resist prevents color (dye, paint, ink) from permeating fabric. In every place where a resist has been applied, the fabric retains its original color, which is revealed when the resist is removed.

Resists are used in almost every technique in this chapter; this page focuses on resists that can be removed with water, and which are colored using textile paints that are set with heat.

Water-soluble resists are easy to use and clean up; they are non-toxic and environmentally friendly. However, using water-soluble resists is time consuming, because the best results are achieved when the resists are allowed to dry thoroughly over many hours. Also, before beginning, the fabric must be scoured to remove sizing or finishes that may bond to the resists; see page 46. After applying the resist, check to see if it has penetrated to the back, or color bleeding may occur. To apply color, brush or spray textile paint between resist lines or on top of the resist, keeping in mind that too much liquid may dissolve it. Before removal, press each side of the fabric with a hot, dry iron to set the color; use a press cloth or parchment to protect the iron.

"School" glue such as Elmer's is the easiest resist to use and is a great way to introduce children to surface design; blue gel glue is preferable. Soy wax is simple to use and remove when doing batik. Make plain flour into a paste and squeegee on fabric before etching or scrunching it prior to applying color. Other dried foods such as oatmeal, rice cereal, sugar and mashed potatoes can also be reconstituted and used as resists; see the Bibliography (page 248).

"SCHOOL" GLUE

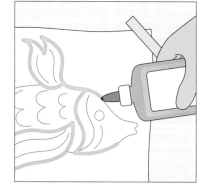

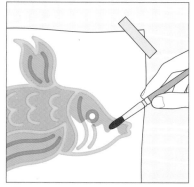

1 Cover work surface with plastic; tape fabric to surface until taut. Apply glue straight from nozzle, holding tip above fabric so it flows smoothly. Allow to set for 1 hour. Check to ensure glue has penetrated back; if not, apply glue to back. Hang to dry overnight.

2 Brush or spray on color. To prevent colors from bleeding, allow each one to dry before applying next one. Air-dry color for 24 hours; press with hot iron to set using press cloth. Soak fabric in warm water for 30 minutes to dissolve glue; machine-wash, gentle cycle.

SOY WAX

1 Use "pillar" form of soy wax, which is harder than pure soy wax. Pages 80–81 provide instructions for traditional batik; follow these directions to work with soy wax except for the melting temperature and wax removal. Heat electric pan to 180–200°F/82–93°C.

2 Melt soy wax until transparent. Apply wax on fabric; ensure that it penetrates to back. Scrunch to crackle when hard. Apply textile paint over wax. When dry, press fabric between newspaper layers to melt wax and set color. Wash in hot water with mild detergent.

FLOUR

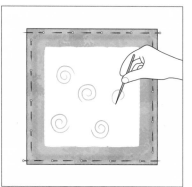

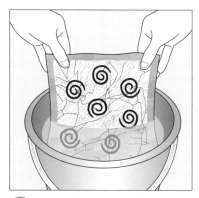

1 Gradually add 1 cup cold water to 1 cup white flour; stir or whisk until it becomes a smooth paste. Pin top edge of fabric to padded surface (page 68). Pour paste on fabric along pinned edge. Use squeegee to spread paste over fabric until evenly covered.

2 Pin other edges to padded surface until taut. For patterning, use stamps or textured items on wet paste, or incise designs with wooden skewer. Ensure that all designs penetrate to fabric beneath. Leave to dry for at least 24 hours or until paste becomes matte.

3 Scrunch fabric to crackle it; shake off dried paste. Apply dark paint, working color into crackled/textured areas. Check the back to ensure color penetrates. Air-dry 24 hours; press with hot iron and press cloth. Soak in warm water so flour dissolves; machine-wash.

ACID ETCHING

Acid etching can be used by art quilters to create a number of effects, both conventional and extraordinary. The technique involves dissolving cellulose fabrics in acid (sodium bisulphate). This isn't as scary or as difficult as it sounds, because a readily available product called Fiber Etch can be used. Fiber Etch can be applied on fabric straight from the bottle through the nozzle. It can also be screen printed, stamped or brushed on fabric. However, use only 100% synthetic threads when acid etching, in a color that will enhance the work, as the threads will be visible on both sides when the fabric dissolves.

Conventional techniques like reverse appliqué and cutwork embroidery can be accomplished chemically with Fiber Etch, eliminating the need to use scissors. Unpredictable and ethereal results can be achieved when fabrics made of different fibers are layered, stitched and acid etched, so that only the cellulose fibers dissolve; see quilt on page 228 and *Layered Etching* below. Protein and synthetic fibers will remain, with only the threads holding the work together.

Health & Safety Rules

- Wear an apron, rubber gloves, goggles and a respirator with an acid gas cartridge.
- Work outside or in a well-ventilated area.
- Pre-wash fabrics to remove sizing and finishes.
- Use 100% synthetic thread.
- Only cotton, linen and rayon fibers will dissolve; protein fibers and synthetics will be unaffected.
- Make test samples.
- Always rinse acid etched fabric.

TECHNIQUE

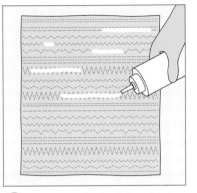

1 Use pre-washed cellulose fabrics such as cotton, linen or rayon. Machine-embroider one or several layers with 100% synthetic thread. Apply Fiber Etch gel on area to be dissolved, rubbing gel into fabric well so it penetrates fibers. Allow to dry or use hair dryer.

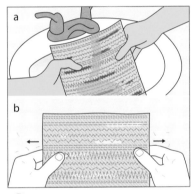

3 When fibers have been etched, rinse fabric well with running water, rubbing with thumb to remove etched areas (a). Acid etched fibers will separate from main fabric and fall off. Stretch fabric and snap between hands to facilitate easy removal of fibers (b).

2 Sandwich fabric between layers of baking parchment. Using dry iron on wool setting, iron fabric firmly to activate acid; also press reverse side. Fabric will discolor in etched areas. Test by scratching with toothbrush—fibers should be brittle and flake off easily.

REVERSE APPLIQUÉ

Stitch cellulose fabric on top of protein or synthetic fabric. Machine satin-stitch a design. Apply Fiber Etch on cellulose fabric, close to stitching in areas to be removed. Finish as described in *Technique*. Fabric within etched areas will fall out when design is rinsed.

CUTWORK

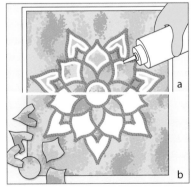

Stabilize fabric with paper. Machine satin-stitch an embroidery design on cellulose fabric with synthetic thread. Run tip of Fiber Etch next to stitching line in areas to be removed (a). Finish as in *Technique*. Fabric and paper will fall off when rinsed, leaving open areas (b).

LAYERED ETCHING

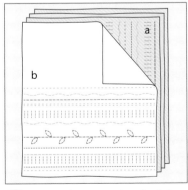

1 Arrange layers or strips of cellulose, protein, synthetic or metallic fabrics on a cellulose base. Sew layers together with decorative stitches using synthetic threads (a). Top with cellulose fabric. Attach top layer with decorative stitches, perpendicular to previous stitches (b).

Layered etching by Kate Crossley.

2 Apply Fiber Etch on stitched surface in horizontal or vertical lines, curves, circles or any other linear pattern. If piece is thick, ensure gel penetrates to back. Finish as described in *Technique*. When dry, piece can be acid etched again for more transparency.

MARBLING

Marbling is a unique monoprinting process that utilizes a thickened medium solution called "size" on which to float colorful textile inks or paints. Because the colors are suspended on the surface, they can be manipulated to create patterns that often resemble marble, hence the name of this process. The design is transferred to fabric that is laid on top of the floating colors.

Suminagashi (floating ink) marbling originated in 12th century Japan, then spread to Turkey where it was known as *ebru*. Originally, marbled art was mainly done on paper used for binding books or picture framing. However, the development of textile paints made it possible to marble fabric, and art quilters embraced this technique with enthusiasm. While no marbled designs will ever be exactly the same, a number of patterns can be created by manipulating the colors in different directions according to set formulas. However, the real joy of marbling is creating something that has never been seen before.

The size medium is made using water and one of the following non-toxic ingredients: Methocel, carrageenan moss, wallpaper paste or Deka Marble Medium. These sizes have their own individual properties; some give better control or more detailed designs, while others have a longer storage life. Experiment with them to see which size you prefer. Follow the manufacturer's instructions for preparing the size, which should have the consistency of egg whites. Weather and temperature will greatly affect the end result. Size needs to cure for several hours or overnight before it is ready.

Use water-based textile inks or paints formulated for marbling fabric. Or use any water-based textile paint, diluted with distilled water to the consistency of whole milk. Too much water will weaken the color, while not enough will cause the color to sink. Some colors (particularly opaque paints) will not spread as easily as others. Apply the color that spreads most first, because using it last will push all other colors aside. The swirling patterning that characterizes marbled fabric is created using combs, rakes, or a stylus such as a toothpick or kebab stick.

Use 100% cotton prepared for dyeing fabric with a smooth tight weave. Pre-wash fabric and cut into pieces that will fit in the marbling tray. Fabric should be pre-treated with a mordant (alum) that enables color to permanently bond with the fibers. When finished, rinse all equipment (particularly the tray) in lukewarm water without soap, as soap residue can contaminate future prints.

EQUIPMENT

You will need: buckets, alum, gloves, clothes pins, hanging line, iron, marbling size, shallow tray to fit entire piece of fabric, newspaper, paper towels, marbling colors, jars for colors, eye droppers, broomstraw (optional), distilled water, stylus, comb or rake, pfd fabric.

SIZE

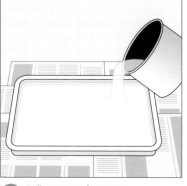

1 Follow manufacturer's instructions to make up the size medium. You may need to make it the day before using. Pour size into a shallow tray to depth of 2–3"/5–7cm; if possible, use a white tray, which will allow you to see colors clearly.

TECHNIQUE

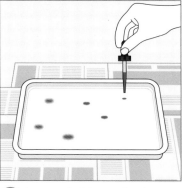

1 Pour textile inks or paints into individual jars; thin with distilled water to consistency of whole milk. Using an eye dropper, gently drop first color on size, either in rows or randomly. Color should disperse rapidly on surface.

ALUM

Fill a bucket with hot water; add 3 tablespoons alum for each quart/litre. Stir until dissolved. Soak fabric in alum for 20 minutes. Wearing gloves, remove fabric and hang to drip-dry so fabrics do not touch or overlap. When dry, press with a dry iron.

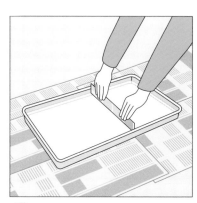

2 Allow size to settle after pouring. Using newspaper or cardboard, gently scrape surface of size to clean away any dust particles and break up the surface tension; this will allow the colors to disperse nicely. Prick any bubbles with a sharp pin.

2 Add drops of the second color either on top of or next to the first drops. Color will sink if too thick, so thin with distilled water and try again. Continue adding drops of color to size; the final color will be most prominent.

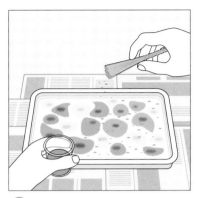

3 For a more random effect, cut lengths of broomstraw bristles and tie them together with string to make a small brush (one for each color). Dip tips of the brush into paint, then gently tap paint onto size using your index finger.

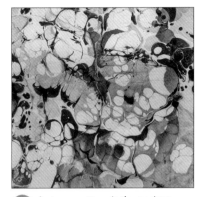

4 A stone pattern is the easiest marbling design. Apply random drops of paint onto surface of size in a variety of colors, then print fabric without combing or swirling the colors. *Fabric marbled by Ursula Schmidt Troschke.*

SWIRLING

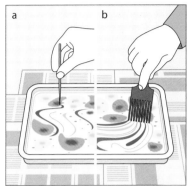

1 Using a stylus (a) or comb (b), swirl colors gently. You will notice many secondary designs developing; these can be further encouraged by careful manipulation with the stylus or comb. Vigorous swirling may cause colors to blend, which isn't desirable.

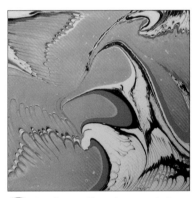

2 Combing will produce myriad effects, depending on how many swipes are taken and in what manner. Judicious combing on small areas can form images of crashing waves or stratified rock, depending on the colors used. *Fabric marbled by the author.*

RAKING

1 Complex all-over patterns can be achieved using a rake. Start at one edge and run rake through colors along entire length of tray. You can make several swipes in same direction, or alternate directions for a more intricate design.

2 Get Gel is a basic raked design; other marbled patterns are based on variations of this one. It is done in 4 swipes—the first 2 pushed and pulled along length of tray, and the second 2 pushed and pulled across width. *Fabric marbled by Ursula Schmidt Troschke.*

PRINTING

1 With an assistant, hold a corner of prepared fabric in each hand; center over size. Lower fabric smoothly onto surface in one fluid movement. Gently pat any areas that are not in contact with the size. Allow to rest for 10 seconds.

2 Carefully peel fabric off size, dragging it over rim of tray to scrape off excess; rinse in cool water. Squeeze gently; air-dry for 24 hours. Press reverse side with hot iron to fix color. Rinse again to remove any remaining alum. Air-dry and press.

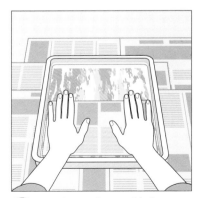

3 To make another marbled print, clean surface of size before adding new colors. Lay sheets of newspaper onto any paint that remains on surface. Carefully scrape surface as before. Color that has sunk will not affect subsequent prints.

MARBLING WITH SHAVING FOAM

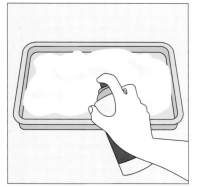

1 A quick and easy method to marble fabric uses shaving foam. Spray inexpensive shaving foam into base of a plastic tray large enough to hold entire piece of fabric. Use a scraper to flatten foam to an even ¾"/2cm thickness.

2 Using an eye dropper, lightly dribble small drops of fabric ink or runny fabric paint onto the shaving foam. Use more than one color as desired, but do not use too much ink or paint.

3 Use a very fine comb or a stylus such as a toothpick to delicately swirl the inks or paints, creating an interesting pattern. Do not swirl too much or you will lose the marbling effect and the colors may blend or get muddy.

4 When satisfied with design, carefully lay fabric directly on top of marbled foam in one movement—do not allow fabric to shift or it will smear the design.

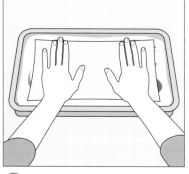

5 Gently pat the fabric in place without shifting it. Check to remove any air bubbles trapped between fabric and foam, which will show up as white patches on fabric. Allow fabric to rest on surface of foam for 20–30 seconds.

6 Peel fabric off foam in one movement and lay foam side up on newspaper or paper towels. Gently scrape all foam off fabric using a scraper, making as few swipes as possible as edges of scraper may leave faint lines.

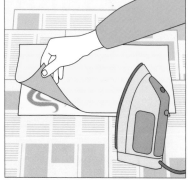

7 Air-dry fabric; press with hot iron to fix inks/paints following manufacturer's instructions, using pressing cloth to protect iron. Hand-wash, rinse, then press again when dry. You can reuse foam left in tray, adding more ink/paint for subsequent prints.

⬆ Suilven Hill in Sutherland—©Kitty Watt, Stockport, UK. Photo by Stuart Watt. Quilt designed from a sketch by the artist's son when he reached the top before his father. Foam-marbled cotton and microwave-dyed fabrics. Machine quilted. 15 x 19"/38 x 48cm. 2011.

➲ Beach Blues—©Hildegard Braatz, Essen, Germany. Photo by Peter Braatz. Ursula Schmidt Troschke's hand-marbled fabrics are featured in this patchwork quilt inspired by the sea; the "windows" show the different weather conditions at the beach. Hand-marbled cotton fabrics. Machine pieced and hand quilted, embellished with glass beads. 31 x 43"/80 x 110cm. 1998.

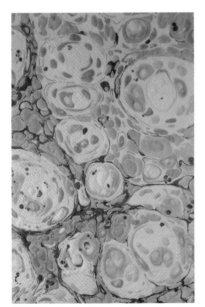

➫ Nature 1: Rock Garden (detail)—©Dean and Linda Moran, Tucson, Arizona. Photo by Dean Moran. The traditional stone marbling pattern creates a riverbed of stones, much like the dry riverbeds of the southwestern United States. Hand-marbled unpolished white satin. Machine quilted with variegated threads. 25 x 45"/63 x 114cm. 2003.

➲ Mandala 1: Core— ©Dean and Linda Moran, Tucson, Arizona. Photo by Dean Moran. Hand-marbled fabric simulates the restlessness of the earth's core in this wholecloth wall hanging. For hanging, raw edges were folded over a curved flexible ruler that was sewn to the back of the work to maintain a round shape; balsa wood was inserted in a sleeve sewn halfway down the piece. Hand-marbled unpolished red satin. Machine quilted with variegated threads. 24"/61cm diameter. 2003.

RUSTING

If you have ever accidentally rubbed rust on your clothing, you'll realize how difficult it is to remove from fabric. Rusting is permanent, and depending on how the rusty items are treated, will create wonderful colors and impressive patterns. Collect a variety of objects for rusting fabric: nails, wire, tools such as a saw or hammer head, tin cans, old locks—the list is endless.

Rusty items can be used again and again. The way you secure the fabric to the item, the amount of time it is left and how warm the atmosphere is while the fabric is rusting will affect the finished outcome. Rusted fabrics vary greatly, but that's half the fun. Even if you have a disappointing result, there is nothing to stop you from rusting that fabric again; reposition iron items to create multiple layers of color. You can stamp, stencil or paint rusted fabric or dye it again with other colors. Rusted fabric looks wonderful when overdyed with indigo.

It's best to use cotton or silk for rusting, but some synthetics also work well. Always pre-wash the fabric to remove any chemicals or finishes that might prevent the rust from penetrating the fibers. Sprinkle the soaked fabric with salt to hasten rusting. While plain water will cause rusting over time, vinegar will accelerate the process; pre-soak fabric in a 50:50 vinegar/water solution. Rusting takes time, but if fabric is kept in a warm place it will react in just a few hours, so check it often—if left too long the fibers can rot. Always wear rubber gloves when rusting to protect your hands from the vinegar as well as the rusty objects. Avoid breathing dry powdered rust by wearing a mask. When finished, tumble rusted fabric in a clothes dryer for a softer hand.

PREPARE OBJECTS

Select a good variety of iron objects. For pale lemon and orange colors, clean objects thoroughly with wire wool and water. If using objects that are already rusted, the results will be darker.

Alternatively, wrap dry fabric around an iron pole or long iron object, pleating or scrunching the fabric, and secure with string or wire. This will create a resist pattern of lines. Soak in a 50:50 vinegar/water solution.

TECHNIQUES

Soak fabric thoroughly in half water, half vinegar solution. Arrange on a flat plastic-covered surface; scatter with iron objects. Roll or scrunch fabric, including more objects in each layer. Tie bundle with string or wire.

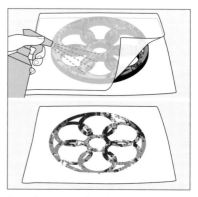

For a direct transfer, place a patterned iron artifact on a piece of dampened fabric in a tray. Place second fabric on top, spray with plain water or sprinkle with salt and spray with vinegar water. When bagging as described below, keep fabrics smooth and flat.

RUSTING

1 Place fabric bundle or wrapped object in a plastic bag or on a flat tray covered in plastic. Leave plenty of room for air as rusting needs oxygen to work. Place bag or tray in a warm area and leave for 12–24 hours.

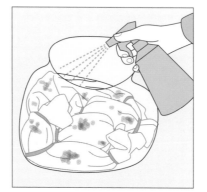

2 Check at intervals and re-wrap to rust areas that need more patterning. Spray with more water or vinegar solution to keep fabrics damp so that the process can continue. Don't leave too long or the fabric may rot.

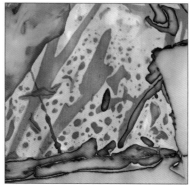

3 Leave to rust until fabric has desired color or pattern, then remove iron items. Rinse fabric well in plain water, then wash in warm soapy water. Soak in a mild soda ash solution for 10 minutes to neutralize; rinse in cold water. *Fabric rusted by Jo Budd.*

⬆ Male/Winter—©Jo Budd, Bungay, Suffolk, UK. Collection of the Victoria & Albert Museum, photo ©V&A. This piece (detail left, photo by Brian Excell) was exhibited in London in *Quilts: 1700–2010*, and is part of the Museum's permanent collection. Rusted fabrics, hand-dyed cotton, silk and synthetic fabrics. 70 x 126"/179 x 320cm. 2008–9.

SNOW DYEING

Snow dyeing is unpredictable, which is what makes it so much fun. The dyeing is accomplished slowly as snow melts over the fabric. Because fiber reactive dyes work best at room temperature, combining them with snow will cause some dyes to separate into their component colors, creating special textural effects and unexpected results. Prepare Procion MX dyes; see page 47. Do not use dyes that are labeled "manufactured colors" as these will not separate when chilled. Allow dyes to cool before using so they do not melt the snow too quickly. Blue/turquoise dyes work best in warm conditions, so they will produce pale colors when snow dyed.

Don't worry if you live in an area without snow. You can use chopped or crushed ice, or make snow using a snow cone machine, which is a bit grainier but gives good results.

The way that you twist, pleat and fold the fabric will affect the outcome, as tightly compressed areas will resist the dye. The twisted fabric must rest on a raised surface to prevent the melted snow from soaking into it and destroying the textured effect. You can do this by clamping plastic netting to the sides of your dye basin. Or use a screen or tray with drainage holes, propped up with plastic pots as shown in step 2. Alternatively, set the tray at a slant so the snow will melt into the basin.

When all snow has melted, drain off liquid and cover fabric with plastic so it doesn't dry out. Allow dye to set on the fabric for at least 4 hours or overnight in a warm place. Rinse fabric several times in warm water. Wash in hot water, adding a few drops of Synthropol or dishwashing liquid, and rinse until water runs clear.

TECHNIQUE

1 Soak fabric for dyeing in a soda ash solution for at least 15 minutes; see page 47 for preparing this solution. Mix the dyes you wish to use, keeping dyes well away from the soaking fabric in case of splashes.

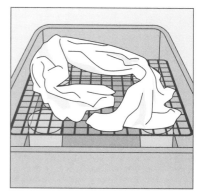

2 After soaking, wring out the fabric, wearing long gloves. Scrunch, pleat, fold or twist the fabric and tie with string or thread if desired. Place on a screen or tray so snow can drain into the dye basin without touching the fabric.

3 Place a mound of clean snow approximately 3"/7cm deep on top of the fabric in the tray, covering all edges and corners. Snow containing twigs or some dirt particles will be fine as the fabric is rinsed several times after dyeing.

4 Pour or dribble prepared dye over the snow, using more dye than you would for conventional dyeing. If desired, apply more than one color dye to the snow. Keep the dyes separate or intermingle them to create additional colors.

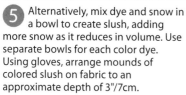

5 Alternatively, mix dye and snow in a bowl to create slush, adding more snow as it reduces in volume. Use separate bowls for each color dye. Using gloves, arrange mounds of colored slush on fabric to an approximate depth of 3"/7cm.

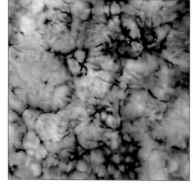

6 Cover snow and tray loosely with plastic; allow snow to melt slowly. When fully melted, set dye and rinse as described in main text. This fabric was snow-dyed using one dye which separated into a mixture of colors. *Snow-dyed fabric by Penny Armitage.*

7 Using several dye colors will create dramatic and unexpected effects. Be careful not to mix the dyes too much on the snow, as this may result in muddy colors. *Snow-dyed fabric by Lisa Reber.*

⬆ Moonriver—©Wil Opio Oguta, Almere, The Netherlands. Photo by Linda Seward. Title was inspired by the patterns created by the snow dyeing process. Machine quilting and beads highlight the patterns on the fabric. Snow-dyed cotton fabric, rayon thread. Free-motion machine quilted, embellished with seed beads. 12 x 20"/30 x 51cm. 2012.

CYANOTYPE

Cyanotype or sun-printing is one of the first examples of a process that we all take for granted: photocopying. It was developed by Sir John Herschel in 1842, when he was experimenting with the chemical processes that produce photographic images. His experiments later led to the establishment of blueprints used by architects and shipbuilders. Although cyanotypes are actually photographs rather than dyed creations, the process does not require traditional photographic equipment or a darkroom. The preparation of the solution is the challenging part of the procedure because of the care that must be taken when handling chemicals. Chemicals, equipment and solutions should not be prepared or used in a kitchen or food preparation area. Always wear appropriate protective gear. If you are unsure about working with chemicals, you can always purchase pre-treated fabric (page 245).

The cyanotype method produces shadow prints using overlaid objects, so the resulting image is exactly the same size as the object that created it. The process should be done on pre-washed, dry natural-fiber fabric such as cotton, linen or silk. Cyanotypes are usually printed on white fabric; using colored fabric will produce stunning results.

The fabric is impregnated with a light-sensitive solution of iron salts. After drying, objects are arranged on the surface. When the treated fabric is exposed to the sun or an other ultraviolet light source, a chemical reaction takes place; depending on the strength of the light, this can take from 5 to 45 minutes. After exposure, the fabric is rinsed in plain water. A white impression of the object remains on the fabric, while all exposed areas turn a lovely Prussian blue—this can take up to 24 hours to develop fully.

Use any natural or man-made objects to create cyanotype prints. Select items with open designs or interesting shapes or edges. Sharp images will result when flat objects are used, as no light will leak around the sides to blur the image. However, 3D items give wonderful reproductions that appear to have depth. You can replicate photographs by using old negatives or by printing digital images on acetate (page 95).

Work with dry objects and hands because water will adversely affect the chemicals. While the images are permanent, only wash cyanotypes with mildly acidic non-phosphate liquid soap; alkaline solutions will leach out the images. (Hard water is alkaline, and can be mildly acidified for rinsing and washing using a few drops of white vinegar in a bucket of water.) Press finished work with a medium/cool iron.

EQUIPMENT

You will need: newspaper, cardboard or foam board, fabric, tape, brushes, objects for printing (leaves, feathers, lace), non-UV-blocking glass and bulldog clips (optional), the sun or UV light source, plastic clothespins, plastic washing line, cleaning cloths, apron.

2 Wear face mask, goggles, apron and rubber gloves. Using 8 fl oz/250ml warm distilled water for each, make two separate solutions: one of potassium ferricyanide and one of ferric ammonium citrate. Stir each with a different spoon until dissolved.

FABRIC

Cut fabric; tape or pin corners to cardboard or foam board base. Working in a dimly lit room, paint solution on fabric with brush, coating fabric evenly. Remove from board. Hang to dry in a dark place. Solution will appear yellowish on fabric.

SOLUTION

1 For the solution: 1 oz/25 grams ferric ammonium citrate (green), ½ oz/14 grams potassium ferricyanide (red), warm distilled water, measuring jug and scale, plastic spoons, face mask, goggles, rubber gloves, 3 glass containers, 3 brown glass bottles, funnel.

3 Blend equal proportions of the solutions together in the third container. Solutions will keep well when stored separately, but will not last long after mixing. Use mixed solution promptly. Store solutions in labelled brown glass bottles in a dark place.

OBJECTS

Working in dim light, arrange objects on treated fabric; if necesssary pin them in place so they don't blow away. For a crisp image, secure flat objects under glass with bulldog clips so there is a tight contact between the objects and the fabric.

PHOTOGRAPHS

Reproduce digital photographs or scans in cyanotype. On your computer, convert photo/scan to high-contrast black and white; invert image to make it negative. Print image on acetate using inkjet or laser printer. Place acetate on treated fabric under glass for sharp image.

PRINTING

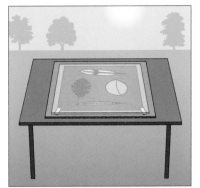

Expose treated fabric to the sun or another ultraviolet light source for 5–45 minutes, depending on brightness of the light. Ensure that fabric is perpendicular to light source for an even exposure. Remove from light when exposed areas turn slate gray color.

WASHING

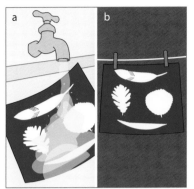

Remove glass (if using) and objects or acetate, then rinse fabric in cold water for at least 5 minutes until water runs clear (a). Hang to dry out of direct sunlight (b) or lay flat to dry in a dark place. Press finished cyanotypes with a medium/cool iron.

The Phosgene Fusiliers—©Cathy Corbishley-Michel, London, UK (detail). Cyanotype on cotton using digital negative from scan of original 1919 photograph. Title was written on back of negative by the maker's grandfather, Sergeant George Corbishley of the Gas School, Royal Engineers, who stands on the left. Free-motion machine quilted. 8 x 10"/20 x 25cm. 2009.

Lace, Pins and Ginkgo Leaves—©Cathy Corbishley-Michel, London, UK. Cyanotype on cotton using antique lace, safety pins, ginkgo leaves and a child's tiara. Free-motion machine quilted. 18 x 20"/46 x 51cm. 2008.

Endurance 3, Dr. Alexander Macklin—©Cathy Corbishley-Michel, London, UK. Cyanotype on cotton using digital negatives made from scans of photographs by Frank Hurley of the Endurance expedition to the Antarctic, 1914–16. Dr. Macklin was one of the two doctors on the ship. Quilt made as a commission for his son, Richard Macklin. Photographs used with permission of Royal Geographical Society, Scott Polar Research Institute and the Macklin family. Free-motion machine quilted. 32 x 34"/81 x 86cm. 2011.

IMAGE TRANSFERS

Art quilters embrace innovation, and nowhere is this more evident than in the process of transferring images to fabric. While the concept of using digital technology to create designs and transfer the results onto cloth may seem intimidating, anyone with a computer or scanner and a printer can do this with relative ease. The best part about this technique is that personal photos and artwork can be readily featured on art quilts without the worry of copyright infringement.

Inkjet printers are most commonly used at home. The inks are generally water based and use either dyes or pigment (archival) inks as the colorant; both will provide good results on pretreated fabric or on heat transfer paper (Transfer Artist Paper (TAP) or T-shirt Transfer Paper). Many print shops operate color laser copiers (CLC's) that use toner rather than ink; CLC's print transfer images on special paper.

Use high quality, smooth white cotton fabric to achieve the most vibrant colors. The simplest way to transfer an image is to print a photo or artwork on transfer paper and then iron the image onto fabric. Transfer papers designed for CLC's and inkjet printers are not interchangeable, so be sure to buy the right paper. (Also, never iron on top of a heat-transferred image without protecting it.) To inkjet-print directly on fabric, buy pretreated fabric or treat the fabric yourself. Image transfers can also be done with inkjet transparencies using a gel medium and a burnisher.

Before beginning, become familiar with your machines. Read the manuals, then experiment with photos and other images. Print on scrap paper before moving on to fabric. Built-in adjustments such as cropping, contrast, saturation, tint and temperature can be found in most computers and scanners. Try these to create different photo effects, but remember to save each test as a separate file, keeping the original intact. Image quality is affected by resolution, image compression and file type. For professional photo alterations, purchase software such as Adobe Photoshop, Photoshop Elements or Corel PaintShop; these all come with instructions.

Art quilters who enjoy image transfers find that a scanner is an indispensable machine. It can be used to copy printed photographs, fabrics and even textured items. Better still, artists can create a virtual collage on a scanner or copier and print it on fabric; see page 163. An all-in-one scanner/printer/copier fulfills multiple functions and is an economical choice; some will allow the artist to print directly on fabric without the use of a computer.

IMAGES

Use your own scanned drawing or a high quality digital or scanned photo. If desired, alter image on computer; add contrast and increase saturation by 20–25% to give brighter colors on fabric. Test print on paper to check size, alignment and resolution.

CLC TRANSFER PAPER

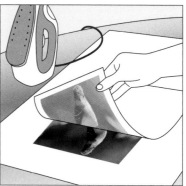

Use a color laser copier (CLC) to print an image on special transfer paper. Place fabric on firm ironing surface; place image face down on fabric. Iron image slowly and firmly with hot iron and strong pressure. Lift corner to check transfer; peel off paper when done.

HEAT TRANSFER PAPER (TAP & T-SHIRT PAPER)

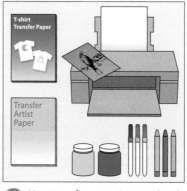

1 Heat transfer paper is coated with a polymer that accepts inkjet printer inks and other art materials such as markers, crayons and paints. When heated, the coating combines with the color and fuses permanently onto fabric, making a washable, lightfast image.

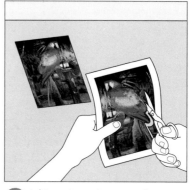

2 Inkjet-print an image or draw on transfer paper with paint, ink, markers or pens. Images transfer in reverse, so if direction is important (such as text), ensure image is printed or drawn in reverse. Do not scratch polymer coating. Trim off surplus background.

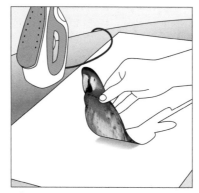

3 Place fabric, right side up, on firm ironing surface. Position transfer paper image on fabric. Place parchment or fiberglass press sheet over transfer. Using dry iron preheated to highest setting, iron image firmly for 20–50 seconds without shifting image.

4 Peel back a corner to check if image has transferred; if not, replace and continue pressing. Peel off paper following manufacturer's instructions (some peel hot, others cold). Cover image with parchment and press for added pliability and permanence.

BUBBLE JET SET PRINTING

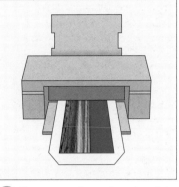

1. Cut fabric slightly larger than the size printer will accept. Shake Bubble Jet Set solution; pour into flat tray. Wearing rubber gloves, saturate sheets of fabric, one at a time, in solution, adding more solution as necessary. Soak 5 minutes. Hang to dry.

2. When dry, use dry iron to press shiny side of freezer paper to wrong side of fabric. Press well so there is a good bond with no air bubbles. Rotary cut fabric/paper to correct size for printer. To prevent jamming, trim off corners of one edge (leading edge).

3. Remove any loose threads or lint. Adjust printer cartridge head clearance to allow the fabric to feed through. Working one sheet at a time, insert leading edge of fabric/paper into printer. Print image. Peel off paper without distorting grain. Dry 24 hours.

PRETREATED FABRIC

An easy and reliable way to transfer images is to buy pretreated fabric, already backed with paper. Though expensive, it gives good consistent results. Ensure that size is compatible with printer. Follow manufacturer's instructions to print.

COATED FABRIC

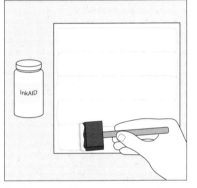

Use inkAID (white or clear Precoat) or Golden Digital Grounds to pretreat fabric for inkjet printing. Stir product well. Apply thin, even coating on fabric with foam brush. Air dry overnight; apply second coat and dry overnight. Iron freezer paper to back; inkjet print.

RINSING

If printing with pigment (archival) inks, skip this step: just air dry. For dye-based ink prints, pour cold water and a little Ph-neutral detergent in tray; swish individual fabrics in liquid. Hang to dry or put in dryer on medium heat. Protect important work with a UV spray.

TRANSFERS WITH ACRYLIC GEL MEDIUM

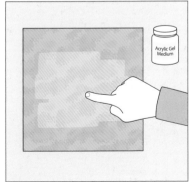

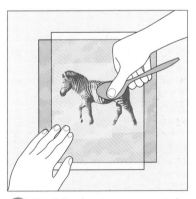

1. Purchase transparencies for inkjet printers from an office supplier. Print image on right side, which will be rougher and less shiny than wrong side. Set transparency aside to dry, printed side up. For background, use white, colored or printed fabric.

2. Brush thin, even coating of acrylic gel medium on fabric, covering an area about same size as image. Work quickly as medium must remain moist for transfers. Run finger over surface to check that all areas are evenly moist and smooth, but not tacky or slippery.

3. Carefully place image on coated fabric surface, ink side down. Do not allow image to slide or it will smear. Use back of a spoon to rub transparency with an even pressure in a circular motion until image transfers. Lift off transparency; allow fabric to dry thoroughly.

IMAGE TRANSFERS: IDEAS

Once image transfer techniques are mastered, there are limitless ways to create distinctive fabrics. Transfer onto commercial prints or fabrics that already have surface design, such as dyed, rusted or marbled pieces. For extra complexity, transfer one image on top of another. Print unique yardage by scanning your own artwork, found objects, or even a fabric that you need but can no longer find (as long as it's for personal use). To impart an aged look, wet an image that has been printed, place on a plastic surface and scatter instant coffee granules or walnut ink crystals on the surface. If an image is not successful, enhance it with embroidery, embellishments or by using any of the surface design methods covered in this chapter. When inkjet printing, always pretreat fabric as described on page 97.

FAUX APPLIQUÉ

Designed, printed on canvas, and quilted by Alicia Merrett.

You can create a fake appliqué by printing it on fabric. For this piece, the artist made a paper collage, photographed it and manipulated the image in Photoshop. She printed the result on fabric and highlighted the "appliqués" with quilting.

SHEERS

If heat-transferring an image onto a sheer or open-weave fabric, some of the ink may transfer to the surface below. Place another piece of fabric beneath to absorb the excess ink and create a secondary image.

LABELS

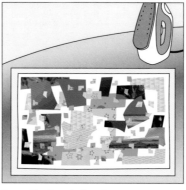

Document your work by printing personalized labels. Include information about the quilt, and a photo of yourself and/or the recipient. Heat transfer sheets make a mirror image, so reverse the design before printing, especially if it contains text.

TRIMMINGS

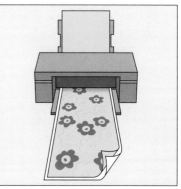

Save all colored trimmings or scrapings of TAP or T-Shirt Transfer Paper. Store in a tightly sealed plastic bag. When there is enough, arrange scraps on piece of fabric to create a spontaneous collage. Cover with parchment; press to transfer to fabric as described on page 96.

BANNER SETTING

Some printers and software programs have a banner setting, enabling the printing of a long continuous strip, up to 40"/101cm long. If your machine can do this, cut long strip of fabric to correct width; back with freezer paper. Create design to fit length of fabric and print.

⬇ Continuum—©Sandra Meech, Somerton, Somerset, UK. Inspired by the movement of melted ice in the polar regions as a result of global warming. Cotton fabric, copper shimm, paint. Collage compositions and photographs were heat transferred using T-Shirt Transfer Paper onto cotton fabric that was dyed and painted, free-motion machine quilted. 71 x 24"/180cm x 60cm. 2012.

⬆ Fashion Lines—©Gloria Hansen, East Windsor, New Jersey. The artist tore pages out of fashion magazines and collaged them together on paper. She photographed the collages and digitally manipulated them in Photoshop before printing the images onto cotton sateen fabric using an Epson Stylus Pro 7900 printer with archival Ultrachrome HDR pigment ink. Shadows were emphasized with fabric pastels and acrylic paints. Cotton sateen fabric, fabric pastels, light touches of acrylic paint. Free-motion machine quilted, machine quilted using twin-needles. 20½ x 24½"/52 x 62cm. 2012.

HEAT DISTRESSING

Using heat to melt or burn fabric is an exciting, creative process that imparts fabulous texture to art quilts. Because the results are generally unpredictable, there is a remarkable freedom to this technique. Whether singeing the edges of a silk appliqué or using a heat gun to melt layers of sheers, spunbonds, or polyester/recycled felt, you can control the amount of distressing that is done to a material, giving just a hint of flame or creating a bubbled surface.

This process does not come without conditions, however, because you can be seriously burned by the required tools, so great care must be taken when heat distressing. Read the Health & Safety Rules before beginning.

Fibers will react differently to heat, and some will not react at all or will respond only to extreme temperatures. The weight of the material will also dictate how the fibers behave: the lighter the weight, the quicker it will bubble, melt and form holes. Synthetic threads may melt when heat is applied—use cotton threads when stitching projects that will be heat distressed.

Some synthetic fibers will fuse as they melt—use a soldering iron to take advantage of this when layering and cutting fabrics into shapes or attaching a synthetic appliqué to another synthetic surface.

Embellish the ridges and holes of heat-distressed materials with foils or waxes. However, do any sewing first because once heated, many fibers will be difficult to stitch through, and you might break a needle.

Health & Safety Rules

- Work with care on a heatproof surface outside or in a well-ventilated area.
- Keep children and animals away from work area.
- Wear a respirator mask with a vapor filter when heating.
- Do not use a naked flame or work near combustible materials.
- Do not allow materials to burn.
- When using a heat gun, wear garden gloves and use a knitting needle to hold fabric to prevent burning fingers.
- Prop soldering iron out of the way on its stand or in a non-flammable container when not in use.
- Do not heat-distress fabric decorated with oil-based paints or paintstiks, as toxic fumes will be released.
- Allow heated fibers to cool before handling.

EQUIPMENT

Iron, baking parchment, ironing surface, respirator mask with a vapor filter, heat gun, long knitting needle, garden gloves, soldering iron or creative textile tool, steel wool for cleaning, heatproof surface, small terracotta pot (for soldering iron).

CONTROL TEXTURE

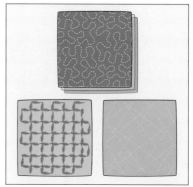

As an optional step, you can control the texture and distortion from heating by stitching thick materials or a few layers of thin synthetic materials together in lines, a grid, or with free-motion curves. Use cotton or rayon threads, and decorative or straight stitches.

DISTRESS TYVEK OR SYNTHETIC SHEERS

(1) Use an inexpensive iron dedicated to heat distressing. Sandwich Tyvek (page 25) or a thin sheer synthetic organza between 2 layers of parchment. Set iron to high heat. Hover iron over parchment, moving iron steadily and continuously as fabric shrinks.

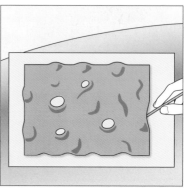

(2) Tyvek and synthetic sheers will shrink away from heat; Tyvek will react much more quickly than organza. Check frequently to prevent over-melting. Use tip of iron to make holes. Remove top parchment. Cool. Release from parchment with knitting needle.

TEXTURE MAGIC/TEXTURE PLUS

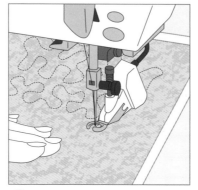

(1) To create texture by heat shrinking with an iron, use a special polyester product such as Texture Magic or Texture Plus. Place on wrong side of fabric to be textured. Stitch layers together in one of the ways shown in *Control Texture* above.

(2) Place stitched piece, polyester side up, on an ironing board. Pin corners to board to prevent curling. Hover a hot steam iron above fabric; steam evenly across entire surface until desired texture is achieved. Synthetic fabric will shrink, crinkling top fabric.

HEAT GUN

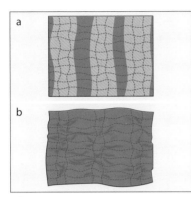

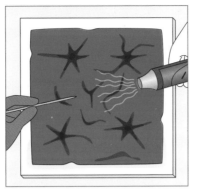

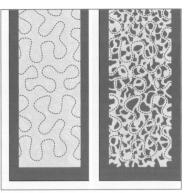

3 To cause differential shrinkage, cut strips or shapes of polyester product and stitch to wrong side of top fabric (a); see *Control Texture*. Hover hot steam iron over synthetic areas to cause shrinkage. Unshrunk areas will pleat softly; shrunk areas will crinkle (b).

1 Use heat gun to distress and/or add texture to Lutradur, Tyvek, polyester felt and synthetic sheers. Place material on heatproof surface. Turn on heat gun; hold at an angle about 1"/2.5cm from surface. Use knitting needle in gloved hand to control fabric.

2 You can create a lacy texture in Lutradur or Tyvek using a heat gun. Free-motion machine stitch synthetic material to a fabric that will not react to heat; see *Control Texture*. Use heat gun to gradually melt little holes in the Lutradur or Tyvek to create a lacy effect.

LAYERING

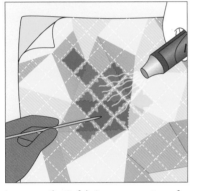

Layer synthetic fabric scraps on top of fabric that will not react to heat; cover with synthetic organza. Stitch layers together; see *Control Texture*. Place on heatproof surface. Use heat gun or side of a soldering iron to melt synthetic fabrics, exposing materials beneath.

SOLDERING IRON TECHNIQUES

Use a fine-tipped soldering iron or creative textile tool. Heat tool for 10 minutes before using. Use tip of soldering iron to cut out shapes from synthetic material on heatproof surface: use metal ruler or stencil, or cut free-hand. Clean tip often with steel wool.

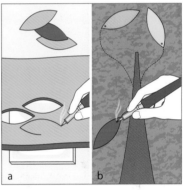

Layer 2 fine synthetic fabrics such as sheer organza on heatproof surface. Cut out shapes with soldering iron (a), which will fuse edges together. Appliqués can be stitched to non-synthetics or adhered to another synthetic with soldering iron (b).

Evolon (page 25) has a soft hand and responds beautifully to heat from a soldering iron. Paint Evolon with water-based paints if desired; allow to dry. Draw a cutwork design on material. Use fine tip of soldering iron to carefully cut out the interior areas of the design.

Pre-plan an art quilt so you can add a border using Lutradur or polyester felt. Create lacy or fantastically shaped outer edges with a soldering iron. *Detail of Forest Fire border by Tilly de Harde; see page 230 for full image of quilt.*

To singe edges of silk, place soldering iron on stand or in terracotta pot so it's pointing upward; heat to full power. Fuse silk to each side of lightweight fusible web. Cut out appliqué. Hold edge of fabric against hot tool to singe; do not allow to burn.

TEXTURE

Using texture is an ideal way to create depth and dimension in an art quilt, while emphasizing the soft, tactile nature of cloth. Just as some painters apply thick daubs to add interest to a picture, quilters can also add a variety of elements that project beyond the flat surface of a quilt to entice the viewer into taking a closer look.

Many of the methods covered here such as pleating, making tucks, gathering, ruching and shirring will be familiar to dressmakers. Adapting these well-known sewing methods to construct an art quilt adds a whole new aspect to a composition. Because texture in an art quilt will usually become a focal point, it should be used judiciously or it may overwhelm the work. Depending on the amount of texture in a quilt, a stabilizer or heavy base fabric should be used so the work hangs properly.

Texture can be used to reproduce realistic effects in a pictorial quilt—such as creating 3D bushes, trees or waves. It can also be used to emphasize a design feature such as a border or sashing between quilt blocks.

Manipulations such as crinkling and shrinking take advantage of the fact that certain fibers shrivel when exposed to heat or hot water. Incorporating a soft sculpture face in a quilt will amuse and surprise, while cutting openings in a quilt will create another dimension, as the viewer looks through and beyond the surface. Try using printed fabrics as well as plaids, stripes and sheers to add further complexity to an art quilt.

Once fabric has been textured, many surface design methods can be used to emphasize the raised areas, creating distinctive patterns. See page 105 for some ways to enhance textured fabrics with surface design.

PLEATING

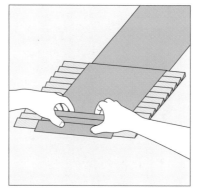

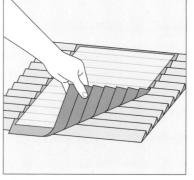

① Use a purchased cloth pleater. Press fabric; place wrong side up on pleater. Use fingers to push fabric evenly into slots. Steam-press frequently to secure pleats. To change size or spacing of pleats, skip some of the slots.

② Steam-press thoroughly when all fabric has been pleated. Place lightweight iron-on interfacing on top of pleats; press to secure permanently. When cool, gently remove pleated fabric from pleater.

ADDING INSERTS

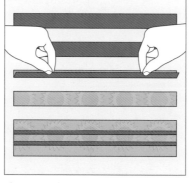

Pleats can also be formed by stitching folded inserts between strips of fabric. Cut 1"/2.5cm wide strips of two contrasting fabrics. Fold one set of strips in half with right sides facing; stitch raw edges of folded strips between other strips to create pleats.

TWISTING

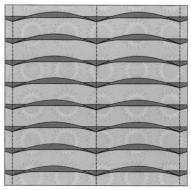

Twist pleats or inserts in different directions and alternate the twisting as shown to create wonderful 3D effects. Use your finger to fold pleats over to one side or the other to see what looks best, then secure with machine stitching or embroidery.

NEEDLE PLEATING

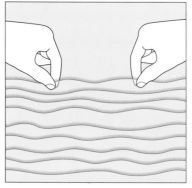

Less structured pleats are sometimes required. Place lightweight or sheer fabric on iron-on interfacing or a base of matching material. Use your fingers to pinch soft pleats in the fabric. Gently press to secure pleats, or hand stitch pleats to the base with matching thread.

CRINKLING

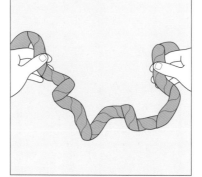

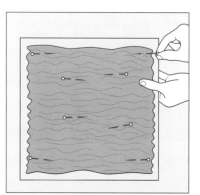

① Wet fabric, wring out and twist it into a tight coil, working from opposite corners. Tie coil into a knot or wrap with string to secure. Leave in a warm place for several days to dry, or tumble in a clothes dryer until thoroughly dry.

② When dry, remove string, uncoil and gently spread fabric open without flattening the crinkles. Arrange crinkled material on base fabric; pin and stitch in place around edges and at strategic points in the middle. Or press iron-on interfacing to wrong side.

SHRINKING

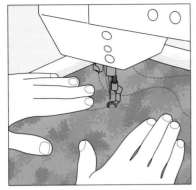

1 For the base fabric, use loosely woven cotton that has not been washed or dried. Pre-wash the fabric to be textured. Free-motion machine stitch fabrics together using thread to match top fabric. You can also use shrinkable thread, which will give stronger results.

2 Wash stitched piece in a washing machine using hottest water temperature available. Tumble on high heat in a clothes dryer until thoroughly dry. Base fabric and/or shrinkable thread will shrink, causing top fabric to crinkle within stitched lines.

3 Remove fabric from dryer. Place crinkled side face down on ironing board. Place iron-on interfacing on top (wrong side) and press lightly to secure crinkles.

MAKING TUCKS

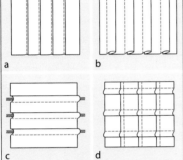

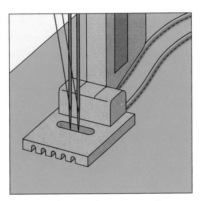

GATHERING

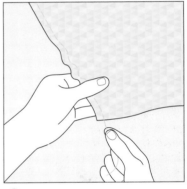

Crease a fold on right side of fabric; topstitch close to fold for pin tuck (a). Stitch further away from fold for a wider tuck (b). Fold fabric around cord; stitch close to cord with a zipper foot to make corded tuck (c). Sew tucks in a cross-hatch pattern (d).

Make mock pin tucks using a twin needle. Read machine manual to find out how to set up threads and tension; twin needles break easily if tension isn't right. Insert a twin needle; stitch carefully. Move fabric gently while stitching to make curved tucks.

1 Gathering is a way to draw up fabric to create even folds. To gather, machine baste across fabric close to an edge or in a pattern. Pull one of the thread ends to draw up the fabric to desired size, making sure you don't pull thread out from other end.

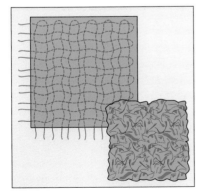

RUCHING

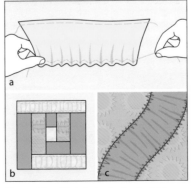

SHIRRING

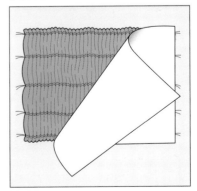

2 Gathering will shrink original fabric, so always cut a piece at least double the required size. Machine-baste in two different directions to create a tightly wrinkled effect—great for imitating trees or bushes.

Cut a strip of fabric to desired width plus seam allowances. Machine baste ¼"/6mm away from each long edge. Draw up threads to gather both edges of fabric to desired size (a). Use ruched strips as patchwork (b) or appliqué pieces (c).

Stitch parallel rows of machine basting; pull threads to gather fabric. When piece is desired size, lightly press iron-on interfacing on wrong side to secure. If cutting shirred fabric into appliqués, machine stitch outlines of pieces before cutting out shapes; see page 105.

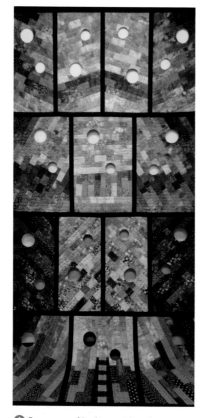

↑ Fragments of Reality—©Rute Sato, São Paulo, Brazil. Inspired by Brazil's skies at different times of day and in different parts of the country: city, forest, back country and beaches. The openings in the quilt show "fragments of reality" by drawing the viewer's eye through and beyond the quilt's surface. Cotton fabrics. Machine pieced, machine quilted, faced openings. 59 x 118"/150 x 300cm. 2012.

FACED OPENING

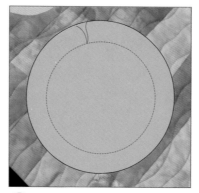

1 To make a facing for an opening, mark shape of opening on wrong side of a fabric that matches the quilt back, adding 1"/2.5cm all around; cut out. With right sides together, place facing over area where opening should be. Machine stitch in place.

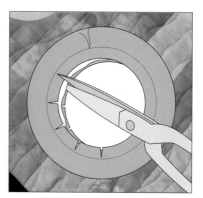

2 Use seam ripper to make a slit in center of stitched area and cut out fabric within stitched area, leaving 1/8"/3mm seam allowance. Clip curves or corners. Turn facing to back of quilt; finger press then hand stitch to quilt back so facing is not visible from right side.

CUT OPENING

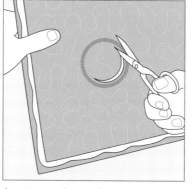

Openings such as circles, squares, hearts or rectangles will draw the viewer's eye through a quilt. Stitch outline of desired shape on quilt sandwich; satin-stitch outline. Cut out fabric/batting inside stitched area. Satin-stitch over cut edges for smooth finish.

PRAIRIE POINTS

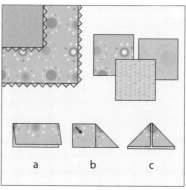

Cut square of fabric, fold in half horizontally, and press (a). Fold each corner over (b) to make triangles (c). Press well. Insert raw edges of prairie points in seams, borders or binding (page 239). Overlap edges or position prairie points side by side.

PUFFING

1 Use a wire rack with a grid. Wet fabric and wring out; place on wire rack right side down. Using eraser end of a pencil, poke fabric through openings in rack, holding previously poked fabric in place with fingers so it doesn't pull out.

2 Place lightweight iron-on interfacing on wrong side of fabric. Press securely in place with iron. Allow to cool thoroughly. Turn rack over so you can see right side of fabric. If desired, apply surface design to puffed fabric (such as color or discharge); see page 105.

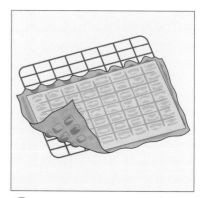

3 Gently pull up corner of fabric to begin removal of puffed work from wire rack; work slowly and smoothly. See page 105 for instructions on how to cut out shapes for use in patchwork or appliqué.

SOFT SCULPTURE FACE

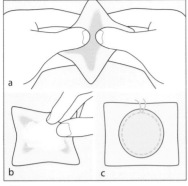

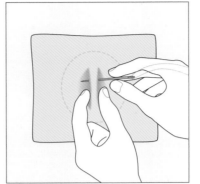

Soft sculpture face by the author.

1 To "sculpt" a face, stretch wrong side of fabric square on the bias with your thumbs until it forms a little pouch (a). Stuff pouch with fiberfill (b). Cover fiberfill with muslin/calico scrap; sew in place with running stitches, making an oval outline for face (c).

2 Turn to right side. Pinch central area to create nose shape. Work invisible stitches from side to side of pinched area, catching fiberfill in the stitches to shape bridge of nose. Make area at bottom wider and make two stitches to pull in nostrils.

3 Once nose is established, pinch stitch upper and lower lips; make line of running stitches between lips for definition. Stitch upper and lower eyelids (leave open space between lids). Stitch eyebrows and ears. Finally, sew a contrasting seed bead in each eye.

ACCENTUATING TEXTURE

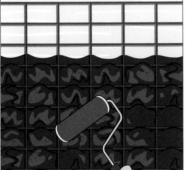

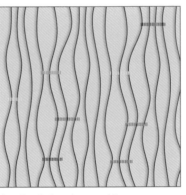

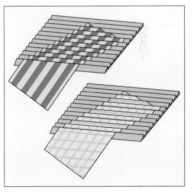

Apply color (page 62) or discharge paste (page 77) to highlight textured areas, using a brush or foam roller. Spread color lightly to only coat raised areas. Uneven surfaces will create unique patterns, especially visible when fabric is pressed flat.

Use simple hand or machine embroidery in a contrasting color to hold down raised areas, such as twisted pleats, the valleys in puffed fabric or parts of shirred or gathered fabrics. The same areas can also be embellished with beads or buttons.

When creating texture by manipulating fabric in the various ways shown on these pages, use commercial fabrics printed or woven with plaids or stripes to add more complexity and interest to the finished result.

CUTTING SHAPES

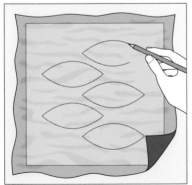

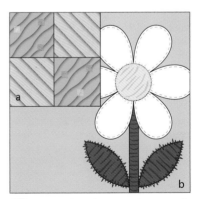

1 To use textured fabrics for patchwork or appliqué pieces, first stabilize pleats, crinkles or gathers with iron-on interfacing. Draw the shapes you wish to cut on the stabilizer, leaving room for seam allowances if required.

2 "Staystitching" by machine will secure edges so texture is not lost when pieces are cut. Staystitch just outside marked line. Cut out each shape, adding ¼"/6mm seam allowance if required. For raw edge appliqués, cut close to staystitching line as shown.

3 For patchwork (a), stitch textured pieces right sides together, making a ¼"/6mm seam; staystitching lines will be hidden in seams. For appliqués (b), zigzag satin-stitch or free-motion stitch outer edges of textured pieces in place using matching or contrasting thread.

CHENILLE/SLASHING

Slashing sounds like a brutal way to treat fabric, but the result is a pleasingly textured surface that is three-dimensional and extremely tactile. In essence, several layers of fabric are stitched together with a series of parallel lines. The channels between the lines are cut with scissors or specially designed rotary cutting tools. The cut edges are roughed up and agitated with water or with a brush to tease and fluff the raw edges, creating an intricate jumble of fibers and colors.

How this technique came to be known as chenille is a bit convoluted. People tend to think of the tufted decorative bedspreads so common in the 1920s–30s when hearing this word. In fact, *chenille* is actually French for "hairy caterpillar" and fuzzy chenille yarns can indeed be likened to these insects. In the 1990s, quilters made a feature of exposing and clipping the seam allowances of simple patchwork quilts, then washing them to create a ragged finish; these became known as "faux chenille" or "rag quilts." However, these were never considered art quilts. More relevant is the simple dictionary definition for chenille of a "pile-face fabric," which does describe the finished effect. So to set the story straight, in this book chenille will be used to describe four layers of fabric stitched together with straight parallel lines and sliced with specialized rotary cutters. A slashed piece, on the other hand, is composed of a variety of fabric scraps arranged in 4–8 layers, and is best cut with sharp scissors.

This method is a great way to use up scraps or fabrics you no longer like because the in-between layers will appear indistinct. Combine cotton, synthetic, sheer or metallic fabrics; juxtapose bright prints with plain materials. However, only use fabrics that are dyed through to the back, as fabrics with an obvious wrong side will diminish the desired effect. The top layer will be conspicuous and set the tone for the piece so choose this carefully. The base layer must be firmly woven, as it is easy to cut through a flimsy material; it should be a color that will gleam through all the layers. The thread is also significant, as it will be visible when the piece is finished. Position stitching lines so that cuts will be mainly on the bias; cuts made on-grain will shred into long strands rather than create the preferred tangled effect.

If planned carefully, chenille or slashed fabrics can be stitched together to create wall hangings, cushion covers and clothing—extend unlayered fabric at the side edges so pieces can be seamed without the bulk of the other layers.

CHENILLE

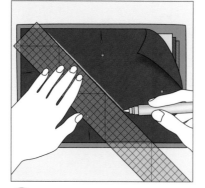

1 Arrange 4 layers of fabric right side up on base fabric with grain lines running in same direction. Press, then pin layers together. Using a ruler and chalk or fabric marker, draw a straight 45° diagonal line across the middle along bias of fabric.

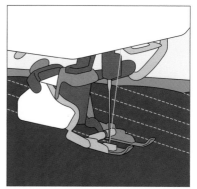

2 Stitch on marked line using walking foot or free-motion stitching; keep fabric layers from shifting. With stitched line and edge of machine foot as a guide, sew parallel lines about ¼"/6mm apart from edge to edge along entire fabric.

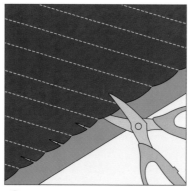

3 After all lines have been stitched, use small sharp scissors to snip upper 4 layers of fabric at one end of each channel. Do not snip through base fabric.

4 Insert chenille rotary cutting tool into snip at beginning of channel. Holding fabric firmly on flat surface, slide tool along channel to slice upper 4 layers. Repeat for all channels. Use scissors to cut short channels, centering each cut between rows of stitching.

SLASHING

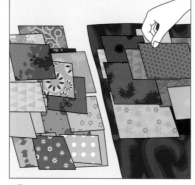

1 Layer wide variety of fabrics right side up in all shapes and sizes on base fabric, overlapping pieces and creating about 4–8 layers, depending on thickness of fabrics. Ensure there are roughly the same number of layers across entire base; leave no bare spots.

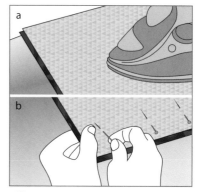

2 Place top fabric right side up over all the layers. Carefully transfer to ironing board without disturbing layers and press (a). Pin layers together around all edges (b). If using a large number of small scraps, baste layers together horizontally, vertically and diagonally.

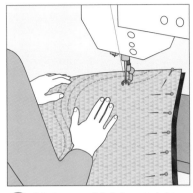

3 Stitch across fabric in a straight or wavy line along approximate bias using walking foot or free-motion stitching. Stitch parallel lines ¼"/6mm apart. You can vary direction of lines, but do not stitch over channels already sewn.

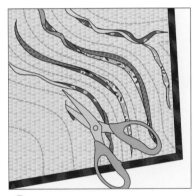

4 Using sharp embroidery scissors, snip through all layers to base fabric without cutting through base (hold a finger beneath area to be snipped so you can feel scissors). Continue for all channels, cutting from middle of channel out to each edge.

⬆ After Summer I—©Karina Thompson, Selly Park, Birmingham, UK. Photo by Richard Battye. Inspired by the changing color of trees on a busy highway in central Birmingham. Mixed cotton, polyester, acetate, wool and Lurex fabrics. Stitched, slashed and appliquéd. 59 x 63"/150 x 160 cm. 2010.

ROUGH IT UP

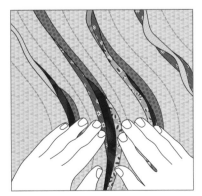

5 Check each channel to ensure that all cuts have penetrated to the base fabric. If not, carefully snip through last layer using small sharp embroidery scissors, working slowly and carefully so as not to cut through the base fabric.

1 Immerse chenille or slashed piece in warm water, or wash in washing machine. Tumble in clothes dryer on medium heat until completely dry. Shake to fluff cut edges; trim any long loose threads.

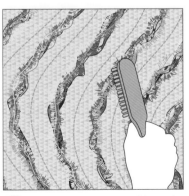

2 Alternatively (or as an additional method for rigorously roughing the cut edges), spray with warm water and rub a specialized chenille brush or a clean hard-wire brush (used for preparing surfaces for painting) along the cut edges. Trim any long threads.

SLASHING VARIATIONS

TOP FABRICS

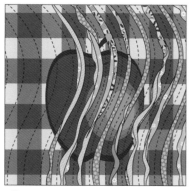

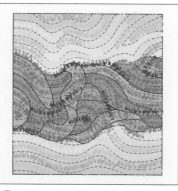

1 Choose top fabric carefully as it will be highly conspicuous, setting the tone for the piece. Appliquéd designs and prints will seem to float above the slashes, creating a secondary design. Or, choose a solid fabric for the top to highlight layered fabrics inside.

2 Use patchwork or appliqué for top fabric. Following colors of top fabric as a general guide, layer a variety of same color fabrics beneath—when slashed, the slight color differences will add depth and sparkle to overall design.

CIRCULAR DESIGNS

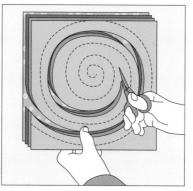

Layer fabrics for slashing or chenille as described on previous pages. Machine-stitch circular or oval design, keeping lines roughly parallel and ¼"/6mm apart. Snip layers along middle of channel between stitching lines. Rough up raw edges.

GRIDS

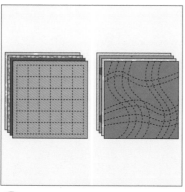

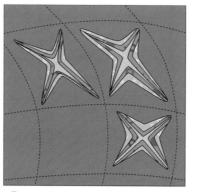

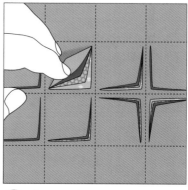

1 Layer fabrics for slashing or chenille as described on the previous pages. Stitch criss-crossing lines through all layers. Lines can be straight and perpendicular, creating a grid of even squares, or can be curved, creating sinuous diamond or rectangular shapes.

2 Using sharp embroidery scissors, cut an X in each square or diamond of the grid, snipping through the layers out to the corners. Take care not to cut through the background or the stitching lines of the grid.

3 Alternatively, use sharp embroidery scissors to cut an L shape in each square or diamond of grid. To create different effects, change position of the L's, moving cuts to different corners of grid. Check that cuts have penetrated all layers to the background.

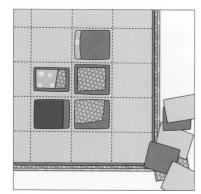

4 Another option for cutting grids is to selectively cut away the top and middle layers to reveal the fabrics beneath. Save the scraps for another project.

COMBINE

Draw rough outline of a design on top fabric, combining circles and grids in the same pattern. Layer and stitch, then slash and cut to create a complex result. Embellish, if desired, after the piece has been roughed up.

EMBELLISH

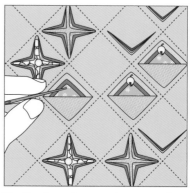

Use tip of needle to catch corners of L's. Bend back fabric(s) and secure in corner of grid with a stitch to reveal underlying layers; use double thickness of thread. Add a bead to embellish each corner if desired. You can also stitch beads inside the X's.

SLASH/QUILT

1 Use slashing as part of a quilting design. Decide on placement of slashed area; layer fabrics to be slashed right side up over batting and back. Place top fabric over layers; outline with chalk to indicate the exact area to be slashed. Baste the quilt sandwich.

Slashed and beaded by the author.

2 Machine-quilt grid or channels for slashing in area you have outlined. After quilting, use sharp embroidery scissors to carefully cut through fabrics, taking care not to snip through to the batting. Rough-up the cut area with a brush or by hand. Embellish if desired.

SLASHED IMAGE

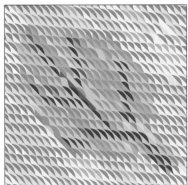

Careful placement of fabric layers can create an image that "appears" beneath the slashed upper fabrics. Make a collage picture using layers of fabrics to create a recognizable design. Slash carefully and selectively to reveal the image.

⬆ Springtime in the Rockies—©Carol Ann Waugh, Denver, Colorado. Photo by Gregory Case. This piece was inspired by photo of a single purple flower poking through the snow in the mountains of Colorado. Commercial cotton fabric, cotton thread. Slashing, free-motion machine quilted. 32 x 78"/81 x 198cm. 2012.

  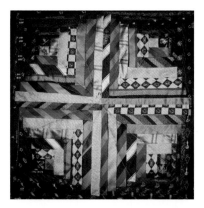

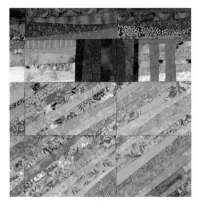  

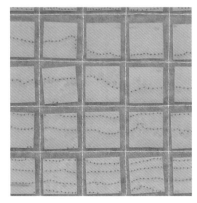  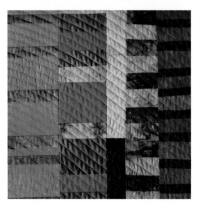

4 PATCHWORK

rotary cutting
foundation piecing
freezer paper
freeform curves
crazy curve flying geese
exposing the seams
Pojagi cross-cutting

4

4

PATCHWORK ART QUILTS

The beautiful art quilts produced today have certainly traveled a long way from their modest beginnings as utilitarian bed coverings. While these early quilts of recycled fabric were an effective way to manage modest resources, the results of quilt makers' efforts were rarely considered to be of any artistic merit. What a contrast with the motivations and results of today's quilt makers, who are buying and even creating fabric specifically to construct a "patchwork" of art.

⊙ Why?—©Janet Steadman, Langley, Washington. Photo by Michael Stadler. The traditional flying geese pattern evolved into a block that resembles a Y. Cotton fabrics hand-dyed by the artist. Machine pieced, machine quilted using a walking foot. 41 x 61"/104 x 155cm. 2010.

This long road of innovation has come both in small steps and at times in giant leaps. Early quilt makers did well to break free from the mold of traditional wholecloth or medallion styles when they embraced patchwork block quilts. But today, new mediums and techniques seem to be exploding from art quilters, who are exploring the limitless possibilities now available through the use of modern equipment and fabrics. The repetitive patterns of antique block quilts have evolved into works that surpass mere geometry. Patchwork art quilts are making strong individual statements on anything from personal reflections to political proclamations, and include materials from woven fabric to paper, wood, and even metal.

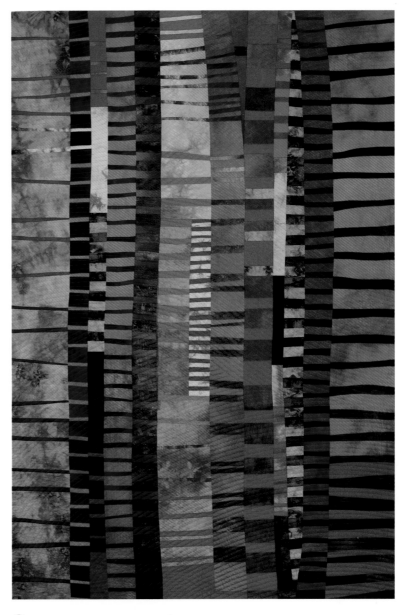

Red Clay Road 2—©Christine Restall, Hamble, UK. Photo by Mike Watson. Inspired by the red clay roads of Alabama, and the quilts of Gee's Bend. Hand-dyed cotton fabrics. Machine pieced, machine quilted. 75 x 50"/190 x 127cm. 2005

➡ Does the Dark Matter?—©Kate Findlay, Reading, Berkshire, UK. Photo by Richard Sedgwick. This quilt was inspired by dark matter and deep space and the circular structure of the Large Hadron Collider. It uses ideas from the simulations of particle collisions in the Collider, but is also a play on words. Cotton fabrics, satins, silks and synthetics, with a centerpiece constructed from card. Foundation pieced with couched cords. 51 x 51"/130 x 130cm. 2010.

⬇ Marking Time—©Linda Beach, Estes Park, Colorado. Photo by Ken Sanville. When driving through the farmlands of Colorado, the artist is intrigued by the open, rolling landscape punctuated by the occasional stand of ancient cottonwoods that often signal the presence of an old homestead. Commercially printed cotton fabrics, cotton and synthetic threads. Machine pieced, free-motion machine quilted. 66 x 38"/168 x 96cm. 2012.

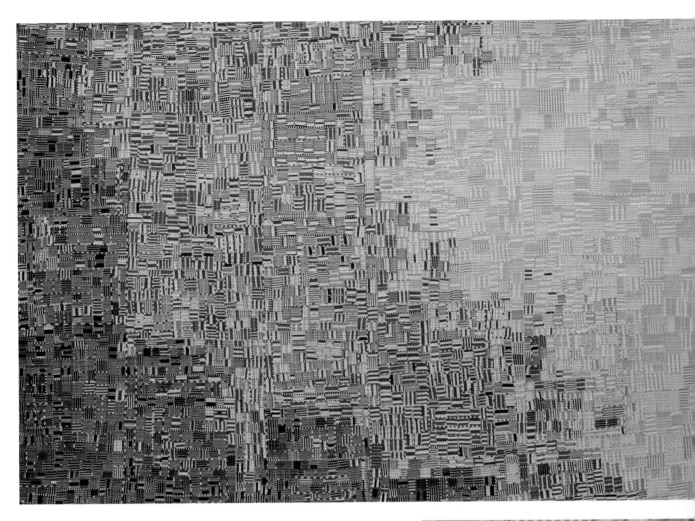

Propelling this movement along, the invention of the rotary cutter has played an integral part in the progression of patchwork from a predominantly utilitarian concept to a more artistic medium. Its ability to rapidly and accurately cut precise fabric pieces has enabled quilters to work expeditiously and with great accuracy, thus freeing them to concentrate more on design and color. This experimentation has led to adaptations of traditional designs that have morphed into stunning, complex patterns that our quilting ancestors could never have imagined.

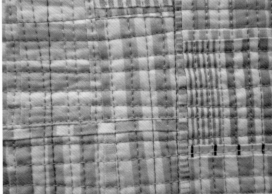

⬆ Crazed 16: Suburban Dream—©Kathleen Loomis, Louisville, Kentucky. Photo by George Plager. The crazed surface of old china gives a name to this series of quilts depicting some of the things that we cannot control or have allowed to go out of control. Commercial cottons. Machine pieced, machine quilted with a walking foot. 81 x 55"/206 x 140cm. 2012.

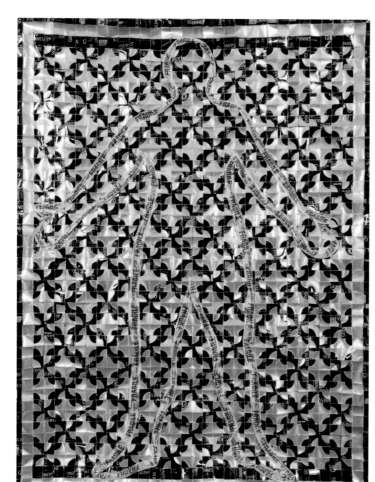

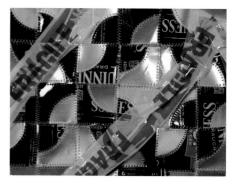

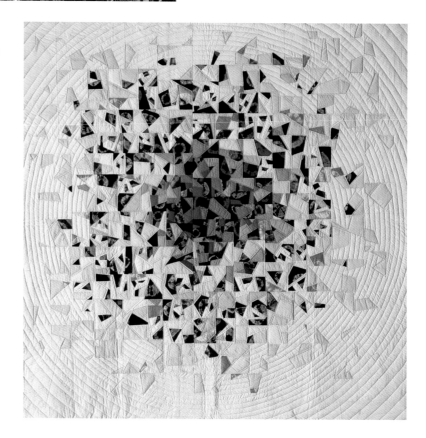

Drunkard's Path—©Becky Knight, Borth, Wales, UK. Photo by Steve Bailey. After seeing the large amount of tin cans that had been used by a friend, the artist started collecting cans, and when she discovered the traditional quilt pattern "Drunkards Path" she had her design. Aluminum drinks cans, cut and machine sewn to old cotton sheet, used blanket for the backing, hand sewn blanket-stitched edge. Machine sewn with life-sized figure picked out in packing tape. 60 x 77"/152 x 196cm. 2010.

The Wind—©Kim Misik, Seoul, Korea. This work expresses the artist's feelings when surrounded by wind on a breezy day. Hand-dyed cotton. Machine pieced, hand quilted. 67 x 71"/170 x 180cm. 2006.

← Veil III—©Kyoung Ae Cho, Milwaukee, Wisconsin. Inspired by the materials, traditional Korean windows and maps. Wood, burn marks, silk organza, ramie, thread. A paper-thin layer of wood veneer was sliced then burned with a wood burning tool, placed between layers of silk organza, secured with hand stitches and framed with ramie.
36 x 60"/91 x 152cm. 2001.

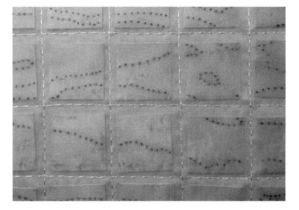

← Manpower—©Tom Phillips, London, UK. Photograph courtesy of Flowers, London. Made with Alice Wood. Inspired by the silhouette of the Stealth Bomber, its fearful symmetry translated into the terms of a quilt design. The title conveys how the toys of war are also men's playthings, with the show of military might an equivalent of sexual display. Prostitutes' advertising cards fused on cotton backing cloth, then hand stitched together.
80 x 80"/204 x 204cm. 1997.

First light—©Ann Brauer, Shelburne Falls, Massachusetts. Photo by John Polak. Inspired by the moment just before dawn when the sky lightens in the east and the birds seem to pause their singing. The artist loves the anticipation of waiting for the burst of light and the promise of the new day. Commercially printed cotton fabrics. Machine pieced in quilt-as-you-go method. 45 x 45"/114 x 114cm. 2009.

The photographs on these pages illustrate the diversity of work that patchwork art quilters have achieved. You will see that while many art quilters have embraced flawless exactitude, others have taken the same tools and media to create pieces that revel in their unpredictability through the use of curves and asymmetry. The concept of patchwork now allows the quilter to combine many different types of fabrics and colors in one piece—and this exploration has led to playing with fragmentation, texture, light and shadow and the use of unusual materials and seam treatments.

This chapter will cover many of the tools and techniques that contemporary quilt artists are using as they create these patchwork pieces of art. Some of the non-textile methods depicted in these photographs have not been included in the step-by-steps as the methods are specialized and exclusive to the artists who made them. These quilts are featured to demonstrate the limitless potential of patchwork. As you read the pages on rotary cutting and other ways to achieve precision piecing using foundations and freezer paper, think about how you can experiment with these techniques and materials to make your own distinctive statement.

⬆ In the Pink—©Cher Cartwright, South Surrey, BC, Canada. Photo by Ken Mayer. Made after 9/11, a dark time for many people. When spring came, the artist's sense of gloom lifted and she once again felt "in the pink." This quilt expresses the joy felt with the return of spring, happiness and hope. Hand-dyed cotton fabric, rayon thread. Machine pieced within hand-cut templates, machine quilted. 52 x 36"/132 x 91cm. 2002.

ROTARY CUTTING

Rotary cutting enables quilters to accurately cut layers of fabric smoothly, quickly and easily, and it revolutionized patchwork when it was introduced to the quilt world in 1979. Rotary cutters have since become standard tools used by quilt makers and have transformed the working routines of many art quilters. As quilters adapted to using the rotary cutter, they developed quick methods for making patchwork with rotary rulers and accurate measurements. Other quilters utilized the rotary cutter without a ruler, creating sinuous curving designs and a more freeform approach.

A brief history of the rotary cutter puts this essential tool into perspective. In 1956 Yoshio Okada invented a blade cutter for his family's paper cutting business, that had segments that could be snapped off when the working edge became dull. Over the years, he and his brother developed their paper cutting tool business, and in 1967 they made all their tools yellow so users could find them easily in toolboxes. In the late 1970's Mr. Okada watched a tailor cutting silk with bulky scissors and noticed the frayed edges that resulted. He determined to invent a cutter for fabrics and in 1979 he and his development team presented the world with the rotary cutter, which changed quilt making forever.

Resembling a pizza cutter, the razor-sharp tungsten-steel blade slices effortlessly through fabric. Rotary cutters will efficiently cut 4–6 layers of fabric at one time, depending on the thickness. Because the blade is extremely sharp, a rotary cutter must be closed every time it's put down to prevent accidents. Handle the blade with care when cleaning or changing it—even a dull blade can cause injury. Dispose of blades in the case in which they were purchased.

Over the years, a growing number of manufacturers have developed different cutters as well as the rulers and mats necessary for rotary cutting. There are literally hundreds of rotary rulers made for different purposes in every size and shape. Rotary mats are essential when using a rotary cutter. The durable self-healing plastic mat enables the quilter to make multiple cuts on its surface without dulling the cutting blade, or leaving any permanent cuts on the mat. Mats are usually double sided, with different-sized grids on each side. The grids help line up fabric, but they aren't accurate enough for measuring or cutting; use a ruler for that. Working on a large mat will make cutting easier and quicker. Mats warp easily; keep them out of direct sunlight and away from heat.

ROTARY CUTTERS

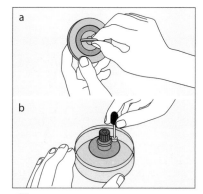

1 Rotary cutters come in a variety of sizes with a choice of blade size, type of handle and locking mechanism. 45mm and 60mm blades are best for cutting fabric for quilt making.

2 Blades must be extremely sharp to work properly. There are devices (a & b) for sharpening used blades, but blades should be replaced when they become blunt or damaged. Do not knick blade against ruler or run it over a pin, or it will become unusable.

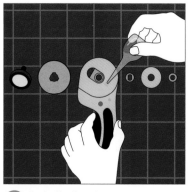

3 Periodically, take rotary cutter apart, laying out parts in a row so it can be reassembled correctly. Remove any lint that has accumulated; clean blade using nail polish remover. Add a drop of sewing machine oil to help blade turn easily.

4 After reassembling, wipe off excess oil before using on fabric. Test blade by rolling it along cutting board. If it wobbles or jams, take cutter apart and reassemble. Do not over-tighten retainer nut on holder. A smoothly turning blade will ensure successful cutting.

CUTTING CIRCLES

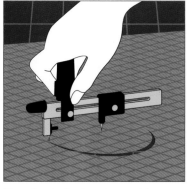

There is a device for rotary-cutting circles of all sizes that uses an 18mm blade. Place cutter on one or two layers of fabric and rotate cutter, holding the ratchet with a gentle downward pressure.

POINT CUTTER

You can use a rotary segment point cutter for clean fray-free pattern cutting or for removing small interior spaces, such as for appliqué. The device can also be used as a seam ripper.

OTHER BLADES

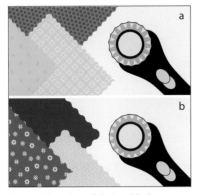

You can install undulating blades to create special effects such as pinked (a) or wavy (b) edges, which may be useful for appliqué or collage. Turn the cutting mat over to the back side when using these blades as they can sometimes leave scars on the mat.

CUTTING MATS

① Purchase a self-healing cutting mat specially made for rotary cutting. Place the mat on a flat surface, at a comfortable height for cutting. It's best to stand when rotary cutting so you can put the necessary pressure on the cutter and ruler.

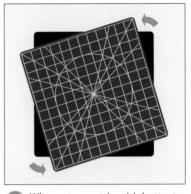

② When rotary cutting, it's better to turn the mat or move around the cutting table rather than pick up and reposition fabric—when you move fabric it can shift out of position. Spinning cutting mats, which turn 360°, make cutting much easier.

③ Rotary cutting mats will require occasional cleaning. Threads and bits of fabric that become caught in the surface will adversely affect future cutting. Run a lint roller over the entire surface of the mat after each cutting session to remove loose fibers.

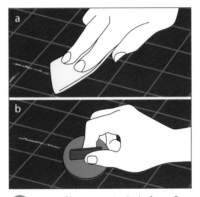

④ Some fibers, particularly from fine fabrics such as silk, may become embedded in the cuts. If this happens, clean your mat by rubbing it with a specially-made scrubber that comes in plastic (a) or metal (b).

⑤ Clean and condition rotary mats to maintain flexibility. Place mat in bathtub with ¼ cup/60ml white vinegar per gallon/4 liters tepid water; add some mild dishwashing liquid. Scrub gently with soft bristle brush. Rinse; air-dry flat on a towel.

ROTARY RULERS

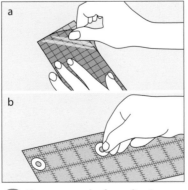

① Use thick, acrylic transparent rulers marked with numbers and lines or a grid. Most useful are a basic 6 x 24"/15 x 60cm ruler and a square ruler. Most rulers will feature additional lines to enable you to cut 45° or 60° angles.

② To prevent ruler from slipping as you cut, buy one with a non-slip reverse side, or affix non-slip vinyl (a) or sticky dots (b) to underside. Try to find clear dots that won't interfere with marked lines on ruler.

③ Rotary rulers are available in every size and shape imaginable. Rulers designed for a specific shape or purpose make cutting easier by indicating the precise size and shape to cut, thus reducing mistakes.

ROTARY CUTTING

PREPARING FABRIC

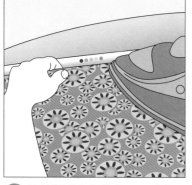

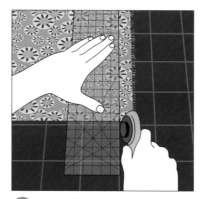

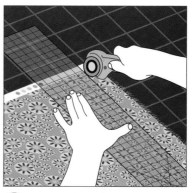

1 Fold fabric in half along straight grain, matching selvages; steam press layers together. Fold in half again, offsetting folded edge from selvages by ¼"/6mm to create 4 layers; steam press. Carefully pick up fabric without unfolding; place on cutting mat.

2 To straighten raw edges, place ruler on fabric, aligning one of ruler's vertical lines with pressed edge opposite selvages to create 90° angle. Pressing firmly on ruler with fingertips, place cutting blade exactly against ruler as shown, starting just off edge of fabric.

3 Pressing down firmly on rotary cutter, run blade along edge of ruler and smoothly off fabric at opposite edge. This will trim and straighten edge of fabric. Place pinky finger on fabric along edge of ruler for extra stability as shown.

CUTTING TIPS

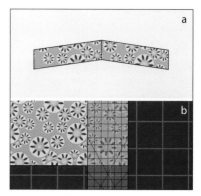

4 Close cutter and set aside. Before removing ruler, pull away fabric that has been cut, checking to ensure that you have a clean cut. If you move the ruler and find that you've missed a spot, it is difficult to re-align ruler accurately.

Always cut away from your body. If right-handed, grasp rotary cutter in right hand and hold ruler with your left. Reverse if left-handed. Never cut toward your body or across top or bottom of ruler. For awkward cuts, turn mat or move around cutting table.

Periodically check cut strips to ensure they are straight. If strips bend in middle (a), it means the angle has shifted and is no longer a perfect 90°. Realign ruler; square up edge so it makes a 90° angle (b). Cut; check strip. If still uneven, refold and press again.

BORDERS, SASHING

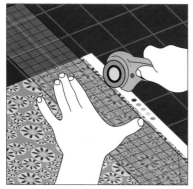

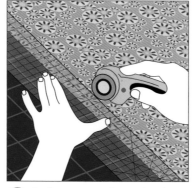

BIAS STRIPS

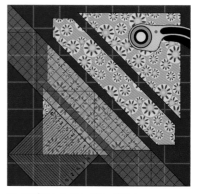

1 Cut borders, sashing and other long pieces along the lengthwise grain if possible, as lengthwise grain is stronger and less stretchy. Fold fabric so cuts will be parallel to the selvage. Trim away selvage and make successive cuts, measuring from the first cut.

2 For long cuts, inch your hand forward as you cut, creeping it along slowly so an even pressure is maintained on ruler at all times. Only cut the distance your hand has moved. Make sure ruler markings remain properly aligned with edge of fabric.

To cut bias strips, place fabric on cutting mat. Align 45° angle on rotary ruler with edge of fabric as shown. If ruler isn't marked, use a square rotary ruler to determine 45° angle. Cut along edge of ruler, then cut strips of desired width.

SQUARES

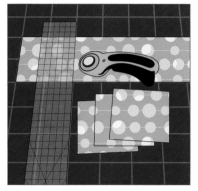

For perfect squares, cut a strip to the desired width of finished square plus ½"/12mm for seam allowances. Trim to remove selvage; then cut strip into square sections exactly the width of the strip.

FOUR-PATCH

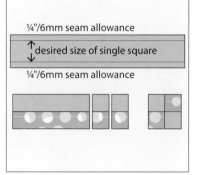

1 To make quick four-patch units, cut 2 fabric strips to desired size of a single square plus ½"/12mm for seam allowances. Sew together; press seams toward darker fabric. Cut pieced strip to size of square plus seam allowance. Reverse one pieced strip and stitch.

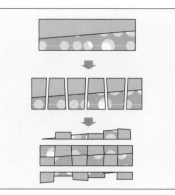

2 To make a wonky four-patch strip, cut two strips at an angle as shown; sew together, then cut into angled pieces. Rearrange pieces so fabrics are opposite one another; sew together, matching seams. Trim top and bottom edges straight or curved.

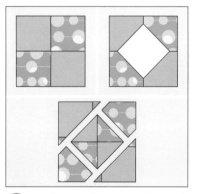

3 Use four-patch unit to make quick quarter-square unit. Cut a template same size as one square of four-patch unit. Center template on patchwork, matching corners of template to seams. Cut off each corner to make quarter-square unit; all edges will be on bias.

NINE-PATCH

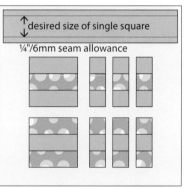

1 For quick nine-patch units, cut 3 strips in contrasting colors to desired square size plus ½"/12mm for seams. Sew strips together in 2 groups as shown; press seams toward darker fabric. Cut pieced strips to size of square plus seam allowances.

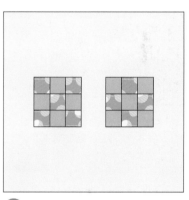

2 Arrange strips as shown to make 2 different nine patch units. Stitch together making a ¼"/6mm seam allowance. Press.

RECTANGLES

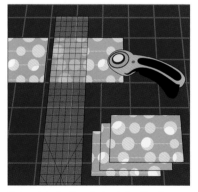

Cut a strip to the desired depth of the rectangle plus ½"/12mm for seam allowances. Trim one edge of strip to remove selvage. Then cut strip into sections of the desired width of the rectangle.

DIAMONDS

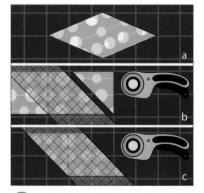

1 For short diamonds (a), cut strip to desired width plus seam allowances. Align 45° line on ruler with edge of strip as shown and cut (b). Rearrange strip on mat, align 45° angle of ruler on edge, same width as strip; make second cut (c).

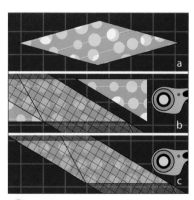

2 For long diamonds (a), cut strip to desired width plus seam allowances. Align 60° line on ruler with edge of strip as shown and cut (b). Rearrange strip on mat, align 60° angle of ruler on edge, same width as strip; make second cut (c).

HALF-SQUARE TRIANGLES

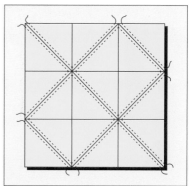

1 To cut half-square or right angle triangles, cut a square to desired size of triangle plus ⅞"/2.2cm for seam allowances. Cut square in half diagonally to make 2 triangles. Long edge of each triangle will be on bias; short edges will be on straight grain.

2 To cut quick half-square triangles from contrasting fabrics, use pencil and ruler to draw a grid of squares on wrong side of fabric. Draw each square to desired finished size of triangle plus ⅞"/2.2cm. Trim fabric edges with rotary cutter on outside lines.

3 Draw a diagonal line through each of the squares as shown. Cut contrasting fabric same size as marked fabric. Place fabrics right sides facing; steam press. Sew ¼"/6mm away from each side of each diagonal line; take care not to pucker fabrics as you sew.

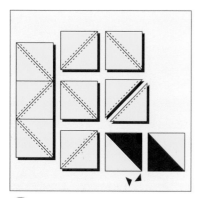

QUARTER-SQUARE TRIANGLES

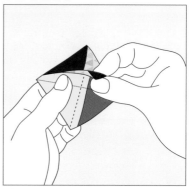

4 Cut out along each marked line. Open square and press seam allowances towards the darker fabric to prevent show-through. Trim away points at the ends of the seam allowances.

1 To cut quarter triangles, cut a square to desired size of triangle base (longest edge), adding 1 ¼"/3cm for seam allowances. Cut square diagonally in half, then in half again across opposite diagonal. Longest edge of triangle will be on straight grain.

2 For quick quarter-square triangles, make quick half-square triangles as described above. Draw diagonal line perpendicular to seam on wrong side of one triangle unit. Place 2 triangle units right sides facing, matching seams and with colors contrasting as shown.

FLYING GEESE

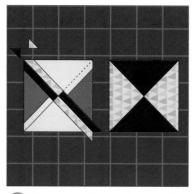

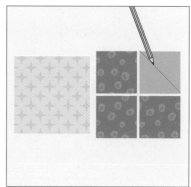

3 Sew ¼"/6mm on each side of the drawn line, the same method used to create the half square units. Cut squares apart on the marked line.

4 Press seam allowances open. Trim away points at the ends of the seam allowances.

1 Choose two contrasting fabrics for the "goose" and "sky". Cut one square of goose fabric, and four squares of sky fabric; see step 2 for sizes of squares to cut. Draw a diagonal line across the wrong side of each sky square.

Finished size of unit	Goose fabric (1 square)	Sky fabric (4 squares)
3" x 1½"	4¼"	2³⁄₈"
4" x 2"	5¼"	2⁷⁄₈"
5" x 2½"	6¼"	3³⁄₈"
6" x 3"	7¼"	3⁷⁄₈"
7.6 x 3.8cm	10.8cm	6cm
10 x 5cm	13.3cm	6.8cm
12.7 x 6.4cm	15.8cm	7.6cm
15 x 7.6cm	18.4cm	9.3cm

2 Decide on finished size of unit required. Add 1¼"/3cm to finished width for goose fabric square (cut 1), and ⁷⁄₈"/2.2cm to finished height for sky fabric squares (cut 4). Or follow measurements in chart. Seam allowances are included.

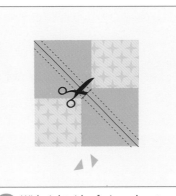

3 With right sides facing, place two sky squares on goose square with diagonal lines forming a continuous line across unit as shown. Trim off tiny triangles where sky squares overlap. Sew a ¼"/6mm seam on each side of the diagonal line.

4 Cut stitched square in half along the central diagonal line. Press sky triangles away from goose triangle.

5 Place a sky square on the remaining corner of each goose fabric; position diagonal line as shown. Sew a ¼"/6mm seam on each side of the diagonal line. Repeat for remaining goose and sky fabrics.

6 Cut each stitched unit in half along the diagonal line.

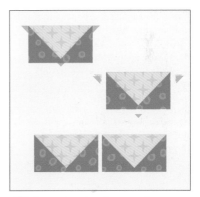

7 Press sky triangles away from goose triangle and trim off points as shown. This method will create 4 flying geese units.

CUTTING TEMPLATES

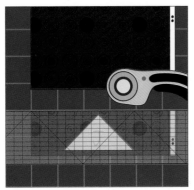

1 Rotary cutters can be used to cut multiple shapes using a template. First, straighten edge of fabric, then place template on fabric ¼"/6mm away from edge for seam allowance. Place ruler over template, adding seam allowance at top edge. Cut strip.

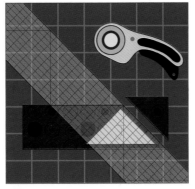

2 Cut off selvage edge. Place template on strip with even seam allowances at top and bottom. Cut around template, adding seam allowances to side cuts. Using a non-grip rotary ruler is best for this, as it will slide over template without shifting it.

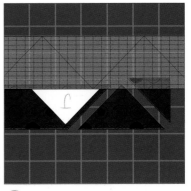

3 Continue cutting shapes from strip, using template. If necessary, turn the template after each cut to utilize fabric strip effectively. Remember to always add ¼"/6mm seam allowances when cutting around templates.

FOUNDATION PIECING

Making patchwork on a foundation is similar to that childhood hobby of painting by numbers, although "sewing by numbers" is a bit more complex. Foundation piecing is worked on a paper base, which is removed before the patchwork is layered for quilting. This means that real accuracy and precision can be easily achieved, particularly when sewing patterns that have very small pieces and fine details such as sharp points or oddly angled shapes. Each piece is numbered and must be joined to the foundation in that order with a single straight seam.

Some quilters prefer to use a foundation of soluble fabric that dissolves in water. Others use lightweight interfacing, which does not need to be removed at all, thus eliminating a step. This hugely popular technique is serviced by many suppliers who sell base paper, pre-printed designs on fabric, and tailor-made gadgets. Books and computer programs are also available with foundation pieced patterns. Art quilters, however, will have their own ideas, so this section will illustrate foundation piecing from an original design.

Because the design is worked from the back, the resulting patchwork will be the reverse of the drawn pattern. While this isn't important for a symmetrical design, it must be kept in mind when creating an assymetrical piece. Alternatively, if your pattern is assymetrical and your paper is sheer enough, turn it over and work from the back side—in which case your design will come out exactly as drawn. It's important to be able to see through the foundation for accurate placement of fabric pieces, so paper or fabric must be transparent enough to do this.

Use a size 14/90 needle in your sewing machine. Sew foundation pieced seams with a stitch length of 18–20 stitches per inch/2.5cm to make it easier to remove the paper after sewing. However, these tiny stitches make it difficult to rip out a seam if you have made a mistake, so keep that in mind. Test your machine to find the longest stitch length that will allow paper to rip off easily (but not too easily or it will come off before you have finished working!) If you are using a water soluble base or interfacing, sew with a normal stitch length.

When sewing through paper, the sewing machine needle becomes dull quickly, so change your needle often. Sew all designs with a ¼"/6mm seam allowance, unless the design is in miniature or has a very sharp point; in this case a ⅛"/3mm seam allowance will be sufficient.

PREPARING THE FOUNDATION

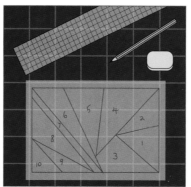

1 Draw pattern on lightweight tracing paper, interfacing or soluble fabric. Patchwork will be mirror image of this design unless you turn the foundation over and sew from the other side. Determine sewing order of the pieces; mark pattern accordingly.

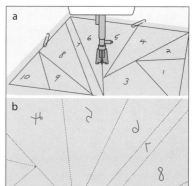

2 If making several blocks, secure up to 12 sheets of paper with paper clips (a). Using a large unthreaded needle, sew along lines to transfer design to other papers; number pattern pieces on smooth side. Back of foundation (b) will feel rough.

TECHNIQUE

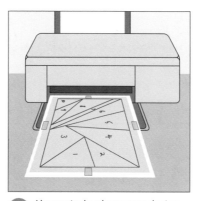

3 Alternatively, photocopy design on lightweight tracing paper or interfacing, using tape to fix it securely to regular paper. Hand feed individual sheets from the top to prevent jamming. Do not photocopy a copy; it could compromise accuracy.

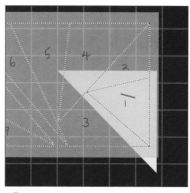

1 Rough cut a piece of fabric large enough to cover the first piece, making sure there is enough fabric all around for seam allowance. Place wrong side of fabric in position on back of foundation; pin to secure.

2 Place postcard on foundation with edge exactly along first stitching line; bend foundation back along line to expose rough cut edge of first fabric piece. Using a postcard as a guide will ensure fold is straight and accurate.

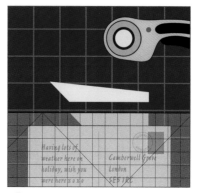

3 Cut away excess fabric using a rotary cutter and ruler, leaving a ¼"/6mm seam allowance above the paper. This will provide an accurate placement line for the next piece.

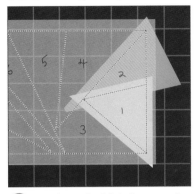

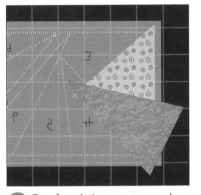

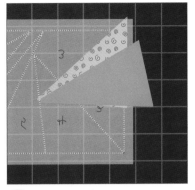

④ Rough cut the fabric for second piece and place wrong side up, in position against the back of the foundation. Ensure that all edges of the second pattern shape are amply covered in fabric.

⑤ Turn foundation over to reveal fabrics. Note that the fabrics are roughly overlapping by at least ¼"/6mm for the seam allowances.

⑥ Fold second fabric over onto the first as if turning the page of a book, so right sides are facing and raw edges are aligned. Pin in place if desired, then move carefully to sewing machine without disturbing the pieces.

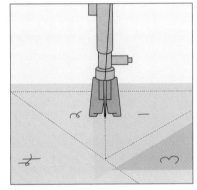

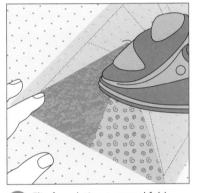

⑦ With foundation right side up, stitch together exactly along marked line. (Note: Black thread is being shown in all these illustrations for clarity. You should choose a thread that blends well with the fabrics you are piecing.)

⑧ Flip foundation over and fold second fabric piece over to right side. Using a dry iron (steam will cause paper to curl), press firmly in place.

⑨ With foundation right side up, use edge of postcard to fold foundation back along line of the seam you have just sewn, revealing raw edges of pieces that were just joined. Cut away excess fabric, leaving ¼"/6mm seam allowance.

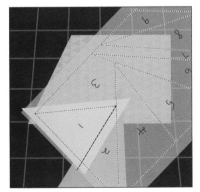

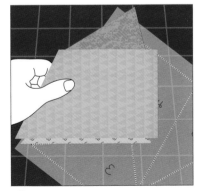

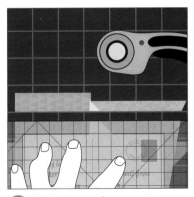

⑩ Turn foundation so next seam to be sewn is horizontal. Fold foundation back and trim that seam allowance to ¼"/6mm. Rough cut piece of fabric large enough to cover next pattern piece; position in place with wrong side facing back of foundation.

⑪ Turn foundation over, then fold back fabric for next piece as if turning the page of a book. Pin in place if desired, then move carefully to sewing machine without disturbing the placement of the fabrics.

⑫ Stitch seam and press as in steps 7 and 8. Use postcard to fold back foundation; trim seam allowance to ¼"/6mm. Repeat in same manner to attach pieces to foundation in numerical order until patchwork is finished.

FOUNDATION PIECING

THICK SEAMS

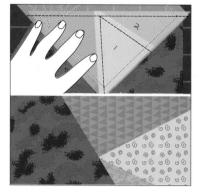

When foundation piecing you will sometimes sew across thick seams as shown here. Stitch exactly on the line, and carefully avoid wobbling your stitches over the thicker areas. Perfectly straight seams and sharp points will result.

STITCH BEYOND

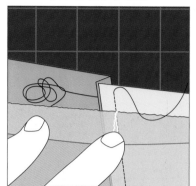

Sew beyond end of line at beginning and end of seams; you do not need to backstitch. As a result, stitching will extend into paper in areas that require trimming. Gently rip paper from stitches until fabric lies flat, then trim seam normally.

CHAIN STITCH

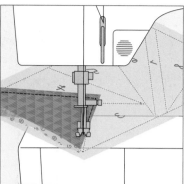

If you are making several blocks in the same pattern, work in a chain, doing the same step for every block before moving to the next step. However, always check first block of chain before continuing to make sure everything fits correctly.

CORRECTING MISTAKES

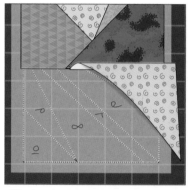

1 It's easy to make mistakes when foundation piecing unless you pay strict attention to what you're doing. Often, a new fabric piece won't quite manage to cover the required area; this is either because the fabric slipped, or the seams shifted slightly.

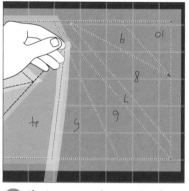

2 If using paper, place a strip of magic tape on the foundation over incorrectly sewn seam. Rip out stitches carefully from fabric side using a seam ripper; tape will hold foundation together.

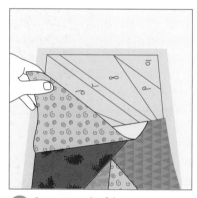

3 Reposition the fabric piece carefully to ensure that the entire area will be covered with a generous ¼"/6mm seam allowance. Stitch in place. Corrected seam can be stitched right through the tape.

DIRECTIONAL FABRICS

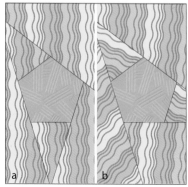

1 If using fabrics with a directional print, take care to place fabric carefully on the foundation to maintain a consistent direction (a) unless you wish to create a random effect (b). The following steps describe how to maintain a consistent direction.

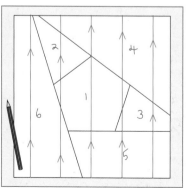

2 Using a different color pencil, draw lines on foundation to indicate direction of fabric print. If print has a definite top and bottom, also draw arrows on the foundation so you know which way to place the fabric.

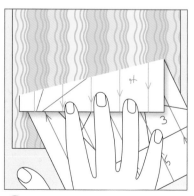

3 When placing fabric on the foundation, make sure it is running in the same direction as the lines/arrows on the pattern. Position remainder of fabrics carefully so as to maintain the direction of the print.

FINISHING

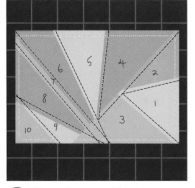

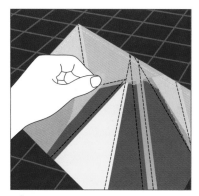

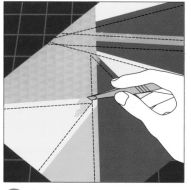

1 When all pieces of fabric have been stitched to the foundation, give the block a final press. Trim outer edges of block, leaving a ¼"/6mm seam allowance on all sides.

2 When ready, remove the foundation paper by gently pulling it away from the stitched seams. Try not to rip the paper away forcefully, as this might pull out some of the stitches.

3 Use tweezers to remove any small bits of foundation paper from the seams. If using water soluble foundation, immerse in warm water until foundation has dissolved. Dry on a towel, squaring up the edges. Press thoroughly when almost dry.

JOINING UNITS

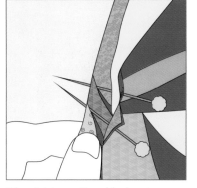

When joining units or blocks, pin matching points and seams, then machine-baste together. Check to see if everything matches perfectly, then stitch the seam. Press seam allowance to one side where it naturally falls. For bulky areas, press seam open.

CURVED FOUNDATION PIECING

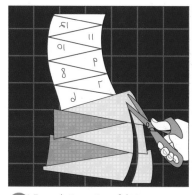

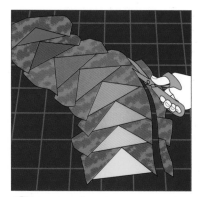

1 Curves add dynamism and energy to an art quilt. First draw a gently curving segment with parallel lines on the foundation. Divide that segment into shapes such as the triangles shown here. Number each piece to indicate order of sewing.

2 Foundation-piece fabrics on segment, following directions on pages 126–127; work from bottom of segment upward. When entire segment is complete, trim outer edges with scissors, following curve of foundation, and leaving ¼"/6mm allowance.

CURVED FLYING GEESE

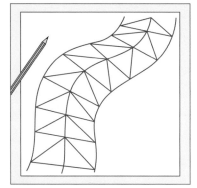

1 Draw a gently curving segment with parallel lines on foundation. Draw a line dividing segment exactly in half. Next draw lines across segment for each individual unit as shown. Finally, draw angled lines from outer edges to central line, creating goose triangles.

2 Begin piecing at bottom end of segment. Cut fabric for first triangle; pin in place. Following instructions for foundation piecing on pages 126–127, sew sky triangles to each side of goose triangle. Leave extra fabric at side edges for seam allowance.

3 Continue foundation piecing the geese and sky units until segment is covered, then trim off excess fabric along each side, leaving a ¼"/6mm seam allowance.

FREEZER PAPER

Freezer paper is commonly used for wrapping food products, but quilters discovered its amazing properties about 30 years ago and have been using it ever since. When pressed with a medium-hot dry iron, the waxy plastic coating on freezer paper will adhere to fabric, making it very stable and easy to handle. After the quilt project is complete, the paper peels off without leaving any residue, and can be reused several times before it loses its "stick" from accumulated fibers. Freezer paper is semi-transparent, so is ideal for tracing designs. It is also excellent for "fussy cutting" pieces for patchwork or appliqué, as its transparency makes placement on fabric very easy.

Freezer paper templates are used as stitching guides to create accurate seams and sharp points. When doing patchwork or appliqué with freezer paper, it is not necessary to rip paper off the back of the block when finished, as stitches do not penetrate the paper and it simply peels off. An immensely versatile substance, freezer paper can also be utilized for transferring quilting designs as well as for fabric printing.

Templates cut from freezer paper are actual-size without seam allowances, so a ¼"/6mm seam allowance must be added around all edges when cutting fabric. Grain is not a problem, as freezer paper will keep bias edges from stretching out of shape while the pieces are being stitched. However, because freezer paper is ironed to the wrong side of the fabric, all asymmetrical pieces will be in reverse. If this is a problem, draw the designs in reverse on the freezer paper. For patchwork, do not remove any paper until you are finished with the entire block. Freezer paper should be removed from appliqués before making the final stitches, or after the appliqué is in place when the background fabric can be carefully slit to remove the paper from the back of the work.

In addition to normal freezer paper purchased from the supermarket, heavy-duty sheets are available from quilt manufacturers in sizes to match computer paper, so they can be easily run through an inkjet printer in order to print on fabric or make labels. Do not use freezer paper in a laser printer as the heat generated from printing will melt the waxy surface and ruin the printer. Buy the best freezer paper you can afford, as the higher the quality, the more times you can reuse it and the stronger it will be. Always wash fabric first to remove sizing and starch or the freezer paper may not stick firmly enough.

CUTTING FREEZER PAPER

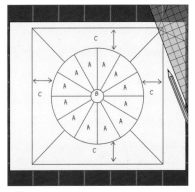

1 When cutting freezer paper from a roll, hold paper flat with two rulers. Use scissors or a rotary cutter only used for cutting paper. Once the freezer paper from a roll has been ironed, it will no longer curl.

2 Cut freezer paper shiny side up to prevent ruler from sliding. To prevent pressing paper on the wrong side and ruining your iron, label matte side with pattern numbers, color and grainline (if using a directional print).

PATCHWORK

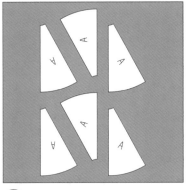

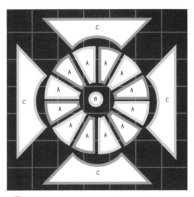

1 Trace, print or scan pattern on matte side of freezer paper; do not add seam allowances. Scan or print from original design (not from copy) to prevent distortion. Cut out templates. Press shiny side to wrong side of fabric; leave space for seam allowances.

2 Cut out each template using a ruler and rotary cutter or scissors, adding ¼"/6mm seam allowance at each edge. Arrange all cut pieces on flat surface in correct placement for assembly.

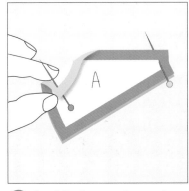

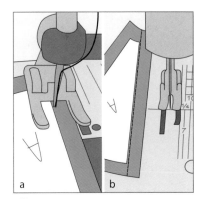

3 Carefully pin two units together, inserting the pin exactly at the corner point of one piece, and matching it up to the corresponding point on the second piece.

4 Stitch seam very close to edge of paper (a), avoiding actually stitching on paper (b). Press seams open, keeping paper in place. When entire block is finished, peel off the freezer paper.

QUILTING

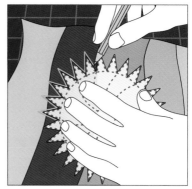

Trace or print quilting pattern on matte side of freezer paper. Cut out pattern and press shiny side on fabric in exact position for quilting. Trace outlines with your preferred marker. Remove pattern after marking and reuse in new position.

STENCILING

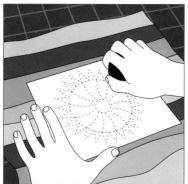

To make quilt stencils, iron 2 pieces of freezer paper shiny sides facing. Draw quilting pattern on one side. Machine-stitch along lines using large unthreaded needle. Use quilt pounce chalk and perforated stencil to transfer design to quilt top.

LONG PATTERNS

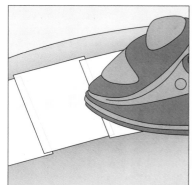

If using freezer paper for long quilting patterns, such as for a border or sashing, iron the edges of several pieces to each other in a row until the sheet is long enough to mark the entire design.

APPLIQUÉ

1 Trace or print appliqué shapes on matte side of freezer paper. Cut out shapes; place shiny side on wrong side of fabric, leaving space for seam allowances. Press with hot dry iron. Cut out appliqués, adding ¼"/6mm seam allowance around edges.

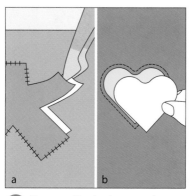

2 Press appliqué edges over freezer paper; clip into seam allowance as necessary. Stitch to background, leaving opening. Use tweezers to pull out template (a); finish stitching. Or, after sewing, slit then trim fabric behind appliqué; remove paper (b).

INVISIBLE APPLIQUÉ

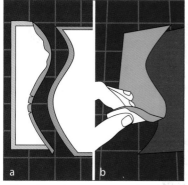

1 Join curved edges using invisible thread and a blind hem or zigzag stitch on sewing machine. Prepare curved patchwork with freezer paper. Press seam allowance of one curved edge over freezer paper (a); lap pressed edge over matching edge (b); pin.

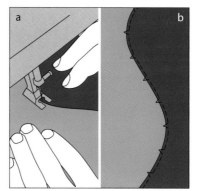

2 Set stitch width and length to 1, then slowly and carefully blind hem stitch or zigzag over fold, just catching outer fold of uppermost fabric to secure seam (a). Illustration shows stitches in black (b), but with invisible thread they will not show at all.

OTHER USES

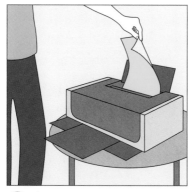

1 If inkjet printing a design or photo on prepared fabric (see page 97), press freezer paper on wrong side of fabric to stabilize it. Paper can be used several times. Ensure there is a secure bond between fabric and paper so printer doesn't jam.

2 To write on fabric with a permanent fabric pen or marker, press freezer paper behind the area to stabilize it. Press gently but firmly when writing. This is useful for signature quilts, labels and for adding handwritten text.

FREEFORM CURVES

Although a rotary ruler is a marvellous piece of equipment, you don't always need to use one when cutting fabric. In fact, cutting "freeform" without using a ruler will liberate your patchwork considerably. It's surprisingly easy to sew curved edges together, as the curves are usually slightly on the bias and will stretch to accommodate each other. The key is to sew slowly, ensuring that the sewing machine needle is in the down position when you stop so that the fabrics do not slip or shift out of position. The most difficult part of this technique is remembering how to position the fabrics when cutting—they must both be right side up and side by side, so that you are creating a kind of jigsaw in which the pieces fit together.

Sewing the curves is really simple and quick; you don't even need to pin the fabrics before stitching. When you start sewing, don't worry about matching the entire seam, just stitch slowly and concentrate only on the small area that's ahead of the foot, adjusting the fabric edges so they match perfectly. Experiment with cutting different curves—the gentler the curve the easier the seam will be to sew.

Freeform curved patchwork can take many forms. Sew strips together in earth tones, graduating upwards to blue and you've got a ready-made landscape; the more fabrics you incorporate the better. You can use the landscape as it is for a quilt, or cross-cut into it to add trees. Cross-cutting will create a complex piece of abstract patchwork. Try making some diagonal cuts to add excitement and movement to the piece. If you are going to cut across seams, always sew with smaller stitches so the seams don't unravel.

TECHNIQUE

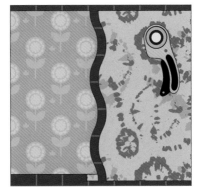

1 Lay two fabrics right sides up and adjacent to one another on cutting board; overlap edges by about ½"/12mm. Making a gentle curve, cut through both pieces at the same time with a rotary cutter. Separate fabrics and remove narrow offcuts.

2 Flip one fabric over the other so they are right sides together. Note the concave and convex curves that don't seem to match at all. Pick up pieces gently without shifting them out of place, and take to the sewing machine.

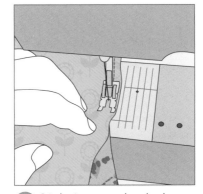

3 Stitch pieces together slowly, gently tugging and stretching fabrics to ease them together in curved areas. To secure pieces as you manipulate them, have needle in down position. Take only a few stitches at a time before readjusting fabrics.

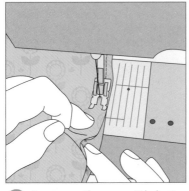

4 As you sew the curves, it helps to keep a finger on the lower fabric, pulling and stretching it to fit the curve of the top piece.

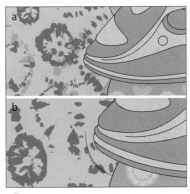

5 Steam-press curved seam carefully (a). A good steam press will forgive a multitude of sins, but if you have sewn a pleat into the seam (b), the only recourse is to rip it out, press carefully and sew it again.

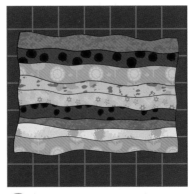

6 Continue to add strips in the same way until piece is desired size; press carefully so it lies flat.

TIP

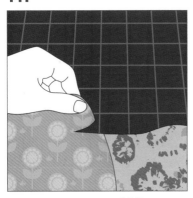

If you are cutting strips of different lengths, make a small cut into the longer strip with your rotary cutter or scissors so you know exactly where to line up the pieces when you are sewing them together.

CROSS-CUTTING

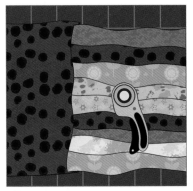

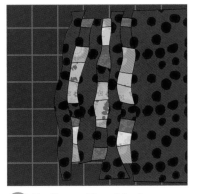

1 You can create a more complex design by inserting contrasting curved strips running in the opposite direction to the freeform curved patchwork. Turn patchwork piece; place fabric adjacent to it and cut as you did in step 1, then sew together.

2 Continue cutting strips in different widths. Insert same fabric or a variety of different fabrics. Alternate direction of pieced strips as shown to add more complexity to the design.

3 Cut an undulating curve across a patchwork block at an angle and insert a curved strip to add excitement and movement to a design. You can repeat this several times across the block, or add another diagonal cut in the opposite direction.

LANDSCAPE

Make several large pieces of freeform curved patchwork in different configurations using earth and sky colors. Cross-cut each piece into gently curving strips. Intersperse strips so seams do not match. Judicious color placement will evoke a landscape.

BLOCKS

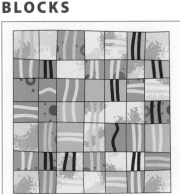

Create several large pieces of freeform curved patchwork in a variety of colors and cut into squares or other geometric shapes. Sew together to make a quilt or wall hanging.

APPLIQUÉ

To spice up a boring appliqué block, insert a few curved strips in a contrasting fabric. Add more interest by piecing the curved strips in a variety of fabrics as shown.

SASHING/BORDERS

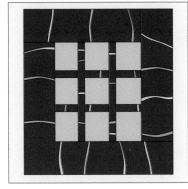

Add some curved strips to make your sashing and borders more exciting. These don't need to be too complex—insert a curved piece every now and then so as not to compete with the blocks of the quilt.

Eternal Lines to Time—©Alicia Merrett, Wells, Somerset, UK. Inspired by Shakespeare's Sonnet 18, "Shall I compare thee to a summer's day?" This quilt was part of an exhibition based on the sonnet. Freeform patchwork, screen printed text, machine quilted. 18 x 48"/46 x 122cm. 2006.

CRAZY CURVE PATCHWORK

The object of crazy curve patchwork is to create a large square of crazy fabric using a rotary cutter but no ruler. This will result in a fluid arrangement of pieces with no straight lines. The crazy fabric is then cut into smaller pieces that are rearranged and sewn together. The finished effect cannot be predicted, and no two results will ever be alike.

Select a number of fabrics that work well together. As you cut and stitch, change the widths, curves and placement of the fabrics, keeping the curves as sinuous and graceful as possible. While these instructions show the crazy fabric cut into squares, you can use it in the same way as plain fabric, cutting out triangles, rectangles or any other shapes. Crazy curve patchwork can even be used to create clothing—just make your piece slightly larger than the clothing pattern, and trim to fit.

TECHNIQUE

1 Cut paper template about 10–12"/ 25–30cm square. You will be using this template as a guide for the finished size of the patchwork, and will not sew fabrics to it. Set paper template aside for now. Rotary-cut a curved corner shape from a piece of fabric as shown.

2 Press the curved edge ¼"/6mm to the wrong side, folding it over with your index finger as you press, and keeping the curved edge smooth with no pleats, tucks or sharp points.

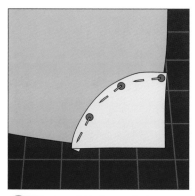

3 Pin the pressed curved piece onto the right side of a second piece of fabric in a contrasting color.

4 Trim the second piece in a smooth curve of any size or shape using a rotary cutter.

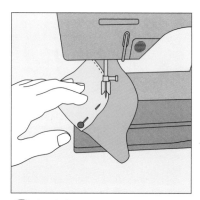

5 Stitch first two together close to fold, removing pins as you sew. If you have it, utilize the needle-down position on machine so you can sew along the curve smoothly and easily without making crooked stitches.

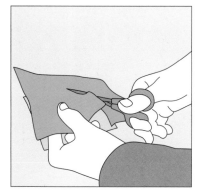

6 Turn the piece over and trim away any excess fabric from the second piece, leaving a ¼"/6mm seam allowance. Then press the raw edge of the second piece under as in step 2.

7 Pin pressed edge of second piece to a third piece of fabric and cut a pleasing curved shape using a rotary cutter. Stitch pieces together close to fold. Trim away excess fabric of third piece from back, as in step 6.

8 Pin and stitch the curved edge to a new fabric in the same way. Remember to trim away the excess fabric on the back. Continue adding fabrics in this way until your piece is size of template you cut in step 1.

STITCHING OTHER EDGES

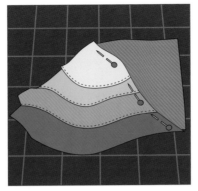

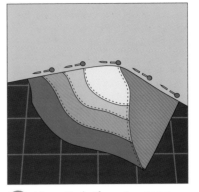

1 For a dynamic design, you can add pieces along the other edges of the crazy curve piece you have been working on. Trim one of the side edges into a smoothly curved shape using your rotary cutter.

2 Fold and press the cut edge ¼"/6mm to the wrong side and pin to a new piece of fabric. Stitch and trim as before.

3 Alternatively, if crossing many seams, you can cut a new piece of plain fabric into a curve, press the edge ¼"/6mm to the wrong side and pin it on top of the pieced fabric as shown. Stitch and trim, then cut the raw edge of the new piece in a curve.

GETTING UP TO SIZE

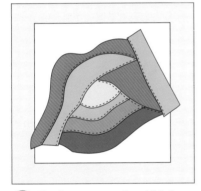

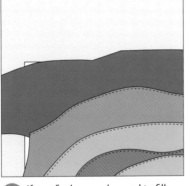

1 Check your crazy pieced fabric against the paper template from time to time to see where you need to add new fabric, and how much bigger it should be.

2 If you find you only need to fill in a small area, use a scrap of previously trimmed fabric to do this.

3 When crazy fabric is the size of paper template, trim the edges and cut into a square (or whatever shape you have chosen to work with). Alternatively, you can cut out the shape in curving lines.

FINISHING

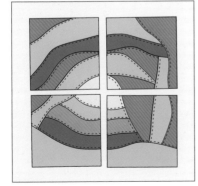

1 Rotary-cut the square into four pieces using a ruler to get straight edges as shown. Alternatively, rotary-cut the pieces in gently undulating curves without using a ruler.

2 Make several more crazy squares until you have reached the desired size of your finished piece, using some different fabrics in each new square for variety. Cut each crazy square into four squares of the same size as you did in previous step.

3 Arrange squares on flat surface in a pleasing composition. Stitch together in rows, then stitch rows together. If you cut curved edges, press one edge under and stitch over adjacent edge (see *Invisible Appliqué* on page 131). Finish as desired.

EXPOSING THE SEAMS

Art quilters searching for a way to inject new life into their work should look no further than exposing the seams of their quilts, revealing the basic structure of patchwork: the seam allowances. And precisely because this concept is so simple, the technique itself becomes risky and somewhat frightening. Revealing the "wrong side" of a quilt means there is nowhere to hide, and the quilter must rely instead on the precise size and positioning of the seam allowances to make a work of art rather than a messy fabrication. In this technique, the threads from the fabric edges are an essential part of the design, to be celebrated rather than trimmed away as in normal patchwork.

Exposing the seams becomes an exercise in the manipulation of color, which isn't easy for many quilters, and thus a very good reason to try it. The freedom of working instinctively with color should also translate into the patchwork, so try to cut the fabric strips without any particular agenda in mind and create the designs spontaneously, seeing what develops as you sew the pieces together. However, because the seams are on view, take more care than usual with accurate stitching and the positioning of the seam allowances. Press the seam allowances in the same direction after sewing the strips together. Use solid color 100% cotton fabrics, preferably hand-dyed. Select one thread color and use it throughout the piece as a unifying factor.

Light and shadow are created by the protruding seam allowances, producing another dimension usually met by the quilting stitches. In this method, the quilting should be unobtrusive, playing a functional rather than artistic role, so stitch in-the-ditch with invisible thread.

TECHNIQUE

① Select a range of fabrics that blend well; avoid using fabrics with a light or white wrong side. Decide on an appropriate strip width; measure and cut fabrics into strips of equal width using scissors or rotary cutter. Repeat until you have a large number of strips.

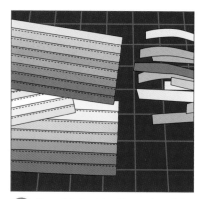

② Press fabric strips flat and straight, then stitch together in various color combinations, making several pieced "striped" fabrics in different colorways. If fabrics have a right and wrong side, sew with wrong sides together.

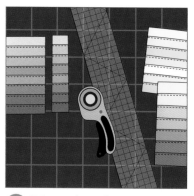

③ Using a ruler and a rotary cutter or scissors, cut the "striped" fabric into pieced strips; strips should be same width as original strips cut in step 1. Repeat for the other striped fabrics you have constructed.

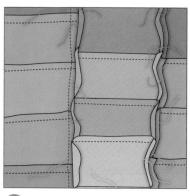

④ Arrange strips on flat surface or design wall, intermingling the different colors. Stitch together, matching seams perfectly, or shifting them so that the seams don't match at all. Ensure seam allowances face same direction along length of each strip.

OTHER OPTIONS

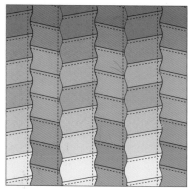

① When cutting pieced strips, make the first cut at a slight angle so subsequent strips are also angled. Stitch together, offsetting the seams to create more movement in the finished piece.

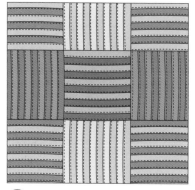

② Create square or rectangular blocks of any size using the pieced strips. Arrange blocks on a flat surface or design wall and sew them together to make a quilt top, turning the seams in various directions to make an interesting arrangement.

FINISHING

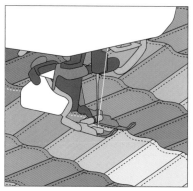

Layer quilt top, seamed side up, with batting and a back. Machine-quilt along the seamlines using invisible monofilament thread so the quilting stitches are not obvious.

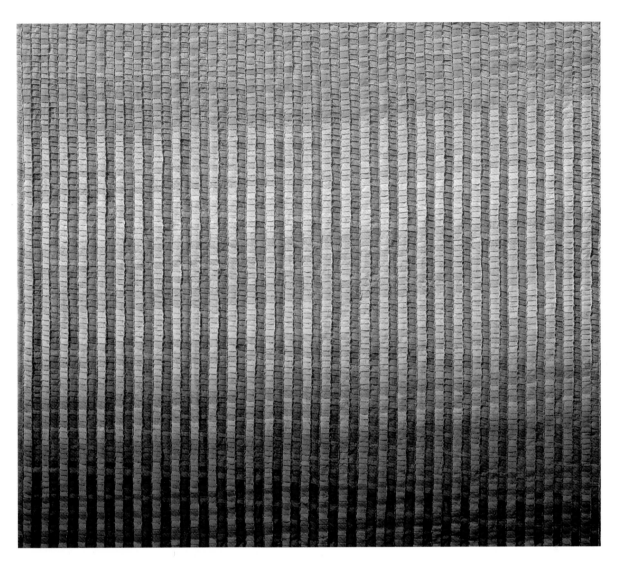

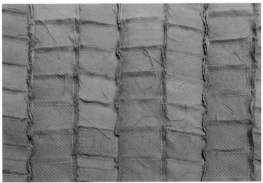

⬆ Sunset/Broadstairs, Kent—©Inge Hueber, Cologne, Germany. Photo by Roland Hueber. Inspired by memories of looking at the sea in Broadstairs over the past 30 years. Hand-dyed cotton fabrics. Machine pieced, machine quilted. 68 x 74"/173 x 187cm. 2009.

⬅ Detail: Broadstairs, Kent—©Inge Hueber, Cologne, Germany. Photo by Roland Hueber. Hand-dyed cotton fabrics. 2010.

POJAGI: KOREAN PATCHWORK

Pojagi (pronounced poh-jah-ghee) is a traditional form of Korean patchwork that has been handed down from generation to generation since its inception during the Chosun Dynasty (1392–1910). Made by ordinary people for use in everyday life, *pojagi* recycles waste scraps of whatever material is available to create pieced fabrics for wrapping gifts, carrying possessions or covering food. In *The Wonder Cloth*, *Pojagi* collector Huh Dong Hwa says, "Depending upon the occasion, [*pojagi*] is also used for decorative and religious purposes, and in some instances as a symbol. Compared to wooden boxes and chests, the *pojagi* is easier to make, costs less and does not require any special skill to make." In homes with limited space, *pojagi* provided the perfect solution for a variety of needs.

Koreans believe that blessings and good fortune, which they call *pok*, are protected if held in a wrapping, which is why *pojagi* are so commonly used in daily life, even to this day.

Though *pojagi* are utilitarian in nature, the myriad patterns created by the makers are stunning in their simple, bold beauty. Utilizing that essential element of patchwork, the seam, and emphasizing it through the use of transparent or two-sided fabrics, this technique elevates patchwork out of the realm of craft and straight into another sphere. Because the seams entirely encase all of the raw edges, *pojagi* are completely double sided. The encased seams add stability to the textile, and create secondary linear designs that may remind the viewer of stained glass or the paintings of Piet Mondrian and Paul Klee.

Transparent fabrics with no obvious right or wrong sides are preferable for this technique. Materials such as ramie, silk, linen, hemp—even paper—are used to make *pojagi*. Ramie is a coarse natural fiber that has been in continuous use since the Egyptians employed it for mummy wrapping thousands of years ago; because of its open weave it has gorgeous translucent qualities. Silk organza and handkerchief linen are also widely used for making *pojagi*.

Traditionally, *pojagi* are constructed by hand with a triple sewn *kekki* seam. However, many of today's *pojagi* artists sew by machine, and both methods are acceptable. The exact type of seam used depends on the weight and weave of the fabrics being recycled and upon the inclination of the maker. If you wish to make the seams even more of a design element, use cotton embroidery floss or sewing thread in a contrasting color.

HISTORY OF POJAGI STYLES

Minpo pojagi were worked in ramie or hemp in neutral colour schemes for use by ordinary people. The remnants used often varied in age or yellowed at different rates. The makers worked those subtle color variations into unique compositions.

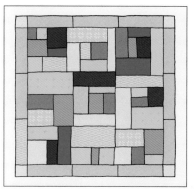

Kungpo pojagi were used by the upper classes and royalty. These were usually composed of richly colored silks, many of which were also embroidered.

Shikjipo pojagi were used as decorative coverings for food, with oiled paper placed beneath fabric to protect it. A small ribbon was attached to aid in lifting the fabric off the food. Fabrics were lightweight and loosely woven for ventilation.

USES

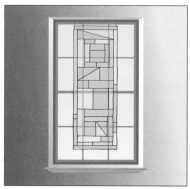

Pojagi are usually made from transparent or double-sided fabrics, so the work looks finished on both sides. Curtains, room dividers, ceiling hangings and scarves are successfully made with this technique, and can look different in various lighting situations.

SEAMS

Because seams are essential to the design, *pojagi* often give the impression of stained glass. When only one color is used, the seams become the focus of the design. Various types of seams that can be employed to make *pojagi*.

MALEOBAKKI SEAM

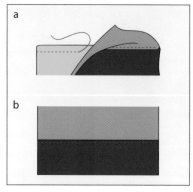

(French Seam) With wrong sides facing, sew a ⅜"/10mm seam; trim to ⅛"/3mm. Fold fabrics so right sides are together; stitch ¼"/6mm away from fold, encasing raw edges in seam (a). Press seam to one side; topstitch in place on right side (b).

KEKKI OR *GEKKI* SEAM

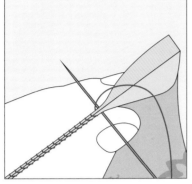

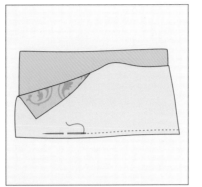

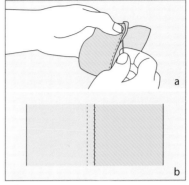

1 Traditionally, *pojagi* is hand-sewn with a rolled triple-stitched *kekki* (or *gekki*) seam that is fine and highly flexible. Place fabrics with wrong sides facing and whip-stitch the edges together with tiny stitches.

2 Refold fabrics so right sides are together and press lightly. Sew a running stitch ⅛"/3mm seam from edge.

3 Roll seam allowance to one side and slipstitch in place with tiny stitches (a). While this method is time-consuming, it will give a delicate result that is quite sturdy. The seam looks finished on the wrong side (b), making the work reversible.

GEOBEOBAKKI SEAM

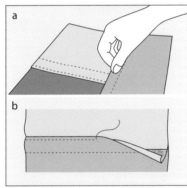

(Flat-Fell Seam) Place fabrics right sides facing; stitch ½"/12mm seam. Trim one seam allowance to ⅛"/6mm. Press both allowances to one side, covering trimmed seam. Fold raw edge of wider seam ¼"/6mm under (a); press. Topstitch in place (b).

CURVED SEAMS

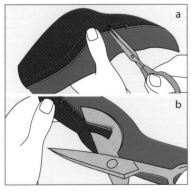

Cut freeform curves in fabric as directed on page 132, so fabrics are on straight grain when joined. Make *maleobakki* seam, clipping into seam allowances at curves so seams lie flat (a). Trim raw edges using appliqué scissors to prevent cutting through fabric (b).

↑ Metamorphosis—©Leonie Castelino, Mahwah, New Jersey. Photo by Seigi Lehman. Inspired by the concept of "breaking boundaries." Commercial and hand-dyed silk organza. Machine-sewn maleobakki and kekki seams. 30 x 60"/91 x152 cm. 2008.

5 APPLIQUÉ

fusible web
raw. edge free cut
mosaic padded
dimensional
landscapes
fabric collage
scrappliqué
confetti

5

5

APPLIQUÉ ART QUILTS

It's quite possible that the origin of the patchwork quilt was actually an appliquéd blanket, though that may seem a contradiction in terms. The first "patched" quilts probably started out as blankets with holes that needed mending; a piece of fabric was applied over the hole and stitched in place—the very definition of appliqué. And as with so many needlework techniques born of necessity, this application of one fabric patch onto another has now evolved into a complex and magnificent genre that we call appliqué quilt art.

➡ Saki—©Yoshiko Katagiri, Nara, Japan. Inspired by the endurance of the sea in northeast Japan after the terrible earthquake and tsunami on March 11, 2011. Hand-dyed sheeting, silk fabrics, satin, rayon, sheers. Hand pieced, hand appliquéd, hand quilted. 79 x 79"/200 x 200cm. 2012.

⬆ Bridge Motel—©Lisa Kijak, Irvine, California. Inspired by a photo by Mark B. Bauschke. Lisa finds inspiration in complex surfaces marked by time and strives to capture her interpretation of them in fabric. Commercial and hand-dyed cotton fabrics, tulle, sheers. Raw edge appliqué, machine quilted. 38 x 38"/96 x 96cm. 2011.

However, there is a major difference between the appliqué quilts of the past and many of those being made today. Previously it was customary to turn the raw edges of the fabrics under to prevent fraying, so appliqués were more difficult and time-consuming to sew perfectly. Curves and points were a particular problem requiring much patience, good light and a meticulous approach. And while the designs could be incredibly elaborate, many were based on simple shapes such as flowers, leaves, and geometrics, resulting in decorative motifs rather than allover pictures. There is no doubt that the antique appliqué quilts we admire today are so well preserved because

⬆ Alberta Rockies #2—©Patti Morris, Alberta, Canada. This original design was created to celebrate the beauty of the Rocky Mountains near the artist's home. Real leaves were used as templates for free-motion quilting. Hand-dyed and commercial cotton fabrics, collaged photographs. Fused raw edge appliqué and collage, free-motion machine quilted. 50 x 63"/127 x 160cm. 2010.

Abu Ali and the Gilded Chairs—
©Jenny Bowker, Canberra, Australia. Photo
by David Paterson. Abu Ali makes gilded chairs
in one of the poorest streets of Cairo, Egypt.
They glow like jewels against the tattered
buildings. Hand-dyed and commercial fabric,
foiled jersey fabric. Raw edge appliqué was
stitched on the face with monofilament in
tiny zigzag, appliqué with foiled jersey was
stitched, then excess cut away with soldering
iron, free-motion machine quilted.
87 x 79"/200 x 220cm. 2009.

they were cherished rather than used. These quilts were carefully stored and only brought out for special occasions because of the huge amount of time it took to make them.

With the invention of fusible web, many of today's appliqué artists no longer choose to turn under the fabric edges, which opens up innumerable possibilites for artistic endeavor and makes the entire process quicker and more spontaneous. Flowing curves and sharp points are easily accomplished. Thin strips and minute accents can be fused in exactly the right place to make intricate pieces that have more in common with paintings than textiles. Featured on these pages are portraits and landscapes that would have been virtually impossible to create by traditional appliqué methods.

➲ Banksia—©Beth Miller, Kambah ACT, Australia. Photo by David Paterson. The brilliant yellow of the banksia flowers contrast with the dark green leaves edged in red, creating a splash of color in the Australian landscape. Hand-dyed and commercial cottons, hessian background. Fused raw edge appliqué outlined in red fabric, machine quilted. 59 x 59"/150 x 150cm. 2005.

⬇ Bimbimbie—©Dianne Firth, Canberra, Australia. Photo by Andrew Sikorski. This quilt was inspired by the view from the residence called "Bimbimbie" over rolling terrain incised by an ephemeral creek. When the creek floods it takes on the colors of the earth. Cotton fabrics, wool batting, polyester thread. Torn strip appliqué, machine quilted, painted. 33 x 78"/83 x 198cm. 2010.

Some appliqué quilt artists are still choosing to hand stitch their pieces, and these magnificent works can be seen here as well. Other quilts depicted in the chapter show alternative techniques such as the use of monofilament thread to stitch the appliqués to a base fabric, with the resulting appearance of hand stitching. Some quilt artists choose to use colorful threads to embroider the edges of their appliqués, making a feature of the stitching. All these examples show the incredible versatility of contemporary appliqué work and how these techniques combine so easily with surface design, patchwork, quilting and embellishment to produce sensational results.

This chapter focuses mainly on these new methods of appliqué and assumes previous knowledge of basic appliqué techniques that are covered so well in other books. Use these pages as a springboard to inspire your own distinct interpretation of appliqué quilt art.

⬅ *Caravanserai*—©Cheryl FitzGerald, Albuquerque, New Mexico. This quilt is based on a photograph by Linda Lucero Hughes of a Turkish *caravanserai*—an inn along the Silk Road where caravans could stop and rest. Cotton fabric. Raw edge appliqué pieces spaced to show base fabrics, machine satin-stitched. 40 x 28"/102 x 71cm. 2010.

⬇ The Untraceable Path of the Butterfly—©Lin Hsin-Chen, Tainan City, Taiwan. Photo by Wu Chung-Yen. The artist is making a statement about how global warming has created environmental damage far beyond our expectations, represented by butterfly migration problems and their reduction in numbers. Commercial fabrics. Hand appliquéd, hand pieced, hand quilted. 118 x 118"/300 x 300cm. 2010.

FUSIBLE WEB APPLIQUÉ

Fusible web appliqué has become the technique of choice for many art quilters. Complex designs with tiny pieces and sharp points can be created because fusible web prevents fabric from fraying. Since fabric edges do not need to be turned, quilters have more flexibility to create realistic and intricate images.

Fusible web is a man-made fiber that melts when heated, bonding two pieces of fabric together. It is sold in prepackaged lengths or by the yard/meter. It comes in a variety of weights, and has many uses, including garment making. For appliqué work, use a lightweight fusible web, as fabrics can become stiff when bonded. Thicker webs will contain more "glue" that will make the finished piece inflexible and could affect the sewing machine needle. Fusible webs without a paper backing are used for fine fabrics that require a soft finish, or as a temporary hold for basting or repositioning. Spray adhesives can also be used to baste the layers of a quilt together.

Special care must be taken when pressing fusible web as it could melt all over your iron and the ironing surface; use parchment paper or a Teflon pressing sheet under your iron. If you get glue on the iron, there are products that will clean away the residue. Alternatively, you can run the iron over a non-scented dryer sheet resting on a fabric scrap, then iron another scrap to remove any oily residue.

Most fusible webs have a paper backing or support which is useful for tracing patterns, keeping in mind that the shapes you are drawing will be in reverse when appliquéd (especially important if creating letters or words). Use a light box when tracing to get as clear an image as possible. Pre-wash the fabrics you are planning to bond to remove any finishes that might prevent the fusible web from melting into the fibers. As fusible webs vary greatly depending on the manufacturer, always read and follow the instructions carefully, and test on small scraps of fabric before beginning.

Sharp embroidery scissors are essential for cutting appliqués from fusible web. Take your time and cut carefully, but don't despair if you accidentally cut off part of the design. If ironed carefully on the background, your mistake will be virtually undetectable.

For art quilts and wall hangings, fused appliqués do not need to be stitched down after bonding. However if your project is going to be well used and laundered, it is essential to secure the edges of the appliqués with machine stitches, quilting or hand embroidery.

TECHNIQUE

1 Use a pencil to draw or trace a simple design on the paper side of the fusible web, keeping in mind that it will be in reverse when cut from the fabric.

2 Cut out the paper pattern, leaving a small allowance around the edges. Place it on the wrong side of the chosen appliqué fabric, paper side up.

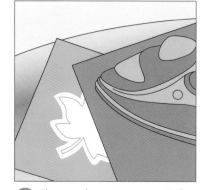

3 Place parchment paper or a Teflon pressing sheet over the pattern. Using a medium-hot, dry iron, press pattern to fabric for about four seconds to fuse them together. A non-steam iron is preferable, as marks from steam holes may transfer to fabric.

4 Using small sharp scissors, cut out the appliqué exactly along drawn outline, making sure that no frayed edges of the fusible web extend beyond the fabric. Handle appliqué gently to avoid fraying the edges.

5 Remove the paper backing by peeling it off. If you have trouble getting it started, score the back with a needle to split the paper, and peel from the slit. A fine adhesive layer will remain on the wrong side of the appliqué.

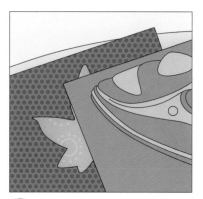

6 Place appliqué, adhesive side down, on right side of background fabric and press using a hot, dry iron and parchment paper or a Teflon pressing sheet. Your appliqué will be permanently fused in place, so make sure the position is right.

FREE CUT

For those who don't wish to use templates, fuse web to wrong side of a piece of fabric, then use rotary cutter or scissors to freely cut appliqués into desired shapes. This is a more liberated way of designing appliquéd art quilts.

PRINTED MOTIFS

1 Feature a motif from a printed fabric with fusible web appliqué. Roughly cut around edges of motif leaving a small allowance and fuse to same size web. Follow steps 2–5 to prepare, fuse and cut out the appliqué. Trim fabric carefully along motif edges.

2 Place the appliqué in its correct position on the background fabric and press until the fabrics are bonded together, using parchment paper or a Teflon pressing sheet to protect the iron.

FINISHING THE EDGES

1 The easiest way to secure a fused appliqué to the background is to sew close to the appliqué edge all around with a simple straight stitch or narrow open zigzag stitch.

2a For a professional finish, machine satin-stitch the edges of the appliqué; add details to the appliqué such as the veins shown here. Try different effects by using any of the decorative satin stitches on your sewing machine to finish the edges.

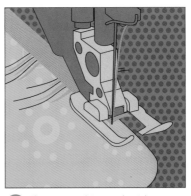

2b If using machine embroidery, make a test piece to ensure that stitches don't cause tunneling (when fabric is pulled or distorted). If tunnelling occurs, place stabilizer beneath area to be stitched or lower machine's upper tension.

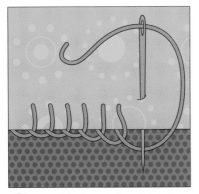

3 Use a blanket stitch to finish the edges by hand. Work from left to right as shown when embroidering with blanket stitch. Pull stitches snugly as you go along so they rest against the edges of the appliqué.

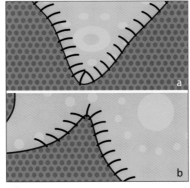

4 You can also blanket stitch the edges using a sewing machine. Work slowly and stop with your needle in the down position. At corners (a) and V's (b), make the last stitch, and pivot the fabric. Make another stitch, pivot again, then continue stitching.

QUILTING

You can secure the appliqués using machine quilting stitches once the quilt has been layered. Make sure that your quilting criss-crosses the appliqués at crucial points to prevent the pieces from coming away from the background.

RAW EDGE APPLIQUÉ

The painterly technique of raw edge appliqué is accomplished using either fusible web or a spray adhesive or by simply pinning and stitching. The main difference between this and traditional appliqué is that the edges are not turned under. This means that precise points are effortlessly achieved, and curved shapes can be organically cut for realistic effects. Every art quilter has a preferred method for doing raw edge appliqué; experiment and adapt these instructions to come up with your own.

To compose an improvisational art quilt, work freely and instinctively, cutting and fusing appliqués onto a background fabric without using a pattern; see pages 148–149 for basic fusible web instructions. Alternatively, create an appliquéd image using a photograph (or a drawing or painting) for inspiration. While a specific image is an excellent design source, don't feel you have to copy it exactly; use it as a starting point and sketch freely to make workable pattern pieces. The key is to simplify the picture while retaining the important elements. Using the right fabrics is also essential. Employ a wide variety of fabrics in various prints and solid colors. For this technique your fabric stash will truly be like a painter's palette.

Arrange and fuse or stitch the appliqués to the base, working from the background to the foreground—the simple overlapping of one fabric on top of another will add a sense of depth and realism to the quilt. Look at the pieces on pages 142–147 to see how some art quilters have made a complete picture in appliqué. If you don't wish to appliqué the entire quilt top, you can make an appliquéd unit, then fuse it to a prepared background as shown on opposite page.

PATTERNS

1 See Sizing & Marking Designs on pages 34–35. Prepare full-size master pattern on tracing paper indicating colors, shadows, directional lines—whatever will help in fabric choice and placement. Number each piece. Transfer all design lines to base fabric.

2 To make working pattern for cutting fusible web, reverse master pattern; trace entire reversed design. Number pieces to match master pattern. Trace pieces of same color onto paper side of fusible web, leaving space for cutting between them. Number pieces.

FUSED APPLIQUÉS

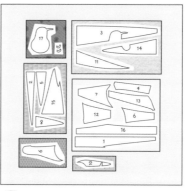

1 Select a large number of fabrics for the appliqués in a variety of prints and solids. Cut out fusible web pattern pieces; fuse to wrong side of fabrics you have chosen for each of the appliqués. Do not remove backing paper yet.

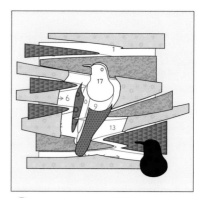

2 Cut out fused appliqués leaving scant seam allowance for overlapping (this can be cut away later if not required). Place each appliqué right side up on master paper pattern. When pieces are in place, study design critically and change any that aren't working.

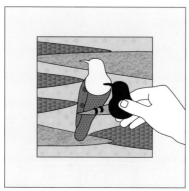

3 When satisfied with appliqués, peel off paper and place in marked positions on base fabric, starting with background elements and working toward foreground. Overlap pieces so no base fabric shows, creating a sense of depth.

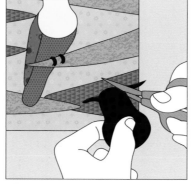

4 Study design again to ensure you are satisfied with the arrangement of all the appliqués. At this point you can carefully trim away any seam allowances that are not required.

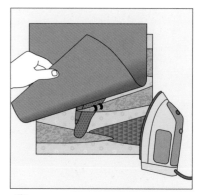

5 Fuse appliqués to base fabric using a hot, dry iron following manufacturer's instructions. Be sure to use a pressing cloth or parchment paper to protect the iron. Work carefully to prevent shifting any unpressed appliqués out of position.

APPLIQUÉ UNIT

Create an appliqué unit and secure it to a previously quilted or painted background; see quilt, below right. Follow instructions on previous page for *Fused Appliqués*. After fusing, trim away base to exact size of appliqué, then fuse or stitch unit to another background.

OUTLINE

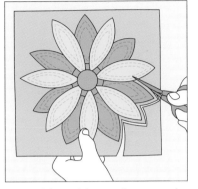

Create delicate fabric outlines around appliqués by allowing base fabric to show (see *Caravanserai* on page 147). Choose base fabric to enhance appliqués. Fuse or stitch appliqués to base and cut out, leaving narrow margin of base fabric showing around edges.

SPRAY ADHESIVE

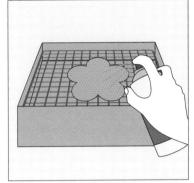

Appliqués can be secured with spray adhesive. Make a spray box using a plastic screen inside a cardboard box. Cut out appliqué, place wrong side up on screen; apply fabric spray adhesive. Position on fabric wrong side down; press as in step 5, page 150.

EDGE TREATMENTS

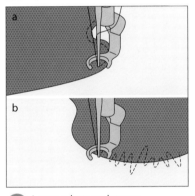

① Leave edges as they are. Alternatively, stitch close to edges, outlining each piece with straight or zigzag stitches (a). On amorphous shapes, you can free-motion machine quilt random zigzag lines over edges to secure them (b).

② Create special effects by fraying the edges of fabric shapes deliberately before fusing them to the quilt background—use fingertips to pull out threads. Try this to create realistic grass in landscapes, froth on waves, hair on people or fur on animals.

⬆ Bird Journal: Magpie Study—©Erilyn McMillan, Palmerston North, New Zealand. All feathers were cut, layered and stitched to a background to make a raw edge appliqué unit. The bird unit was appliquéd on a brocade background with hand-embroidered lettering, which was then daubed with fabric paint. Cotton fabrics, glittered netting. Raw edge appliquéd, hand embroidered, couched, free-motion machine quilted. 17¼" x 17½"/44 x 45cm. 2011.

MOSAIC APPLIQUÉ

Inspired by mosaics made of tile or glass, this appliqué method runs the gamut from simple to complex, depending on the design you choose to make. The technique is relatively simple: small pieces of fabric are fused to a background with narrow spaces in between to create a motif; the background fabric becomes the "grout" between the mosaics. Though time-consuming, mosaic appliqué can be quite absorbing and once any design issues have been solved, the quiet repetition in placing the pieces is very satisfying.

There are three styles of mosaic appliqué: irregular, regular and a combination of the two. Designs can be geometric, abstract, or realistic. Study images of actual mosaics to see how they work and to give you some ideas for your own piece. Looking at real mosaics will enable you to better understand the concept and how the pieces interact with one another. Many churches and museums have mosaics that may spark your imagination; bring your camera along to capture these images for later use, and don't forget to look at the floors, which often feature wonderful geometric designs. Search for ideas in needlepoint or counted thread books and children's coloring books. If your computer can digitize a photo, this would also be useful. Otherwise, choose a photo or other image and study it carefully to see how you can simplify it. Using tracing paper, outline the main shapes, creating key areas of color.

When creating mosaic appliqué, it's important not to show too much of the background, so tiles must be cut with this in mind. However, the color of the background must be chosen carefully as it will have a strong impact on the overall look of the finished piece. Take some time to choose the fabrics for cutting the mosaics as well. Solid colors work best, and hand-dyed fabrics are excellent, as slight variations in color will provide depth and interest. Use cotton, silk or even felt for mosaic appliqué; tightly woven fabrics will ensure against fraying. Use metallic fabrics to add some sparkle to your design, although take care as metallics tend to shred easily and may be difficult to fuse.

Cut the mosaics using sharp scissors; remember to peel off the fusible web backing paper before cutting. For ease in working, separate the mosaic tiles and shards into piles by color and store them in trays or other containers so they don't get mixed up. Use tweezers when working with small pieces. Save any leftover mosaics for future projects, or use them to add highlights to other work.

MOSAIC APPLIQUÉ STYLES

1a Irregular mosaic appliqué uses fabric pieces in different shapes and sizes, herein referred to as shards, as they often resemble shards of broken glass or porcelain. This style is quite free and spontaneous.

1b When creating irregular mosaic appliqué, you can leave uneven spaces between the pieces as shown. The background (grout) fabric is just as important as the mosaic pieces, so choose the color carefully to enhance the rest of the fabrics.

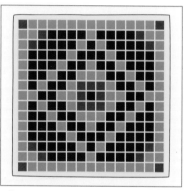

2 Regular mosaic appliqué uses squares or rectangles, herein referred to as tiles, of approximately the same size, creating an ordered design. Try to ensure that the spaces between the tiles are of equal size.

3 Alternatively, you can have a mixture of tiles and shards in the same design. You can also stagger the placement of mosaic tiles like the bricks in a wall.

Gaudi Mosaic Cushion (detail)—©Barbara and Rebecca Weeks, Hertfordshire, UK. Silk mosaic appliqué designed and bonded by Rebecca, machine quilted and finished by Barbara. 2000.

OTHER ARRANGEMENTS

Curves add flow and interest to a design, so gently angle the pieces to create smooth curves—in this case the gap between tiles will be more like a narrow triangle. Trim pieces to fit as necessary.

Cut fabric tiles into special shapes to fill in any unusual gaps that occur in your design, or to add a colorful highlight such as this bird's eye

Don't get rid of any unused mosaics that have been prepared with fusible web. Save leftover fabric tiles or shards to use as accents on patchwork or appliqué projects.

TECHNIQUE

1 Choose a design and enlarge to the size of the piece you wish to make. Use colored pencils, crayons or watercolors to indicate the placement of color on your pattern. Cut a piece of background "grout" fabric slightly bigger all around than the design.

2 Lightly sketch the general outlines of the design on the right side of the background fabric using a pencil or fabric marker.

3 Follow the instructions for fusible web appliqué on pages 148–149 to prepare your fabrics. Peel off the backing paper, then cut into mosaic tiles or shards using scissors. Tiles should be approximately ½–¾"/12–19mm in size; shards can be slightly larger.

4 Working on small areas at a time, arrange the mosaics, adhesive side down, within the marked lines on the background fabric; trim as necessary to fit using small sharp scissors. Position mosaics so grout shows between each piece.

5 When you are completely satisfied with the arrangement, press in place using a hot dry iron and parchment paper or a Teflon pressing sheet. Your "tiles" will be permanently fused to the background, so make sure the positioning is right.

FINISHING

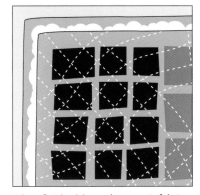

When finished, layer the mosaic fabric with batting and a back; baste and quilt. For extra security, and particularly if piece will be handled or used on a bed, quilt so stitches cross each mosaic tile or shard.

PADDED APPLIQUÉ

A trapunto effect can be achieved by padding appliqués before they are stitched to a base fabric. For the padding, use felt in a matching color to create a subtle effect or use two layers of polyester, cotton or wool batting beneath the appliqué for a loftier result. You may wish to add a stabilizer to the wrong side of the fabric base, especially if you are planning to do machine embroidery. The appliqué edges can be left plain, satin-stitched, machine embroidered or free-motion machine quilted (pages 176–182). You can also quilt the padded appliqué by hand or machine once it has been stitched to a base fabric. Add embellishments such as buttons or beads over the appliqué to emphasize the puffiness. Another option is to free-motion machine quilt individual appliqué shapes, cut them out and sew them to the quilt top.

PAD THE APPLIQUÉ

1 Choose fabric for appliqué and base; add stabilizer to wrong side of base if desired. Layer padding (see text, left) on right side of background. Cut out appliqué shape; place right side up on padding. Use a sewing machine to straight-stitch close to edges.

2 Carefully cut away padding and outer edges of appliqué fabric as close to stitching line as possible, using sharp embroidery scissors. Do not cut base fabric.

SECURE THE EDGES

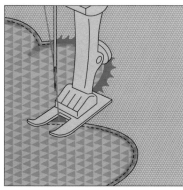

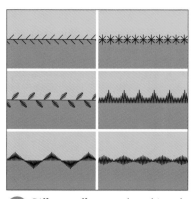

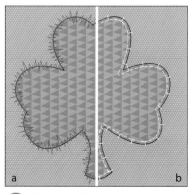

1 Select an embroidery stitch on sewing machine and stitch all around edge, covering straight stitches. Use a rayon or other decorative thread if you wish to highlight stitches. When finished, tear away stabilizer (if using) from base or leave in place.

2 Different effects can be achieved using the various embroidery patterns on your sewing machine to edge appliqués. To expand your repertoire, try using the machine stitches or in an assortment of combinations.

3 Alternatively, layer work for quilting and free-motion machine quilt around appliqué edges (a). Or stitch appliqué invisibly in place using monofilament thread and blind hem (b) or buttonhole stitch on the sewing machine (shown in white thread).

QUILTED APPLIQUÉ SHAPES

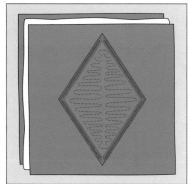

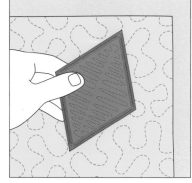

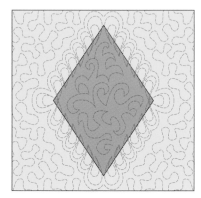

1 Draw outline of appliqué shape on fabric; layer with padding (see text above) and a back. Straight stitch along outline. Free-motion machine quilt motifs or backfill designs (see pages 180–181) within appliqué shape. Machine satin-stitch edges if desired.

2 Cut out quilted shape carefully using sharp scissors. Pin in position on quilt. Hand-appliqué invisibly or machine-stitch using buttonhole or blind hem stitch.

Alternatively, baste quilted appliqué to unquilted top, then layer with batting and a back. Free-motion machine quilt over edges of quilted appliqué to secure.

DIMENSIONAL APPLIQUÉ

To add a sense of realism and fun to appliqué work, think about making some parts three-dimensional. The subtle unexpected addition of a leaf, petal or wing extending from the surface will add a quirky touch to an art quilt. However, too many dimensional appliqués are gratuitous—use restraint and good judgment in their number and placement. Be sure to stabilize the background fabric to prevent distortion or pulling from the extra weight.

Consider dimensional appliqués as an embellishment that should be added last so they don't interfere with the quilting. If using another appliqué such as a tree trunk or insect body to conceal raw edges, lightly stuff the appliqué with fiberfill before sewing it down and quilt it to add dimension. Make invisible stitches to secure appliqués to the background, leaving the edges free.

TECHNIQUE

1 Draw outline of appliqué shape on right side of fabric. Layer with thin batting or felt and a back; back should have right side facing out. Straight stitch along outline, then machine satin-stitch over straight stitches using matching or contrasting thread.

2 Free-motion machine quilt within the shape to delineate design and create texture. Add highlights with fabric paint or dye, inks, pens, etc. Embellish with beads if appropriate. Cut out appliqué with sharp scissors close to satin stitching.

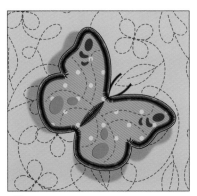

3 Sew center of appliqué to quilt with invisible stitches; leave edges unstitched so they raise slightly away from quilt surface. Where appliqué is attached, cover stitches with machine satin-stitch (as for the body shown here) or appliqué another shape on top.

WINGS

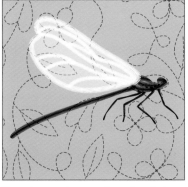

To make translucent wings, fuse 2 sheer fabrics together using lightweight fusible web or soldering iron (see page 101). Machine satin-stitch edges and interior lines with tear-away stabilizer. Cut out with sharp scissors and remove stabilizer. Stitch ends of wings to quilt.

STEMS & BRANCHES

Depending on desired finished effect, cut or rip thin fabric strips, or use narrow strips of lightweight felt in brown or green. Gently twist fabric or felt several times to make a knobbly branch. Pin and hand stitch to background with matching thread.

PETALS

Fuse two different fabrics with wrong sides facing and cut out petal shapes with sharp scissors. Before stitching petal to background fabric, make a small pleat at the bottom so it forms a slight cupped shape; stitch pinched base of petal securely to background.

LEAVES

Make leaves same way as petals (see left). To attach leaves to fabric, machine quilt along veins, leaving edges free. Or attach leaves at the stem only and allow to hang freely. Deliberately fold some edges over; stitch folded areas in place invisibly.

To make a decomposing leaf, cut shape from brown or rust fabric. Raggedly cut out interior areas. Place between two layers of water-soluble fabric. Machine-stitch veins all over leaf, criss-crossing stitches within cut areas. Rinse to remove water-soluble fabric.

LANDSCAPES

Interpreting landscapes in fabric is a pursuit that particularly appeals to art quilters. While only seven basic approaches are shown here, there are countless combinations and permutations that can be tried. Find a style that appeals to you and add your own special flourishes to make it unique. You do not need to be able to draw or paint—rely on the texture and color of the fabrics, the stitches and the embellishments to create a distinctive composition.

Creating a quilt landscape may appear a daunting prospect, but it is actually easy and highly enjoyable. First compose a design based on a photograph, a rough sketch, a painting or on your immediate observations. Crop and simplify that design, selecting a few elements on which to focus rather than trying to make an exact copy. Establish a focal point, then begin picking fabrics.

Fabric color and pattern will impart depth and proximity to your landscape. Use fabrics and elements in the correct scale, making distant objects/prints smaller than those in the foreground. Light cool colors seem to recede, so place these in the background. Warm, dark colors appear closer, so use these in the foreground. Choose fabrics with more detail and texture for the foreground areas, keeping background elements vague and imprecise. Try placing large and small versions of the same object in the landscape to give a sense of scale, positioning the larger object in the foreground or overlapping objects to give a real sense of depth and perspective.

Whether depicting sweeping panoramas or intimate details, landscape quilts can incorporate most of the techniques featured in this book.

LANDSCAPE STYLES

Naive: Interpreting a landscape with traditional needle-turned or machine satin-stitched appliqué will give a tranquil naive result. Keep lines smooth and details to a minimum. Do not strive for realism; indicate different areas of the landscape in a simple way.

Realistic: Fabrics that are ripped and roughly cut will create a landscape that has a more natural appearance. Temporarily secure fabrics to base with a fabric glue stick, which will allow you to move pieces if you are not happy with their position.

Impressionist: Just as Impressionists painted landscapes using daubes of color, art quilters can create landscapes using tiny pieces of fabric, scattered like confetti on a base. Sheer fabric or tulle overlays hold pieces in place before and during stitching (see page 159).

Patchwork: To depict landscapes in patchwork, identify the important elements and break them down into geometric shapes. Try strip piecing, stitch and flip piecing or digitizing an image into hundreds of tiny squares to make a patchwork landscape quilt.

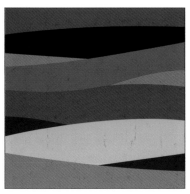

Abstract: Landscapes do not have to be realistic or instantly recognizable. Interpreting a landscape through color, line or just the ambiance of a place is a meaningful and liberating way of creating an art quilt.

Painted: Paint washes of color to represent background areas, then define with appliqué, stamps or monoprints, pens, stitching, embellishments and quilting. Talented painters can use dyes and fabric paints to depict realistic wholecloth landscapes on fabric.

Digital: Photographs of landscapes can be modified and/or enlarged on the computer, then printed on fabric. To make larger images, print overlapping sections on fabric and seam together so elements match. Quilt to highlight key areas and add texture.

DESIGNING A LANDSCAPE QUILT

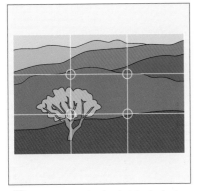

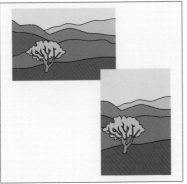

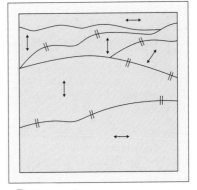

1 As a general rule, divide design in thirds and position the focal point to one side about one-third of the way across horizontally or vertically. Avoid symmetry and centering of the focal point. Simplify image to indicate essential placement lines.

2 A horizontal (landscape) orientation will produce a calmer effect than a vertical (portrait) one. Choose the orientation that reflects the mood you are trying to convey. Include diagonal elements in the design to lead the eye toward the focal point.

3 Enlarge drawing to make master pattern. Decide on preferred style for landscape quilt, and adapt pattern accordingly. If cutting pattern apart, draw grainlines and hatch marks to help match pieces when sewing. Also, make another copy for reference.

FABRIC TIPS

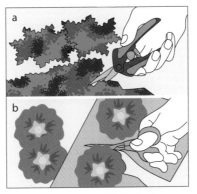

Collect fabrics that portray natural features such as cloudy skies, grass and stones. Also utilize backs of fabrics, which are often paler in color. Use mottled hand-dyed fabrics for blending. Take close-up photos of natural elements; print on fabric.

Ripped or messy-cut fabrics look most natural and should be utilized for realistic landscapes and background areas (a). Fussy cutting is best used for foreground pieces such as flowers, leaves, animals, insects—use sharp scissors to cut precise shapes (b).

When arranging fabrics on a base, begin with the background (usually the sky) and work toward the foreground. Continually step back to review design and determine whether fabrics are working; remove any that look inappropriate.

SHEERS & TULLE

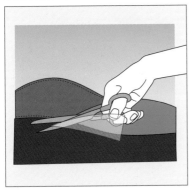

Tone down bright colors or create atmospheric effects such as fog, haze or bright sunlight with sheer fabrics or tulle. Lay tulle or sheer fabric over specific area; machine-stitch outline of area you wish to cover. Cut or tear away excess beyond stitching.

3D SHAPES

For added realism, minimally attach fabric petals, leaves and other "dangly" elements with 1–2 stitches so they have a 3D appearance. See page 155 for instructions on making double-sided leaves.

BORDERS

If adding a border, select fabric so that it complements design in the same way as a frame around a painting. A border will contain the landscape, but you can also include foreground elements spilling out into the border for added depth.

STRIP PIECING

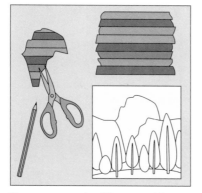

To create more detail in areas with striped features such as fields, water, rock faces and canyons, make strip-pieced fabrics in appropriate colors. Then roughly free-cut the strip-pieced fabrics, or use templates to create that section of the landscape.

STITCH AND FLIP

Use fabric strips to create patchwork landscapes, stitching and flipping them in place onto a background. Place strips right sides together on a base; stitch seam, then turn bottom strip to right side and press. Continue adding strips, angling them slightly for realism.

DEPTH

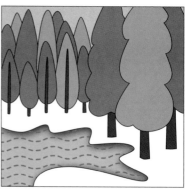

Overlap landscape elements such as trees and bushes to give a stong sense of depth—objects in front of other objects appear closer to the viewer, so utilze this concept. Trim away fabrics to reveal areas hidden underneath, such as the lake shown here.

TEXTURE

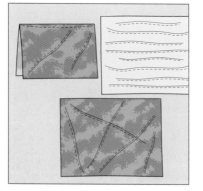

Fold fabric randomly and stitch very close to fold to create small pleats or darts. Parallel pleats can signify ripples on sand and water, or bark on a tree. Overlapping or perpendicular pleats can denote mountain ridges or cracks in the earth.

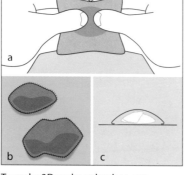

To make 3D rocks or bushes, cut appropriate color fabrics in approximate shapes. Rub thumb on bias of fabric to make a pouch (a). Trim to final shape and appliqué to landscape (b). Stuff pouch with fiberfill before sewing closed (c).

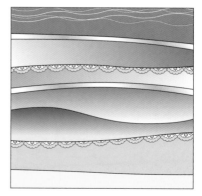

To create sparkly lines on water, fold strips of metallic fabric in half; insert in seams. Alternatively, insert lace in seams to indicate froth. Or fuse some Angelina (pages 214–215) to fabric to simulate the movement of sparkling water.

HIGHLIGHTS

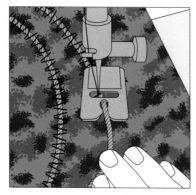

Free-motion machine embroider areas of the landscape, using thread colors that will highlight and enhance the design. Couch thicker threads onto the surface by hand or machine to simulate vines, branches or logs (see page 224).

PAINTING

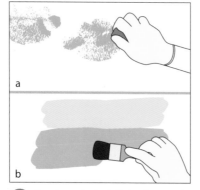

1 Create a wholecloth background for a landscape quilt by sponging (a) or painting (b) fabric with washes of color. See pages 60–65 for ideas and instructions. Skilled artists can paint a detailed landscape that can then be layered, stitched and embellished.

2 Once color is dry, add details to painted background with fabric markers, paintstiks or more color. Use sponge to dab color on bubble wrap, corrugated card or steel wool, then dab on fabric to simulate flowers, grass or shrubbery.

CONFETTI

1 Lay small pieces of similar color fabrics on cutting board. Use rotary cutter to slice them into very small pieces, cutting several times in different directions to make confetti. Set aside and repeat for other colors you intend to use in design.

2 Sprinkle fabric adhesive powder on background fabric. Scatter confetti on background, using a small implement to move pieces to proper position if necessary. When satisfied with arrangement, place parchment paper on top and press with a dry iron.

3 Use sheer fabric/tulle to hold small pieces and obscure edges of confetti. Center it over landscape so cut fabrics are undisturbed. Audition colors as pale sheers/tulle will soften outcome, while darker colors will add intensity. Quilt over the sheers/tulle.

⬆ Autumn— ©Marlene Cohen, London, UK. Photo by Michael Wicks. Made of thousands of hand-cut leaf shapes, fused and applied to a backing fabric. The complete piece was then overprinted with patterns of memory neurones, using a thermofax screen. Cotton fabric, tulle overlay. Appliquéd collage, machine quilted. 27 x 59"/ 69 x 150cm. 2011.

⬆ Looking Up—©Laura Breitman, Warwick, New York. Photo by Michael Needleman. This collage was inspired by photographs taken by the artist's husband of a maple tree in their home town. Cotton fabric, army duck canvas, polymer medium. Fabric collage: hand cut fabric layered and glued on canvas with polymer medium. 19½ x 23¾"/49 x 60cm. 2001.

Piter 1—©Natalya Aikens, Pleasantville, New York. Inspired by St. Petersburg, Russia. The city's architecture has been described as poetry in stone and now the artist has created it in soft textiles. Silk organza, dryer sheets, rayon and cotton embroidery thread, oil paint sticks. Computer manipulation and printing, image transfer, painting, hand stitching. 18 x 18"/46 x 46cm. 2010.

Say It With Flowers—©Laura Fogg, Ukiah, California. Inspired by a coastal scene in Mendocino County, northern California. Raw-edge collage with "zillions" of tiny pieces of printed cottons, sheer fabric and synthetics arranged on batting with no pins or stitching until composition was complete, overlaid with transparent tulle, machine quilted. Signs made with digital photos printed on textured fabric and sanded for a distressed look. Pintucked border was appliquéd and couched with leaves, blossoms and chenille yarn flowers. 41 x 49"/104 x 124cm. 2007.

FABRIC COLLAGE

Fabric collage is not a technique that can be taught. It is a true art form and its success or failure is dependent on the maker's artistry and inventiveness. The examples in this chapter show just how diverse fabric collage can be—from naive assemblages of fabrics and embellishments to pieces that are breathtaking in their complexity and beauty. The quality that all these works have in common is spontaneity and the imaginative use of fabric and other textile elements.

Fabric collage can be so liberating for quilters who have always worked to a specific plan—try to embrace the concept of improvisation and enjoy it. This style of quilt art gives the maker the opportunity to try out any and all of the techniques featured in this book. Experiment and learn something new, then compose a collage with the result—in particular, look at the Surface Design and Embellishment chapters for some ideas with which to experiment. Permit yourself time to improvise and play; this is not a process that can be rushed. It's virtually impossible to make mistakes, as any perceived imperfections can be hidden by fabric, paint or an embellishment.

Although this method may seem simple, successful collages do not just happen. The development and construction of a fabric collage requires some time and thought. Rather than slapping all the elements down and stitching them in place, consider integrating the layers as you work so that the elements link together. Embellishments and mixed media elements will contribute greatly to the finished result, but don't overdo it. Know when to stop.

Lateral thinking and an open mind will contribute to the success of a collage, but because this technique is unstructured, it can be difficult to focus. That's why it's a good idea to have a theme, be it color, texture, a subject or a concept. Memorable collages will always convey some message to the viewer.

Here are a few points to keep in mind:

- limit the color palette
- avoid symmetry
- ignore the rules
- be subtle or bold—not bland
- eliminate elements that aren't working
- strive for a sense of balance and scale
- embellish but don't overwhelm

PREPARATION

Decide on a theme; select fabrics and embellishments. Choose an interesting fabric for the base unless you plan to completely cover it; medium-weight, tightly-woven fabric will keep work flat, or you can use a stabilizer. Tear or roughly cut fabrics for layering.

THREADS

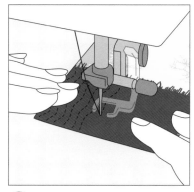

1 Choose threads carefully so they integrate well and complement design. Select cotton, silk, metallic and variegated threads in a variety of colors and thicknesses. Free-motion machine-stitch layers together as you proceed rather than waiting until the end.

PAPER

Add paper elements such as torn newspaper, photographs, photocopies or printed designs. Paper must be made water-resistant or the ink might run. Use a matte spray fixative—apply 2–3 coats, letting it dry between each coat, before using paper.

FABRICS

Arrange fabrics, lace, ribbons etc. randomly on background. Adjust elements until you are pleased with the composition. Temporarily secure pieces to base with fabric glue stick or a drop of fabric glue; keep outer edges free for tucking other pieces underneath.

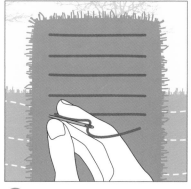

2 Alternatively, stitch or embroider pieces by hand using decorative stitches with threads in contrasting colors. Or machine-embroider using a fine needle with a sharp point to prevent holes in fabric. If you wish, add batting and a back, then quilt-as-you-go.

SURFACE DESIGN

Highlight areas of the collage using paint, crayons, pencils, fabric markers, fabric inks, oil pastels, stencils—anything goes! See Chapter 2 for surface design ideas. Alternatively, if you are unhappy with certain areas, paint, stamp or stencil over them and start again.

SHEER FABRICS

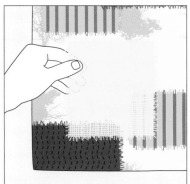

Step back and study collage to assess its progress. Use a reducing glass or take a digital photo and look at it on a computer. Ease abrupt transitions or fill in blank areas with sheer fabric, tulle or cheesecloth, which will also soften the design.

TEXTURE

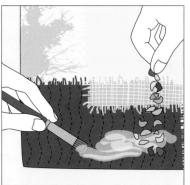

Add texture by featuring fibers, yarns, glitter, seeds, sand, pebbles, broken shells—anything that will add something to the message you are trying to convey in the collage. Stitch or glue in place.

EMBELLISHMENTS

Add dimension and interest to collage with embellishments such as buttons, beads, sequins, twigs, flowers, metal or ceramic charms, feathers, etc. Stick to the theme and keep to scale. Stitch or glue embellishments to collage after all other stitching is finished.

FUSED FABRIC COLLAGE

1 Sketch outlines of design on tightly-woven base fabric (shown in cream); place on parchment paper so collage can be moved for pressing without disturbing the pieces. Cut paper-backed fusible web to fit; center and fuse on base. Peel off paper as shown.

2 Arrange fabric scraps, ribbon, lace, fibers, etc. on fusible web, making a picture or creating random design. Overlap pieces slightly, using tweezers for placement; trim to fit as necessary. Place parchment paper or pressing cloth on top; press with dry iron to fuse.

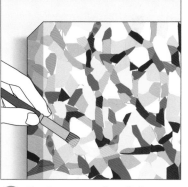

3 Check to ensure that all elements are mostly fused to base fabric. Free-motion machine stitch randomly all over to firmly secure pieces to base fabric. Alternatively, stretch collage on a frame and apply a layer of matte varnish to hold pieces in place.

VIRTUAL COLLAGE

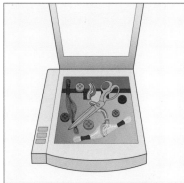

Print a collage using scanner or inkjet copier. Arrange items on glass; items placed first will be in foreground. For colored background, place fabric over assemblage, right side down. Print on paper to check placement; then print collage on prepared inkjet fabric.

FINISHING

1 After collage is complete, you can leave the edges unfinished and irregular, or trim away uneven edges with a rotary cutter and ruler. Another option is to frame the collage with a patchwork or appliqué border.

2 See Chapter 8 to choose best edge-finish and hanging method for your collage. Add a binding or facing, or embroider edges by hand or machine. Secure to a quilted fabric mount as shown here or place in a box frame (ensuring that no elements touch glass).

APPLIQUÉ EXTRAS

There are many different approaches to the technique of appliqué, with new ideas being developed all the time. The more complex procedures are covered earlier in this chapter, but here are some hints and tips you may want to try to help make your appliqué work quicker and easier.

Fabric glue will considerably speed up appliqué work without clogging up your needles. Use colorfast fabrics when working with fabric glue and wash with a gentle laundry detergent when finished. If using glue or fusible web, always cover and protect your work surface and ironing board. When ironing, place an additional sheet of parchment paper or a pressing sheet on top of the work to protect the iron. Check frequently when pressing so you don't accidentally scorch the fabric.

Some technical guidelines are common to all appliqué techniques. Insert a new sharp needle (size 60/8 to 75/11) in the sewing machine for each project; using larger needles may leave holes in the fabric. When sewing, reduce the speed of your machine; this will give you more control, especially around curves and corners. Utilize the needle down position if you have it. Using an open toe appliqué foot on the sewing machine will enable you to see both the edge of the appliqué and the needle position. Use a stabilizer (page 220) for appliqué work to ensure a crisp result and prevent tunneling and puckering, particularly when edging appliqués with machine embroidery. Lightweight stabilizers can be left in the work; paper, tear-away and water-soluble stabilizers should be removed when finished. To highlight machine appliqué stitches, lower the top thread tension so stitches will sit on top of the appliqué instead of embedding in it.

CURVES

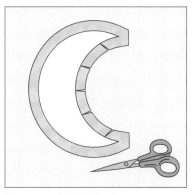

Prepare appliqué using freezer paper (page 131). When turning appliqué seam allowances under, you only need to clip concave curves, like the inside of the crescent moon shown here. Bias edges should turn easily. Gentle curves will require fewer clips than tight curves.

EDGE FUSED

1 Edge appliqués with liquid fabric glue for fusing onto background fabric and to prevent fraying. Glue should run freely but not spread; thin with water if too thick. Run tip of nozzle on wrong side of fabric within marked cutting lines so glue flows evenly.

GLUE STICK

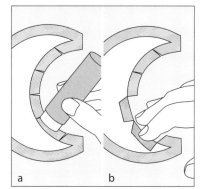

a   b

Use a fabric glue stick to secure seam allowances of appliqués to freezer paper (a). Run glue stick along raw edges on wrong side of fabric, then use fingertips or a cuticle stick to help turn the raw edges to the wrong side—finger press in place (b).

2 Allow to dry, then cut out exactly along marked outline using sharp embroidery scissors. Place in position on background fabric and press to secure with a hot, dry iron, using parchment paper or a pressing cloth to protect iron and ironing board.

FACED APPLIQUÉS

1 Draw outline of appliqué on wrong side of fabric. Choose lightweight interfacing or matching fabric for facing; place right sides together and stitch all around on marked line. Clip curves and angles; trim off points. Cut out leaving ⅛"/3mm seam allowance.

2 Cut slit in facing. Turn appliqué to right side through slit, pushing out all points and corners carefully with a point turner. Smooth and flatten edges with fingers or cuticle stick. Make sure that facing is not visible from right side of appliqué.

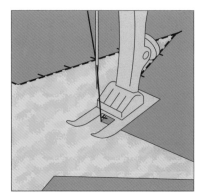

3 Place appliqué on background and stitch in place with matching thread by hand or machine (stitches are shown here in black for clarity). You can use same technique with water-soluble stabilizer for facing. After stitching, wash in cool water to remove stabilizer.

BIAS STRIP APPLIQUÉ

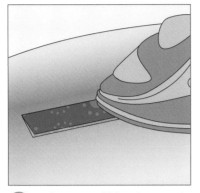

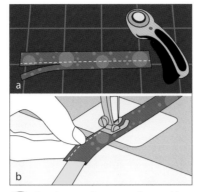

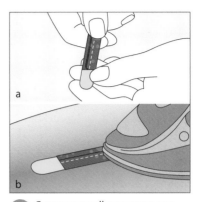

1 Cut bias strip of fabric (page 122) to twice desired width plus ½"/12mm for seam allowances. Press fabric in half lengthwise with wrong sides together, matching raw edges.

2 Stitch raw edges together making a ¼"/6mm seam. Trim seam allowance to ⅛"/3mm (a). For accuracy, use a heat-resistant plastic pressing bar to make equal width bias strips. After sewing a short distance, test to ensure pressing bar fits snugly in opening (b).

3 Center seam allowance on one side of pressing bar (a); press gently. Continue adjusting and pressing seam allowance along entire length of strip, sliding bar along as you press (b).

SCRAPPLIQUÉ

4 When finished, position pressed tube on background fabric and pin in place, seam allowance side down. If making a curve, shape curve with fingertips and press using steam. Stitch to background fabric by hand or with invisible machine appliqué (page 131).

1 This is an excellent way to utilize small scraps of fabric. Cut base fabric to desired size; apply fusible web and remove paper. Arrange fabric scraps on base with edges slightly overlapping so base does not show. Press in place using hot dry iron.

2 Prepare appliqué shapes with fusible web. Arrange on top of scrap background, making sure there is good contrast between appliqués and background; fuse in place. Layer with batting and a back, then free-motion machine quilt all over to secure pieces.

SCRAPPLIQUÉ WITH WATER-SOLUBLE STABILIZER

1 This method does not require the use of fusible web. Cut background fabric in a color that will complement the design; place on a flat surface. Arrange scraps and appliqués on background. Cut piece of water-soluble stabilizer to cover design; pin or baste in place.

2 Using monofilament thread in needle and neutral thread in bobbin, free-motion machine stitch over entire piece, catching at least one corner of each fabric scrap in the stitching.

3 When stitching is finished, immerse design in water or rinse under a tap following manufacturer's instructions to remove stabilizer. Press carefully once all stabilizer is gone. Layer with batting and a back, then free-motion machine quilt to accentuate the design.

6 QUILTING

machine quilting
free-motion
quilting designs
trapunto
longarm quilting
coloring
hand quilting

6

6

QUILTING

Quilting is the vital spark that turns a layered textile into a work of art. As stitches are added, a flat and possibly unexceptional textile is gradually transformed into a textured piece that demands examination and admiration. Quilting has advanced well beyond its original remit as a way of holding the quilt sandwich together. Quilting stitches—tiny or large, manual or mechanized—add the finishing touch to every art quilt.

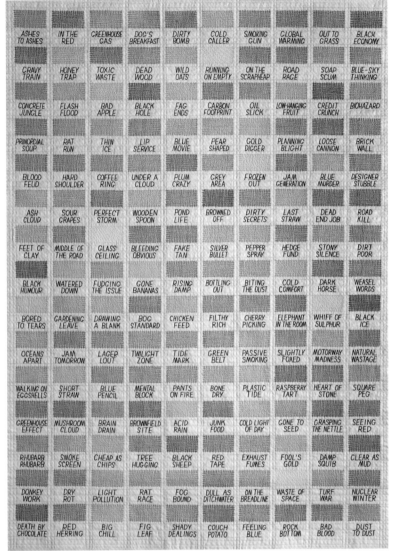

Spoiled for Choice—©Sara Impey, Colchester, Essex, UK. Photo by Kevin Mead. Inspired by color charts, this wholecloth quilt is intended as an ironic comment on today's consumer culture in which people enjoy an abundance of superficial choices but have very little choice about the big issues facing humanity such as climate change, environmental degradation, disease and war. Cotton fabric, polyester thread. Free-motion machine quilted. 32 x 43"/82 x 110cm. 2012.

Fractured Nature 1: Summer—©Deborah Schwartzman, Philadelphia, Pennsylvania. Photo by John Woodin. Inspired by tiled stepping stones that the artist made on Long Beach Island, and by the work of Antoni Gaudi and his mosaic-encrusted surfaces in Barcelona. In this piece the artist celebrates the wonderful array of patterns inherent in cotton fabric and explores the technique of thread painting to achieve the "grout" effect in her mosaic design. Commercial cotton fabric including batiks, silk, heavy-weight cotton thread. Pieced background, fused mosaic tiling, thread painting that also serves as quilting. 30 x 30"/76 x 76cm. 2011.

Quilt makers have embraced the sewing machine since its invention, but today's art quilters are exploiting mechanical possibilities as never before, leaving more time for design and creativity. Free-motion work, using a home or longarm machine, has enabled quilters to virtually "draw" elaborate designs on fabric using thread. Traditional styles, such as wholecloth and trapunto quilts, can be done entirely on the sewing machine, and embroidery has taken the concept of the quilting stitch to a new level. Once the stitches are in place, some adventurous art quilters add color to quilted work, highlighting the texture. This chapter celebrates the quilting stitch as an integral element in the design of an art quilt.

◀ Mt Fuji—©Annabel Rainbow, Royal Leamington Spa, UK. Inspired by the woodcuts of Utagawa Hiroshige. Hand-dyed cotton fabric, acrylic paint. Painted, machine appliquéd, machine pieced, free-motion machine quilted. 36 x 42"/91 x 107cm. 2012.

◑ It's Risky Being a Beer Drinking Mantis!—©Carol Fletcher, Yakima, Washington. Photo by Evans Fletcher. Inspired by a photo, taken by Ted Gamlen, of the foam on his empty beer glass, and by the artist's interest in praying mantises and their habits. Hand-dyed and painted fabrics. Raw edge appliquéd, machine quilted, beaded. 29½ x 52"/75 x 132cm. 2011.

◓ Pearl in a Zen Garden—©Linda Seward, London, UK. Photo adjusted by Kevin Mead. Cotton fabrics. Japanese *kanji* meaning 'pearl' was appliquéd using fabric dyed with fermented indigo by Ken Utsuki of Kyoto, Japan. The quilting represents raked gravel in the Zen gardens of Kyoto. Hand appliquéd, machine quilted: free-motion and using a walking foot. 35 x 50"/89 x 127cm. 2009.

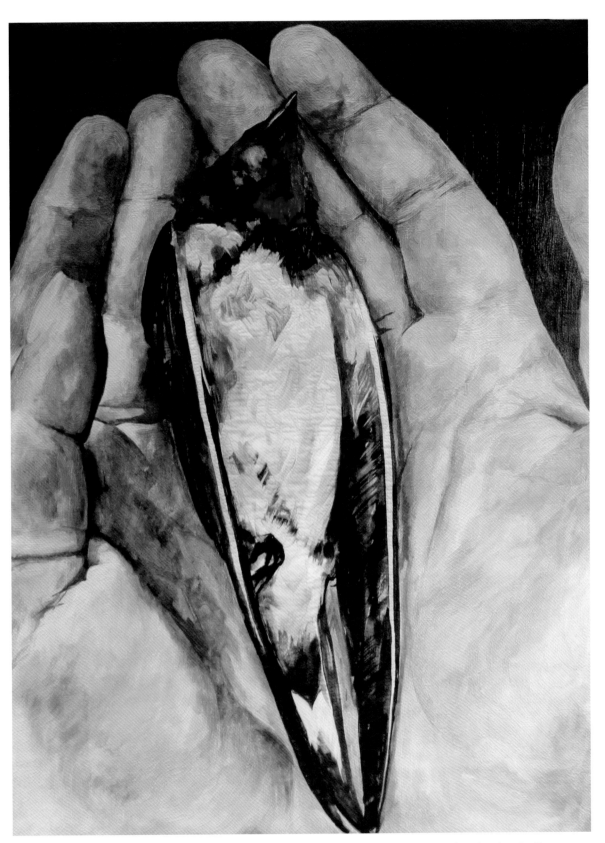

⬆ Don't Go—©Laura Kemshall, Trysull, Staffordshire, UK. This wholecloth quilt is part of a series of works that explore ideas about fragility, protection, love and possession. The image is from an original acrylic painting that was photographed and digitally printed on fabric using a wide format printer. Cotton fabric. Free-motion machine quilted on a longarm machine. 52 x 71"/132 x 181cm. 2012.

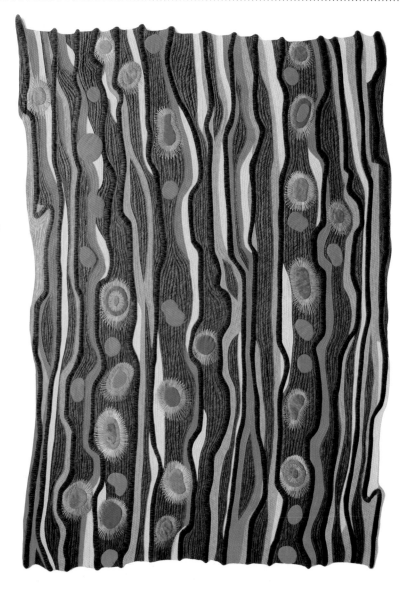

➡ *Joie de Vivre*—©Anna Hergert,
Moose Jaw, Saskatchewan, Canada. Inspired by
a sketchbook border created while researching
Friedensreich Hundertwasser's mark-making
on post-war structures in Vienna. Hand-dyed
and commercial cottons, hand-dyed and
commercial silk and cotton threads.
Machine and hand appliquéd, free-motion
machine quilted, hand embroidered.
48 x 66"/ 122 x 168cm. 2010.

⬇ *Favela – Espaço Aleatório*—©Vivian Wilm
Pinto, Petrópolis, Brazil. Photo by Marcelo
Pinto. Inspired by the landscape seen by the
artist on arrival in Rio de Janeiro: the Sugar
Loaf, the Corcovado, and the massive presence
of the slums—*favela*. While the random and
unplanned growth of the houses is depicted,
the artist also shows the *favela* as a place
where children fly kites and clothes hang
on a line—life following its natural course.
Hand-dyed cotton, linen and hemp fabrics,
embroidery threads. Hand and machine
appliquéd, hand embroidered, free-motion
machine quilted. 18 x 28"/46 x 71cm. 2012.

Unraveled—©Kati Spencer, Salt Lake City, Utah. This Modern Quilt artist finds ideas everywhere. For this piece, she was inspired by a simple DIY stamp—a wooden block wrapped in twine. Cotton fabric. Improvisational machine piecing, machine quilted. 45 x 49"/114 x 124cm. 2012.

Rainbow Drops—©Philippa Naylor, Beverley, East Yorkshire, UK. Photo by Peter Naylor. Collection of Margaret Johnson. An original design based on the theme of a rainbow. Hand-dyed cotton fabrics, rayon, polyester and cotton threads, cotton piping cord. Machine pieced, machine appliquéd, free-motion machine quilted with trapunto, double-folded piped binding. 19 x 26"/48 x 67cm. 2010.

MACHINE QUILTING

Machine quilting is an essential technique for most quilters, and has been developed to a fine art by many award-winning quilt makers. It is a technique that anyone can do, but it takes time and effort to master. Working with the right equipment is important, as is setting up your workspace properly. This section discusses the basics of machine quilting, followed by instructions for the many different types of quilting that can be done on a machine, and patterns for inspiration.

Machine-guided quilting, the most basic form of machine quilting, is where the feed dogs on the sewing machine and a walking foot move the fabric under the needle. The bottom of the walking foot has its own feed dogs, which help to pull the layers of the quilt sandwich evenly though the machine. This prevents the top layer from being pushed ahead of the batting and the back. Set stitch length for 10–12 stitches per inch/2.5cm, depending on the weight of your batting.

When machine quilting anything, and particularly a large quilt, the setup of your work area is very important. Set your machine into a table or cabinet so it is flush with the surrounding area. Then push this table or cabinet against another flush surface to help support the weight of the quilt while you are working; this will take the strain off your neck, hands and fingertips. It will also help with stitch quality, as there will be no pulling or distortion on the quilt sandwich.

Sit erect with your back supported, and ensure you have a clear view of the needle without having to crane your neck. Position your hands comfortably in front of the machine, resting your forearms on the work surface if possible. Your chair should be a proper height so that you aren't reaching up to sew, which will strain your shoulders and neck. Good lighting is important, especially if using thread that matches the fabric. An adjustable lamp will enable you to direct the light exactly where you need it.

Machine quilting is so mesmerising that it is often difficult to stop, but it's important to take breaks. Enjoy what you're doing by staying relaxed. Tensing up will affect your health as well as your stitching, so stay serene and don't strive for absolute perfection, as very few people can achieve this. Stay hydrated, which will also ensure that you take regular breaks! See pages 38–39 for exercises that you can perform during your breaks from machine quilting.

WORKSPACE

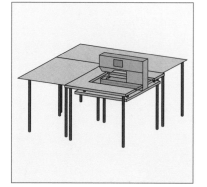

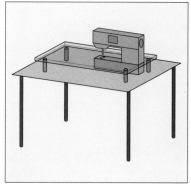

1 Set up your workspace properly. Sewing machine should be flush with a work surface and pushed against a table that will support the quilt and prevent it from dragging as you sew. Another table to left of machine is also beneficial.

2 An acrylic surround is adequate for small projects and piecing, but sewing with your arms slightly raised will eventually put a strain on your shoulders and neck. It's best if the bed of the machine is flush with the work surface.

WALKING FOOT

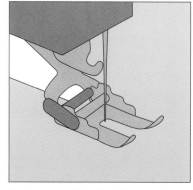

Purchase a walking foot that exactly fits your machine; choose one with an open toe so you can see the stitching easily. Use a walking foot to stitch straight or gently curving lines.

SPACER BAR

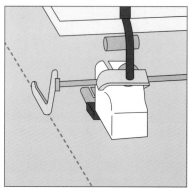

Use a spacer bar to sew parallel lines to a specific width. Read the instructions that come with the walking foot to learn how to attach it. Position bar on previous line of stitching as a guide.

THREAD

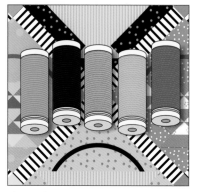

Choose high quality size 40 thread, matching the color in the needle and the bobbin so slight fluctuations in tension are not obvious. Some quilters prefer to use a thread that is lighter in weight in the bobbin, such as a size 50 or even size 60.

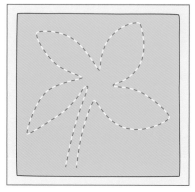

To mimic hand quilting, use invisible nylon thread on top, and contrasting color sewing thread in bobbin. Use clear nylon on light fabrics, and the smokey color on darker fabrics. The dots of bobbin thread will look like hand stitches on right side.

NEEDLES

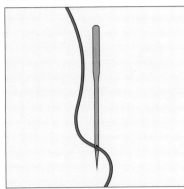

Start each project with a new needle; replace as necessary. Needle size depends on thickness of batting and choice of thread. Use needle size just large enough for thread to pass through eye with minimum friction. A needle that's too big will make holes.

TENSION

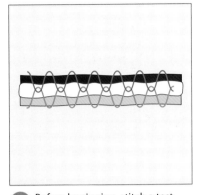

① Before beginning, stitch a test piece on a small quilt sandwich using the same fabrics as in main quilt. Carefully check machine tension to ensure that quilting stitches interlock in middle of quilt sandwich.

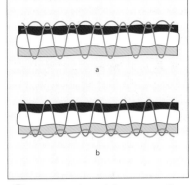

② If bobbin thread shows on quilt top (a), loosen top tension or tighten bobbin tension. If top thread shows on quilt back (b), tighten top tension or loosen bobbin tension. Adjust bobbin tension (page 37) only as a last resort.

BOBBIN THREAD

To begin stitching, lower needle into the quilt at the point you wish to start. Turn wheel by hand to pull up the loop of bobbin thread as shown. Use needle or seam ripper to coax and pull bobbin thread to right side.

STITCHING

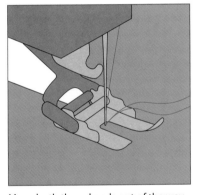

Move both thread ends out of the way of the stitching. Turn wheel by hand and insert needle back into exact hole made by the bobbin thread. Lower walking foot and begin stitching.

STITCH-IN-THE-DITCH

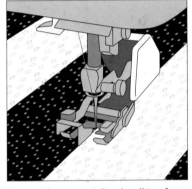

Use regular or specialized walking foot to outline shapes, blocks, borders and sashing; this is known as stitching in-the-ditch. Ensure that you stitch exactly in the seamline, or on the side opposite where seam allowances were pressed.

ROLL QUILT

For ease in sewing long lines of machine-guided stitching across a quilt, roll the quilt sandwich tightly and evenly into a tube; guide tube through arm of machine. Start stitching in the middle of the quilt and work outward towards the edges.

SECURING THREAD ENDS

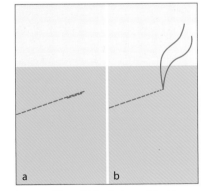

By machine: Make 3–4 small locking stitches, by stitching in reverse, then forward. Cut thread ends close to quilt top (a). Or, set stitch length to 0; make 2–3 stitches in same place. Gradually increase stitch length to normal (b). End stitching line in same way.

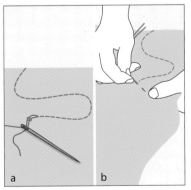

By hand: For a professional finish, knot threads ⅛"/3mm from quilt surface and insert both threads in needle (a). Pull into quilt sandwich, burying knot in batting (b). Trim off excess thread. Repeat at beginning and end of every stitching line.

FREE-MOTION QUILTING

Free-motion quilting is a natural extension of machine-guided quilting, but with infinite potential and scope for creativity. Because free-motion work is done with the feed dogs disengaged, your stitches are not constrained or predetermined in any way, and the quilt is able to be moved freely on the machine bed to create an infinite variety of designs. The feeling of being in full control of the movement of your quilt can be disconcerting, and it will take time to get comfortable with this way of stitching, but the more you stitch the better you will become at it.

In this technique, the stitch length is entirely controlled by the speed with which your hands move the fabric under the foot, regardless of the speed at which the machine is being operated. However, it's best to find a stitch speed that you are comfortable with, and coordinate that with your hand movements to create even stitches. Hand positioning is also important; master all the positions shown on the facing page so you are ready for every situation. Don't feel you have to sew quickly, as this can lead to stress and tension, which is counter-productive. Free-motion quilting is done most effectively when you are calm and in complete control of the machine, so find the speed that works best for you, relax and enjoy yourself.

While a basic mastery of this method of quilting isn't difficult, time and daily practice will combine to improve your stitching considerably. Some quilters give up doing this technique because their stitches aren't as perfect as those they see in shows. However, starting each quilting session with some free-motion exercises will produce gradual and noticeable improvements, so don't give up.

A specialized foot is used for free-motion work. Every manufacturer has a foot specific to their machine, so read the instructions that come with your machine to find the correct foot and how to use it. Insert a single-hole needle plate (for straight stitch) in your machine to prevent fabric from being pulled into the throat plate slot as you stitch. Engage the "needle down" function (if you have it) to hold the quilt in place when you stop stitching since the work is not being secured by the presser foot.

Before beginning a new project, always make a sample sandwich using the same fabrics and batting to test threads, needles, patterns and tension. Use it as a warm-up piece each day for about 10 minutes. This practice is not a waste of time as it will help you relax and make even stitches when you start sewing "for real."

FEET

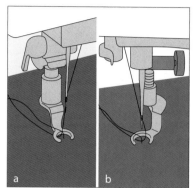

1 An open toe darning foot (a) with a spring on its shaft works best, because the foot "hops" over the fabric, self-adjusting for minor differences in thickness. To easily see behind needle, use an open toe darning foot with an offset shank (b).

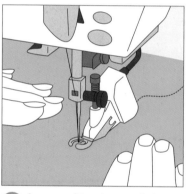

3 Some machines have a stitch regulating foot with a sensor underneath that follows fabric movement to control stitch length. Regulator adjusts length of stitches depending on how quickly or slowly fabric is moved so stitches will always be the same length.

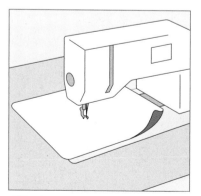

1b Alternatively, use a Teflon-coated sheet with a slick upper surface and a tacky back that sticks to your sewing machine to allow quilt to glide easily. Position pre-punched needle hole under sewing machine needle, and tape down edges if necessary.

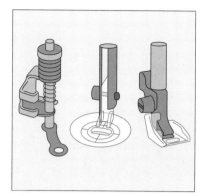

2 Manufacturers have a number of different free-motion feet available. Test several feet to see which one you prefer using. A foot with a closed front area will not give such good visibility when you are stitching as an open toe foot.

PREPARATION

1a A slick surface on which to slide the quilt will make free-motion quilting easier. Wipe down bed of sewing machine to remove any sticky residue that might have accumulated, or spray bed with a silicon-based, anti-static spray.

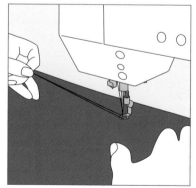

2 Drop feed dogs and set stitch length to 0. Place quilt sandwich under needle. Lower presser foot and ensure that work slides freely under foot. Pull up bobbin thread (page 175) and hold both threads to one side to begin stitching.

POSTURE

Sit with your arms resting on surface in front of machine. Arrange bulk of quilt behind and to the left of the machine; ensure there is no drag on quilt which could cause jerky movements and crooked stitches.

HAND POSITIONS

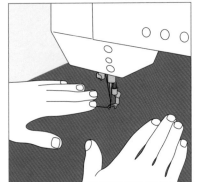

1 Free-motion quilters use different hand positions depending on which area of the quilt is being stitched. Try all of these positions to determine what feels best for you. The basic position is to place hands flat on the quilt on each side of the needle.

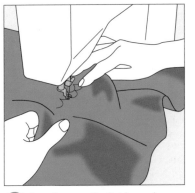

2 For a large quilt, divide work into small flat areas that fit easily within arm of machine. Place hands in a triangular position to spread open and flatten the area you are stitching. Reposition hands as soon as the area is filled.

3a Some quilters like to grip the quilt from the back when they stitch rather than work with it flat. Grasp a fold of the quilt from the back using your right hand.

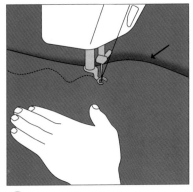

3b Move quilt under needle and stitch while holding fold. Grasping the fold (see arrow) will enable you to use it as a tool for moving the quilt to free-motion stitch. Once area under needle is filled, reposition hand and begin again.

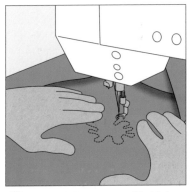

4 Gloves help to grip and hold the surface of the quilt; slipping hands will create clumsy stitches. Find special quilt gloves that are thin and lightweight. Less effort will be needed to move quilt, so use fingertips to guide fabric under needle.

5 If you experience loss of fine motor control with gloves, try using a non-greasy hand cream. Alternatively, place a rectangle or square of an anti-slip mat (available from kitchen supply shops) under left hand to help grip and move the quilt.

6 To quilt an intricate design, use a hoop or quilt halo to stabilize the area and prevent pleats or folds forming on the back. Reposition hoop once area has been quilted.

TIP

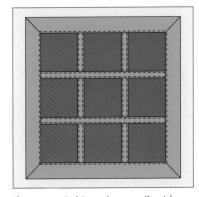

If you are stitching a large quilt with blocks, borders or sashing, stabilize entire quilt by machine-stitching in the construction lines to keep them straight; use a walking foot (pages 174–175). Then free-motion quilt within the stabilized areas.

Many problems encountered in free-motion quilting can be resolved by doing some basic checks on your machine. First, change the needle—chances are that this will immediately solve the problem. In addition, you might need to change the needle size depending on the thread weight being used. Make sure the machine is threaded correctly. Remove the bobbin and brush away lint or threads. Finally, check the tension; it may need adjusting. Refer to Sewing Machine Tips on pages 36–37 for the various ways you can take care of your machine to ensure that problems do not occur.

Removing incorrect stitching isn't impossible, but it is very time consuming and frustrating, so work slowly and get it right the first time. Knots will occur when you hesitate during stitching, so try to stitch at a steady pace. When in doubt, just stop stitching, or the threads will pile on top of one another forming a nasty nest. It's best not to use heavy or decorative thread in the bobbin when free-motion quilting. Use a finer bobbin thread such as 60 weight, in a color to match the top thread; this will prevent the bobbin threads from showing on the front.

Skipped stitches will happen when there is drag on the quilt, preventing it from moving freely. Ensure that no part of the quilt is hanging off the table. Crooked stitches will occur when you leave the needle down in the work and it jumps as you start quilting again. During the seconds it takes to regain control, irregular uneven stitches will result. To prevent this, move the needle to the up position just before starting again. Align the needle's point exactly over the spot where you wish to start; begin stitching slowly before getting back up to normal speed.

If the needle breaks repeatedly, your hands may be moving the work too quickly for the speed of the machine. If the needle isn't moving fast enough it will bend and snap as it passes through the quilt. Either run the machine at a faster speed or slow down your hands.

Excess fabric can form a balloon that may turn into a pleat if it isn't quilted carefully. Release the pressure on your presser foot (if you can) to prevent pushing excess fabric forward, then encircle the puffy area and meander-quilt until the bubble is under control.

Many people believe that quilting is quicker by machine, but this is not necessarily the case. A quilter can spend hundreds of hours mastering this technique and even more learning how to create a successful design. Correcting any mistakes and finishing off threads can also be time consuming. Though free-motion quilting is not a speedy option, it is hugely satisfying.

TIPS

Familiarize yourself with your chosen design by drawing it to the desired size on a sheet of paper. Go over the lines with your finger several times to imprint design in your head. Then test-stitch the design on a small quilt sandwich.

When satisfied with your stitches and thread tension, stitch design on quilt in an unobtrusive area. Stitch same design everywhere it will appear on the quilt before changing to a different pattern. Repetition will impart muscle memory and confidence.

KNOTS

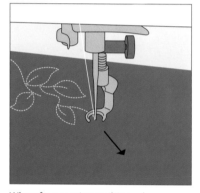

When free-motion quilting, always look ahead to where you want to stitch next rather than looking at the needle. If you lose your focus for a minute, stop immediately rather than stitching aimlessly and possibly ruining your design.

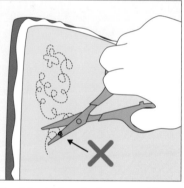

Check back of work often, as problems can arise intermittantly during free-motion quilting. Knots or nests on the back are common. Don't be tempted to surgically cut knots off with scissors, as the line of stitching will gradually pull out.

CORRECTING MISTAKES

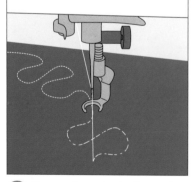

1 If you make a mistake that can't be ignored or disguised, stop stitching immediately. Raise needle; lift presser foot and cut thread. Slide quilt under needle to area on your quilt approximately ¼"/6mm before stitches went awry.

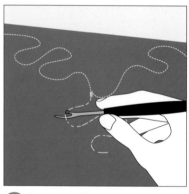

2 Lower needle into a good stitch. Make 2–3 tiny backstitches which will lock end of previous stitching line as well as new line. Continue stitching. When finished, carefully rip out erroneous stitches up to backstitching.

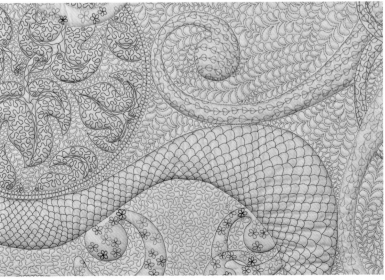

⬆ Silk Fantasy a la Diane—©Sally Gould Wright, Los Angeles, California USA. Traditional nine-patch setting was used to feature all the free-motion quilting designs learned in a class taught by Diane Gaudynski. Silk fabric, silk thread. Machine pieced, free-motion machine quilted. 32 x 32"/81 x 81cm. 2011.

⬅ White Gold (detail)—©Philippa Naylor, East Yorkshire, UK. Inspired by Art Nouveau designs, this wholecloth quilt took 1200–1400 hours to complete. Cotton sateen fabric, rayon and polyester threads. Free-motion machine quilted, machine trapunto. 83 x 83"/211 x 211cm. 2009.

FREE-MOTION QUILTING DESIGNS

Designs for free-motion quilting can be found everywhere. They can be as simple as a random doodle or as complex as a detailed feather. Shapes and lines are freely "drawn" on the quilt using a sewing machine needle and thread instead of a pencil (except in this case you move the "paper" rather than the "pencil"). You do not have the tedious task of marking designs on the quilt top or the challenge of stitching on a marked line. Nothing is prescribed and no one will know that the swirl on a quilt wasn't meant to be there, which is why this liberating technique is so enjoyable.

Set up your machine and read the basic instructions for free-motion quilting on the previous pages. If you're a beginner, work through the exercises in the following step-by-steps to acquaint yourself with free-motion quilting and gain confidence in your ability to stitch. More advanced quilters will already be familiar with these basic designs, and can create their own variations following the patterns on the subsequent pages.

Ideally, designs should be continuous to prevent frequent starts and stops, which can be tedious and time-consuming to finish off. Draw your favorite designs in a sketchbook, finding ways to create them without lifting pencil from paper so you'll be able to stitch them the same way on fabric.

Make a series of small quilt sandwiches and practice stitching the designs. Use a variety of threads and needle sizes so you can determine which works best for you and your machine. Write notes about threads and batting in permanent fabric marker on the back of each block. Dating the blocks will enable you to see how your quilting is improving as time goes on, because practice really does make your stitches perfect. Keep the test sandwiches handy so you can refer to them when designing a new quilt.

The free-motion quilting designs on the following pages can be used on home as well as mid- and longarm machines. Use your imagination to modify and develop these free-motion designs, creating new and unique patterns. Stitch the basic designs until you are comfortable with them, then add little flourishes and changes to individualize the patterns and make them your own.

Evenly distribute free-motion quilting all over your quilt to create a harmonious, balanced design so that the quilt hangs well. However, it's important to include areas on the quilt where the eye can rest, as too much quilting can overwhelm a quilt.

EXERCISES

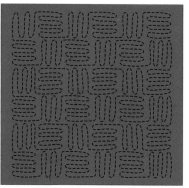

1 Practice sewing a series of curved lines up, down and sideways without turning the fabric. This will accustom you to sewing to the right, left, top and bottom without rotating or pivoting the quilt. Strive to maintain a consistent stitch length.

2 Stitch same design, but make sharp points instead of curves; do not linger at tips of points for too long or stitches will pile up on one another, creating a knot on the back. Just stop for a moment before smoothly stitching in the other direction.

3 Practice same design making a maze of sharp right angles instead of curves or points. Stitch a tight right angle, not a rounded corner. Don't hesitate for more than a fraction of a second when changing direction or you'll create a knot.

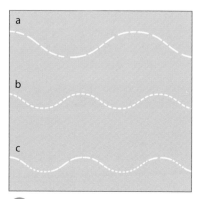

4 Carefully study your stitches. If stitches are really big (a), slow down your hands or speed up the machine. If stitches are really small (c), speed up your hand movements or slow down the machine. Keep practicing until you can make even stitches (b).

5 Next stitch e's and l's, which form the basis for many quilt designs. Practice stitching loops upside-down and sideways without turning the fabric. Try making a simple motif in the middle by connecting 4 loops.

6 Practice free-motion quilting on a printed fabric, outlining and highlighting the shapes and images on the fabric to practice your curves, points and corners. Use a thread that blends well with the print so any errors will not be too noticeable.

BACKFILL STYLES

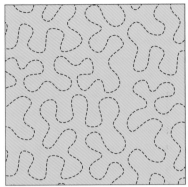

1 Meandering (or vermicelli) is the most basic style of free-motion quilting. A background area is filled with an irregular pattern of spaced curving lines that do not cross each other. Keep lines smoothly flowing with no points and no discernible pattern.

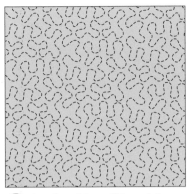

2 Stipple quilting will "ease in" excess fabric or flatten background areas to make patchwork, appliqué or trapunto designs stand out. Similar to meandering, stipple quilting is tighter and takes more time to execute.

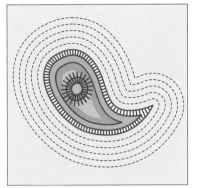

3 Echo quilting is excellent for enlarging a motif to fit a space. Patchwork, appliqué or quilted designs that look too small can be echo-quilted until exactly the right size. Stitching lines must be evenly spaced—uneven spacing will stand out sharply.

4 Echo meandering is an effective way to fill an area and create texture. Find one shape, like a teardrop or crescent moon; echo that shape several times before moving in another direction and repeating it. Position shapes efficiently to fit the space.

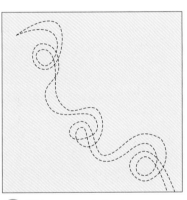

5 Ribbon meandering is characterized by parallel lines that cross each other periodically, creating a 3-D effect. Stitch a gentle curve, then reverse and stitch back to the beginning, crossing over first line at random intervals. Add loops for interest.

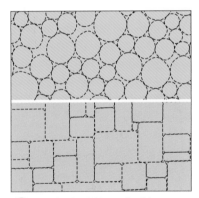

6 Stitched pebbles will add texture and interest to the background of a quilt, and practicing this will enhance your skills in backtracking and looking ahead to fill the next area without being cornered. Vary size and shape of pebbles to add interest.

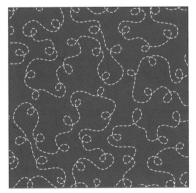

7 Another basic doodling stitch is a loopy meander. However, you'll find that it's a challenge to keep this design looking random, so continually look ahead to see the shape of the space that needs filling; vary position of loops as you stitch.

8 Vines and leaves are natural shapes that are fun to quilt. Sew straight or curly vine, then add one leaf on left and the next on right. Notch the leaves, curl the tips and add a vein down the middle for variety.

9 Patterns from nature form the basis of many successful free-motion designs. In pictorial quilts, imitate the element you are featuring by quilting ripples on water, wood grain on trees, tufts of grass or currents of air in the sky.

THREAD ADVICE

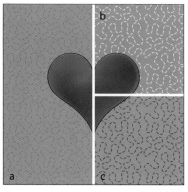

Compress an area with dense (backfill) quilting to make that area recede into the background, creating negative space. To accentuate this, use thread to match background (a). If using colored thread, light colors will leap forward (b) and dark colors recede (c).

If you are quilting with a variety of colored threads, use an invisible monofilament thread in the bobbin to save changing the bobbin thread every time you switch the top thread. Be sure to check the tension first on a test sample.

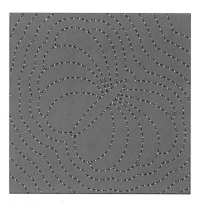

Wind metallic or contrasting decorative thread in bobbin and use thread to match fabric on top. Tighten top tension so bobbin thread is pulled to the quilt top. Free-motion quilt; bobbin thread will create small sparks of color along top thread.

STITCHING ADVICE

Plan your backfill designs so they move continuously into every area. Start in the middle and work outward, filling each quarter of the area before moving on to the next.

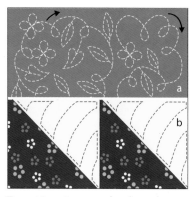

Try not to get cornered—always have an escape route in mind. You can stitch a loopy meander to move to a different area (a) or backtrack along a seam or part of a quilting design to get out of a tight spot (b).

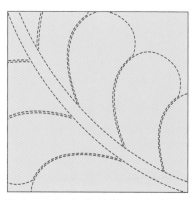

Backtrack (backstitch) along stitching lines of quilt design to move from one area to another. This is best done by stitching slowly and in control using fine thread, as heavier threads will be more noticeable. This is essential for stitching feathers.

OTHER IDEAS

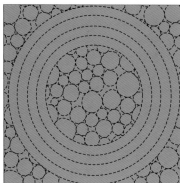

Try free-motion quilting in a contained shape. Use fabric marker or chalk to draw an outline on fabric, such as a circle or triangle. Work free-motion stitches inside drawn shape. Echo-quilt around outline of shape to make it a feature.

To fill a specific area, trace the outline on clear plastic or lightweight tracing paper, then make a rough sketch of the proposed quilting design. Place sketch over area to be quilted; adjust to fit. Mark design (page 35) or refer to sketch while stitching.

Long curved lines are difficult to free-motion quilt without a bit of help. To make it easier, you can sketch long curved lines on the quilt top using a flexible curved ruler and chalk or a fabric marker.

↑ Flower Bouquet—©Leah Day, Shelby, North Carolina. Photo by Paul Huggins. The artist took a vase appliqué workshop with Linda Cantrell of Asheville, NC, and was inspired to try a new design, leaving space to quilt the flowers as filler designs instead of using appliqués. Cotton fabric, polyester thread. Hand appliquéd, machine pieced, free-motion machine quilted. 22 x 29"/56 x 74cm. 2011.

It's good to break down a complicated design into manageable parts. When stitching, use a mantra to keep the pattern in mind such as:

Curl around …

go back and loop one, two, three …

out and curl around again

These quilting motifs can stand alone in a plain block or corner; enlarge to fit the space required. After quilting by hand or machine, try coloring in the different areas; see pages 202–203.

When stitching this lazy meandering floral design, change each of the large flowers so that no two are alike.

It's best to stitch a flower, then fill in around it with loops before setting up the next flower, allowing a good amount of space to lead into the next one.

You have lots of options with this design: change the shape of the feathers to make half circles, pointed leaves or spikes.

The same basic design can look quite different depending on how tight or loose the petals are stitched.

Outline geometric shapes such as this star with feathers, making the feathers even and symmetrical or loose and asymmetrical.

Get into a rhythm when stitching this filler pattern. Keep the design going by always using the starting curl as the spine for feathers or leaves. Vary the design by opening it up or making it tighter; change the soft curves into points or close up each unit (shown bottom right).

BORDERS

Create a continuous spine on this leaf border by looping back tightly, almost touching the previous "valley." Change the outer points to curves to make petals.

You can really have fun with this, changing the length, shape and size of each point to create a bold, exciting border.

Vary the shape of the loops between each flower.

These hanging flowers can loop and curve to create a filler design as well as a border. Make thick, closed stems by backtracking along the previous line of stitches so that only the flowers are open.

Break down the design into manageable "bites."

Stitching loopy hearts is almost like doodling. Change the size and shape of the hearts to add interest.

Clamshells can be mesmerizing to stitch and these borders also make good fillers if you angle the shells in different directions.

Any border design can be adapted to curve around a shape. Remember to break down each design into easy-to-remember sections.

SEASHORE DESIGNS

Use this fish as a starting point for creating your own imaginative sea creature. Add loops and spines and vary the shape of the scales. Keep your stitches continuous, backtracking over previous stitches if you find yourself cornered. Stitch around the eye several times to highlight.

This fish in the sea filler is challenging to stitch. Vary the size of the fish to fit each area you are trying to fill.

Tumbling waves is a wonderful filler that is enjoyable and absorbing to stitch. Just backtrack if you find yourself in a corner. Open it out and make the points into curves to turn this design into clouds in the sky.

DRAGONFLY, BIRDS & BUTTERFLIES

Use the fanciful creatures on these two pages as the starting point for designing your own quilting motifs inspired by nature. Enlarge designs to the appropriate size and sketch the basic outlines on fabric before starting to stitch.

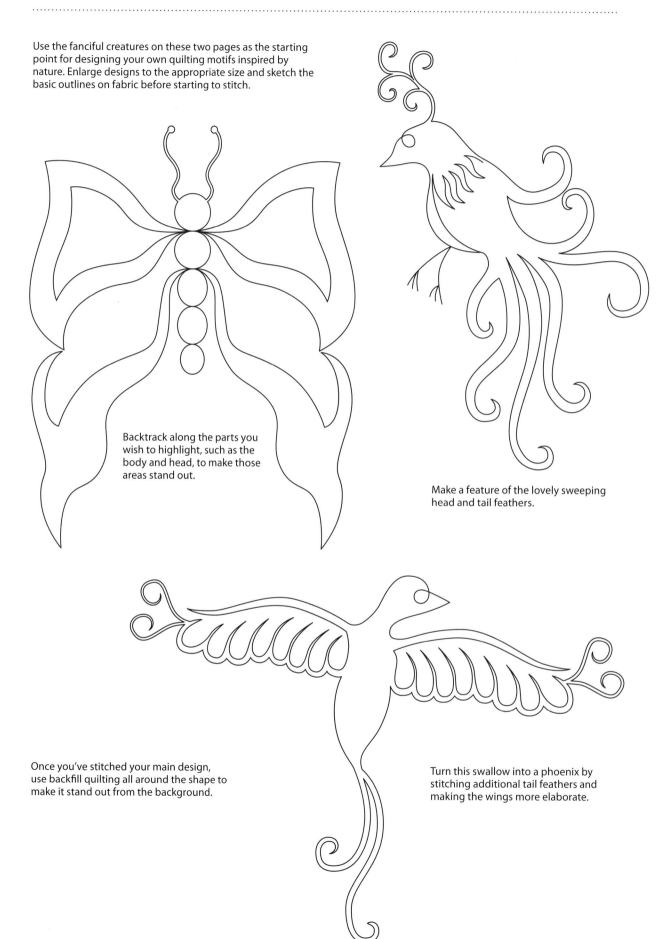

Backtrack along the parts you wish to highlight, such as the body and head, to make those areas stand out.

Make a feature of the lovely sweeping head and tail feathers.

Once you've stitched your main design, use backfill quilting all around the shape to make it stand out from the background.

Turn this swallow into a phoenix by stitching additional tail feathers and making the wings more elaborate.

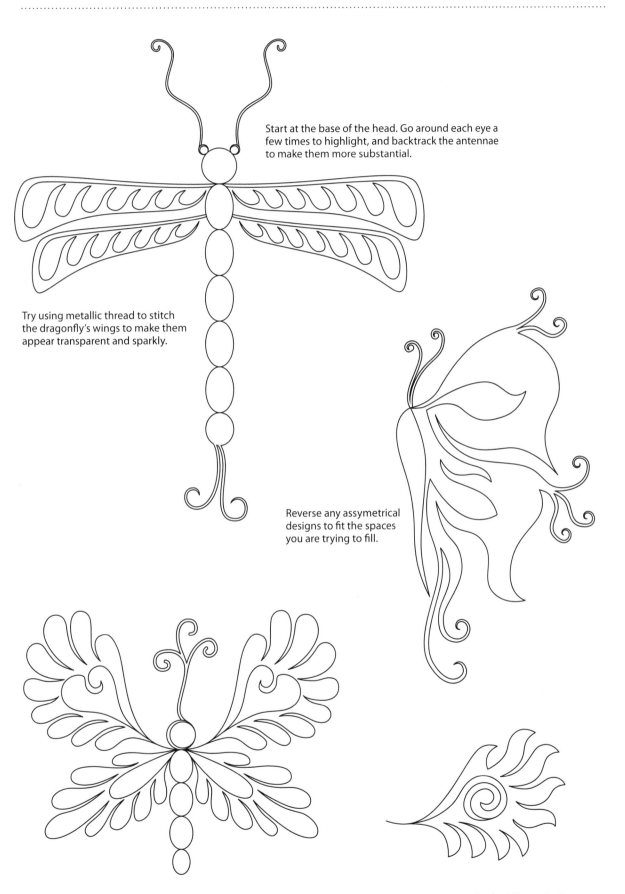

Start at the base of the head. Go around each eye a few times to highlight, and backtrack the antennae to make them more substantial.

Try using metallic thread to stitch the dragonfly's wings to make them appear transparent and sparkly.

Reverse any assymetrical designs to fit the spaces you are trying to fill.

Add color to the wings and body after stitching; see pages 202–203.

For a completely different look, turn curves into points on the wings of birds or insects.

LONGARM QUILTING

Longarm quilting is a mystery for the uninitiated and a revelation for those in the know. It has long surpassed its early reputation as a means to secure quilt layers together with simple zigzag stitches. Longarm machines have now become the instruments by which intricate stitching can be accomplished in countless ways, either using a pantograph, a computer or the imagination.

This summary will not attempt to go into excessive detail about longarm machines as there are many books, videos and training lessons that will teach quilters the fine points of their own particular machine. Different brands will have their own distinct frame setups, and all have diverse features and functionality. Instead, these pages will give a broad overview of longarm quilting to impart a greater understanding and appreciation of this technique, and perhaps entice you to try longarm quilting yourself if you are not already one of the converted.

There are some prerequisites to owning a longarm machine. The first is space: longarm machines can be quite large and require a dedicated work area in order to set up the complete system. The second is price: longarm machines can be costly. The third and ongoing requirement is maintenance: these systems need to be kept in tip-top condition. The machine must be meticulously inspected, cleaned and oiled in preparation for every new quilt that is being loaded.

A longarm machine is usually purchased as a complete system that includes a table frame, carriage and the machine itself. The machine rests on a carriage with four pairs of wheels running on rollers and tracks so it glides effortlessly in any direction across the area to be stitched. Because the quilt layers are attached to rollers, you do not have to rearrange or struggle to fit the quilt layers under the arm of the machine. It is the machine that moves, not the quilt sandwich, which stays steady and under tension. A longarm machine does not have feed dogs or fancy stitches (such as zigzag), although some machines regulate stitch size.

A whole new world of quilting is available to those with the space, money and time to devote to these amazing machines. Alternatively, consider taking lessons in using a longarm machine and renting time on it from someone who already owns one—in that way you will control the making of the quilt from start to finish, which is an important consideration if entering a piece in a contest or exhibition.

PARTS OF THE MACHINE

1 Longarm machines have a 16–36"/ 41–91cm throat space, with an average of 23"/58cm. A digital panel controls preferences such as motor speed, stitches per 1"/2.5cm and horizontal/vertical channel locks. Handles are located on front and back of machine.

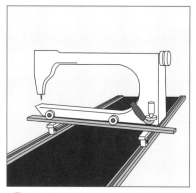

2 Machine sits on a carriage with wheels gliding on tracks; these must be kept clean and lint-free so machine rolls smoothly in every direction. Most systems have a channel lock facility to lock movement in horizontal or vertical direction.

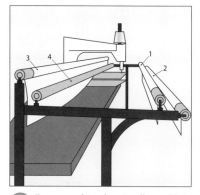

3 Every machine has 3 rollers which act like quilting frames to keep layers under tension. Top roller (1) holds quilt top, back roller (2) holds quilt back, and pickup or takeup roller (3) holds all 3 layers. Some machines have a leveling roller (4) to keep work flat.

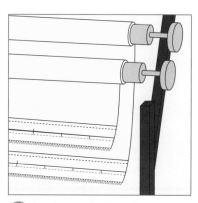

4 Leaders made of sturdy canvas are permanently attached to each roller. Quilt layers are secured to leaders using pins, zippers, clamps and Velcro or snap fasteners. Accurately mark and match center points of all leaders before beginning.

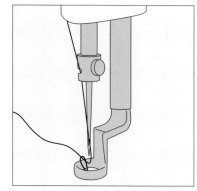

5 The presser foot, called a hopping foot, holds layers down while a stitch is being made, then hops up to move smoothly forward to make the next stitch. Hopping foot should be round with raised edges so it can be used with quilting guides.

6 Use multidirectional industrial needles. Change needle with every new project and often halfway through; if you experience stitch problems, always change needle first. Insert needle in machine following manufacturer's instructions.

THREADS

Thread machine following manufacturer's instructions. Use a bobbin case tension gauge to check bobbin tension; adjust until tension is perfect. Insert bobbin in machine and pull up thread. Move machine to spot where you wish to start stitching.

MACHINE TIE-OFF

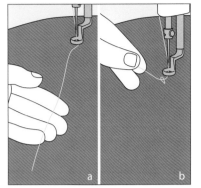

Take one stitch, holding on to top thread (a). Move machine over a few inches, grab bobbin thread that has appeared and pull it up (b). Move machine back to where threads came up; make a couple of locking stitches to tie-off. Snip threads close to quilt top.

HAND TIE-OFF

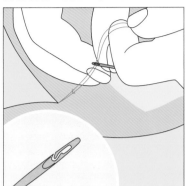

Or, bury thread ends for a professional finish. Pull up threads; knot close to surface of quilt. Slip thread ends through notch of a spiral-eye needle. Insert needle back into quilt where threads have come up; bury knot between layers of quilt. Snip off ends.

LONGARM MACHINE

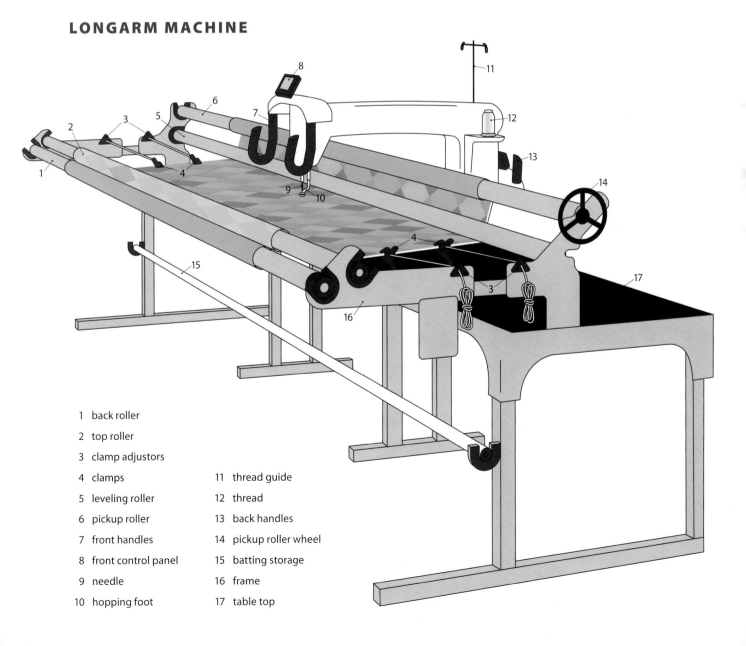

1 back roller

2 top roller

3 clamp adjustors

4 clamps

5 leveling roller

6 pickup roller

7 front handles

8 front control panel

9 needle

10 hopping foot

11 thread guide

12 thread

13 back handles

14 pickup roller wheel

15 batting storage

16 frame

17 table top

While quilting on a longarm machine is quicker than using a home sewing machine, some time must be spent preparing the machine. First the entire machine must be cleaned and oiled. The rollers must be tested to ensure they are parallel. The quilt must then be set up or "loaded" into the machine. The tension on the quilt layers must be perfect, as well as the stitch tension. If the quilting is being done using a pantograph or computer, the patterns must be correctly positioned. Freehand designs may require placement lines. Only then can the quilting commence. When the first area has been stitched, the quilt is rolled-on to expose the next section and the process repeated.

Though all machines are different, there are some basic procedures they all have in common; these are covered here. Don't be put off by the seemingly complicated steps required for loading; these will quickly become second nature. Pin loading is shown here; follow manufacturer's instructions if using zipper or Velcro leaders or the snap method.

Choose a good quality backing fabric to blend with the threads you have chosen; use the same thread in the bobbin and machine. Ensure that all edges of the quilt back are cut on straight grain and the fabric is well pressed. Avoid the use of tightly woven sheets as the needle may bounce off them, causing skipped stitches; the needle might also pierce the threads, thus undermining the fabric's integrity.

Always warm up by making some test stitches, as it's tedious and tiresome to rip out mistakes. The easiest way to test stitches is to make the side borders wider than required and use these areas for testing the stitches and tension before sewing on the actual quilt.

LOADING

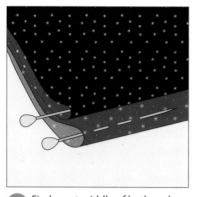

1 Find exact middle of both ends of quilt back and top by folding in half; mark with pins woven in and out of fabric, perpendicular to edge. If quilt back fabric is patterned, make sure quilt top and back are oriented in the same direction.

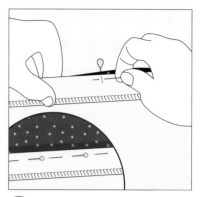

2 With wrong side up, attach bottom edge of back to quilt back roller, lining up center pin with marked center on canvas leader. Pin back to leader along canvas side so pins lie tip to point; pin from center to corner on each side, leaving no gaps.

3 Drape quilt back on pickup roller to hold it out of the way. Keeping fabric straight, roll fabric onto quilt back roller until top edge meets pickup roller. Pin top edge to leader of pickup roller as in step 2. Tighten rollers to remove slack.

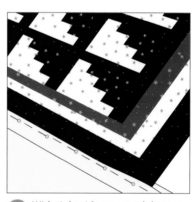

4 With right side up, attach bottom edge of quilt top to quilt top roller in same way as quilt back. Once pinning is complete, roll quilt top onto roller, checking to make sure canvas and fabric are straight and flat. Leave top edge loose for the moment.

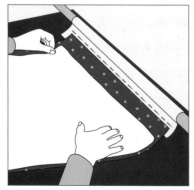

5 Place batting smoothly and squarely on taut quilt back; allow rest of batting to hang free (called a partial float). Set stitch length to 7–8 stitches per 1"/2.5cm. Stitch basting line across top edge 1"/2.5cm from pins, engaging horizontal channel lock.

6 Bring quilt top up to basting line, matching centers, and lining up edges along stitched line; pin to secure. Stitch ¼"/6mm from edge of quilt top, walking your fingers along the edge to keep it straight and even as hopping foot moves along.

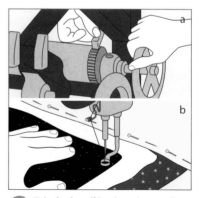

7 Take locks off back and top rollers (a); roll quilt to within a hand-width of pickup roller. Lock back roller, then top roller so quilt is taut. Using vertical channel lock, baste down each side of quilt, walking fingers along each edge as before (b).

SIDE TENSION

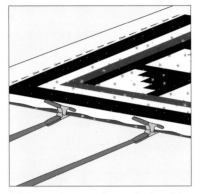

A light tension must be applied to sides of quilt before stitching to prevent the sandwich from flapping up and down. Pin stabilizing straps or clamps with Velcro strips along each side of quilt; attach straps to frame. Check that there is no distortion.

STITCHES

1 Stitch speed is constant, but machine can be set to stitch faster or slower. Stitch length is determined by how machine is moved: move fast and stitches will be long; slow, and stitches will be tiny. Coordinate stitch speed and length to achieve perfect stitches.

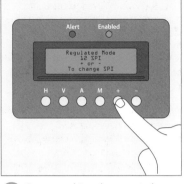

2 Some machines have a stitch regulator mode, which means the stitch length will remain consistent no matter how quickly or slowly you move the machine. You can set the number of stitches per 1"/2.5cm using the control panel.

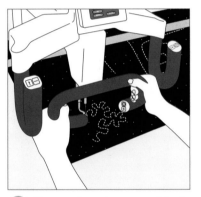

3 Close work can be accomplished by adding micro-quilting handles to the machine. The different handle position enables you to concentrate on a limited area, producing finer stitches with more control.

ROLLING-ON

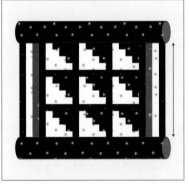

1 Width of area between rollers determines how many times quilt will need to be rolled-on before it is finished—the wider the area, the fewer roll-ons. Rolling-on is time consuming so this width is an important consideration when buying a machine.

2 Once first area of quilt has been fully stitched, quilt must be rolled-on. Remove clamps from sides of quilt, release back and top rollers, then roll quilted area around pickup roller to expose fresh surface. Lock back and top rollers. Reclamp sides of quilt.

3 Every time you roll a quilt on, check that all layers are straight, without puckers. Use ruler or zero-center measuring tape to check center of quilt, sashing, blocks and borders before beginning to stitch again. Baste down each side of quilt when satisfied.

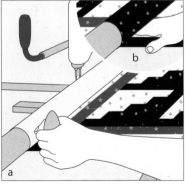

4 As you roll-on, pickup roller will increase in size. Leveling roller keeps work flat so needle is always stitching a level surface. If you don't have a leveling roller, turn crank to raise pickup roller (a) until hand can just fit beneath it each time you roll-on (b).

FINISHING

To finish bottom of quilt, fold quilt top out of the way and smooth out batting. Smooth top over batting, set horizontal channel lock and baste ¼"/6mm from bottom edge, walking fingers along to help straighten edge. Finish quilting final area. Remove from machine.

Stitching with a longarm machine is often compared to painting, such is the freedom with which you can achieve gorgeous designs. The weight of the machine and the ease of movement enables the stitcher to sew smoothly with little effort. The stitches can create texture or can become the entire focus of the quilt.

All-over or edge-to-edge designs can be achieved by using a pantograph pattern, which usually comes on a roll in three sizes. The appropriate-sized pattern is placed on a table at the back of the machine, and a laser light or stylus is adjusted to point at the design lines. The quilter moves the machine to follow the lines of the pantograph pattern with the laser light or stylus which copies the pattern onto the quilt top. The quilter is not looking at the quilt at all, only the pattern, but is in full control of the stitches—they are not done automatically.

Freehand designs can be used to complement and enhance a quilt top or can become a major feature, such as when stitching wholecloth masterpieces. Feathers, flowers and leaves, birds, bees, fish—virtually any design can be accomplished with a longarm machine, although these designs are more challenging and will take a longer time to sew. See pages 184–189 for inspiration. The quilter must take the time to practice in order to perfect this type of quilting, always striving to maintain an even density of stitches across the piece.

"In-the-ditch" designs are not easy to do on a longarm machine because most quilts are not stitched precisely enough to use a horizontal or vertical channel lock, and the quilter must always use one hand to guide the machine. Ruler work enables the quilter to stitch in-the-ditch, and other specialized acrylic templates enable longarm quilters to stitch precise shapes.

Computerized designs on the higher-end machines are very popular, and these can be adjusted and changed to fit any space. The machine will then execute the design with little input from the quilter, regulating the length of the stitches as it sews. However, the quilter still has to ensure that the patterns are positioned correctly and that the top and bottom thread tension is just right.

Because longarm quilting is so absorbing, quilters must take breaks to prevent fatigue and drink water to keep hydrated. The quilter usually stands in order to sew, therefore good posture and comfortable shoes are a must, although some machines allow longarm quilters to sit.

PANTOGRAPH

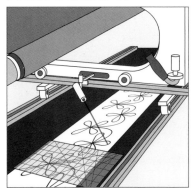

1 Pantograph pattern must be same width as quilt; place on table on back of frame, straight and centered between quilt edges. Place needle in down position on lower right corner of quilt. Set laser/stylus so it points to bottom line of pattern.

2 Move laser/stylus to start of pattern, bring up bobbin thread; tie-off. Begin stitching using laser/stylus to follow lines. Stay relaxed; stitch rhythm will develop and accuracy will improve with practice. Stitch to other edge of quilt; tie-off threads.

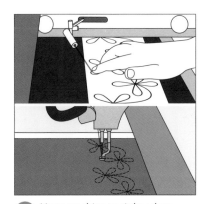

3 Move machine to right edge; place needle in fabric when laser/stylus is at starting point on pattern. Remove clamps, unlock rollers; gently roll pickup roller until laser light is on pattern's start position. Tighten rollers, clamp sides; stitch as before.

FREEHAND

1 It's hard to start stitching in the middle of a blank fabric. Use fabric pencil or marker to sketch some basic outlines or shapes on fabric. Begin stitching marked motif, then continue adding to it; change design elements and add flourishes as you go.

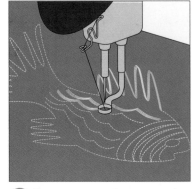

2 To create texture, increase number of stitches per 1"/2.5cm; match thread to fabric. To emphasize stitches, decrease stitches per 1"/2.5cm so more thread lies on surface. To emphasize certain areas or make them stand out, stitch over same line several times.

3 Start with design element, like a bird, insect or flower, and build on it, echoing around the shape and adding swirls or curlicues to make it more interesting. Doodle with stippling (page 181) in the background to make the design pop.

RULER WORK

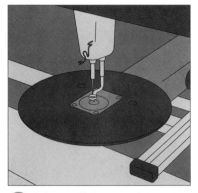

1 Rulers in all shapes and sizes are made specifically for longarm quilting. These are thicker than rotary cutting rulers (which should not be used) so they will not slide under hopping foot. Add an extended throat plate to balance and support rulers.

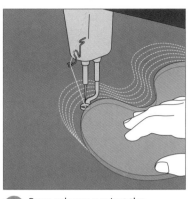

2 Press ruler up against the hopping foot while stitching, and press it firmly into quilt sandwich with fingertips as shown. Keep fingers well away from edge of ruler. Remember that the stitching line will be ¼"/6mm away from ruler edge.

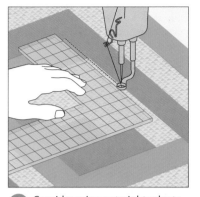

3 Consider using a straight ruler to stitch in-the-ditch or to stitch any straight lines on a quilt. Work slowly, moving the ruler along gently and steadily as you proceed. The ruler is really being used as a guide to keep your stitches smooth and straight.

⬆ Quilting Samples—©Tracey Pereira, Hampshire, UK. Photos by the artist and Stephen Pereira. Selection of original quilting designs inspired by crop circles, classic redwork and the artist's interpretation of creative meanders and stippling. Cotton fabric, 40wt cotton thread (12wt and large-eyed needle for gray/red sample). Free-motion machine quilted on a longarm machine. 2004–2011.

MACHINE TRAPUNTO

An excellent way to add dimension and texture to your quilting is with trapunto. The old method of painstakingly slitting the back of the work to insert stuffing and then resewing the hole thus made was not only time-consuming but yielded a messy result. The methods shown here will create raised stuffed areas without cutting the backing fabric.

The many variations of machine trapunto make this an extremely versatile technique. You can machine-trapunto plain background areas on your quilt or stuff appliquéd areas so that they become more prominent. You can also create a shadow effect by using this technique with silk organza. If your sewing machine does fancy embroidery, place batting beneath the embroidery to give it more texture.

When adding trapunto to a quilt of any size, you will need to carefully plan the design and transfer all the trapunto patterns to the fabric when the quilt top is finished. Machine trapunto is worked before the quilt is layered with batting and a back. For the trapunto areas, choose an 80% cotton/20% polyester batting. You can use either one layer of a thick batting (10–12oz), or two layers of a thinner one. Use any preferred batting for layering the quilt.

An inbuilt hazard of this technique is the ease with which you can cut through the fabric when trimming the trapunto/batting shapes. Duckbill or sharp blunt-nosed scissors are useful at this stage. However, for the final cutting use small, sharp embroidery scissors. Take extreme care as you cut, especially when using sheer fabric for shadow work, as this can't be repaired. Trimming trapunto shapes is a job best done when you can give it your full attention.

PREPARATION

1 Choose a quilting design to trapunto. Enlarge to desired size; transfer to right side of fabric. Cut one or two pieces of batting slightly larger than design; pin to wrong side of fabric. Check to ensure fabric lies smoothly over batting with no wrinkles.

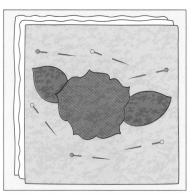

2 Alternatively, trapunto an appliqué to make it stand out. Cut out and fuse appliqué shapes to background fabric following instructions on pages 148–149. Pin batting beneath appliquéd shapes as in step 1.

3 Roughly trim away any excess batting outside the line of pins; you can use large fabric scissors for this step.

STITCHING

Thread a fine sewing machine needle with water soluble thread; use neutral bobbin thread. With large stitches, sew ⅛"/3mm inside marked design lines or inside edges of appliqué; drop feed dogs for curved areas. Do not stitch other lines inside the design.

TRIMMING

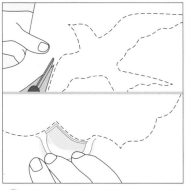

1 Using sharp embroidery scissors and taking great care, trim away thick batting ⅛"/3mm from stitching. If using 2 layers of batting, trim top layer first, quite close to stitching, then trim second layer ⅛"/3mm from stitched line.

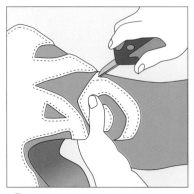

2 If design is large or has more than one element, work gradually to cut away batting, leaving only areas that you wish to stand out in trapunto. Take special care when trimming inside areas. Continue until entire quilt top has been trimmed.

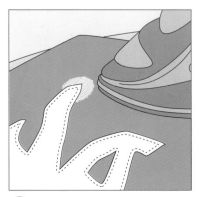

3 If you cut fabric while trimming batting, rip small piece of light-weight fusible interfacing; press over cut area (ripping will make interfacing blend in better). If necessary, use a toothpick to apply drop of anti-fray product to cut on right side.

QUILTING

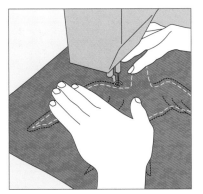

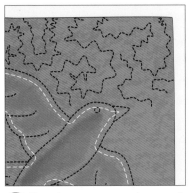

1 When all batting has been trimmed close to the stitching lines of the quilting design or appliquéd shapes, layer the quilt top with batting and a back as for a normal quilt. Secure layers with preferred basting method.

2 Drop the feed dogs. Using thread to match or contrast with fabric, free-motion quilt over marked lines of design or along edge of appliqué; stitches will run parallel to line of water soluble stitches previously sewn. Also quilt along inner design lines.

3 To make trapunto stand out, work free-motion meander quilting all around outside of design to flatten the background. See pages 180–181 for a selection of different free-motion backfill designs.

REMOVE THREAD

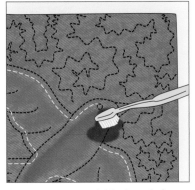

To remove water soluble thread after quilting, either immerse work in a warm bath of water or gently scrub away threads with a moistened soft toothbrush. If fully immersing quilt, spread it out flat to dry, squaring it up carefully as you do so.

PRINTED FABRIC

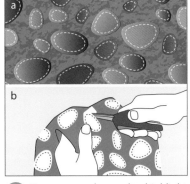

1 Trapunto can be used to highlight areas of a painted, stamped or printed fabric (a). Follow instructions on facing page to prepare fabric, stitching around design elements you wish to highlight. Trim away batting around each of the elements (b).

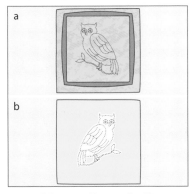

2 Layer fabric for quilting; meander-quilt in between trapunto areas so they stand out clearly. See pages 180–181 for free-motion backfill designs. You can embellish the trapunto with fabric pens or paints to add more dimension.

SHADOW TRAPUNTO

Mark design on sheer fabric. Stitch batting behind design, then trim very carefully as you won't be able to repair any cuts in fabric. Place bright fabric behind organza so it highlights white trapunto areas. Layer with batting and a back; free-motion quilt.

REVERSE SHADOW

Draw design on wrong side of a vibrant background fabric; stitch batting to right side (design will be in reverse when finished). Trim batting, then place sheer fabric on top. Layer with batting and a back; free-motion quilt.

EMBROIDERED

Secure felt or needle-punched batting to wrong side of fabric; place in hoop. Machine-embroider design on right side (a); trim off excess felt/batting around embroidery (b). Layer and quilt, using invisible thread to quilt over embroidered design lines for extra texture.

EMBROIDERED QUILTING

Substituting hand or machine embroidery for the basic quilting stitch has become increasingly popular with art quilters eager to complement their work with a decorative element. Hand embroidery can impart realistic touches, such as stars, grass, or a flower center. It can also be used strategically to ease puffy areas on a quilt.

On the sewing machine, select from the various programmed decorative stitches, and embroider/quilt using a walking foot. Or free-motion embroider delicate designs with specialty threads. You can embroider/quilt motifs with the aid of computer software, either on a home sewing machine with an embroidery module or on a longarm machine. When embroidering intricate designs, some quilters prefer to layer the quilt top with batting only, adding a quilt back later to hide any flaws.

HAND EMBROIDERY TIPS

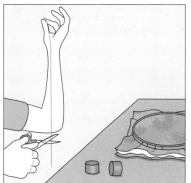

Cut embroidery floss no longer than distance from fingertips to elbow to prevent fraying or tangling. Run floss or threads over beeswax, before threading in a small chenille needle that has a sharp point and large eye. Hoop quilt to ensure an even result.

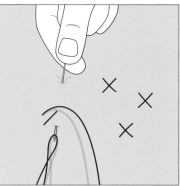

To begin a line of stitching, knot end of thread or floss and bury knot in the batting by popping it through the quilt top. When travelling from one area to another, run the thread or floss through the batting as shown here, so the back of the quilt looks as good as the front.

HAND EMBROIDERY STITCHES

Straight stitches worked in a random pattern (known as seeding) can be an effective way to quilt large areas or flatten any puffiness in a quilt (a). To imitate flowers or the sun, work straight stitches in a circle (b). For grass, vary the length and angle of the stitches (c).

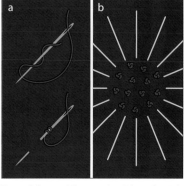

French knots Wrap embroidery thread 2 or 3 times around the needle close to tip; insert tip into quilt and pull through, with knot close to surface (a). Embroider cluster of knots for a flower center (b) or stitch random knots to hold quilt layers together.

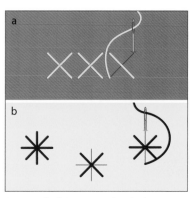

Cross stitch Scatter individual cross stitches on a quilt to add a folk art touch while anchoring the quilt layers together (a). To create a star, make two diagonal stitches over a cross stitch as shown (b); vary length of stitches for each star for extra interest.

PROGRAMMED DECORATIVE MACHINE STITCHES

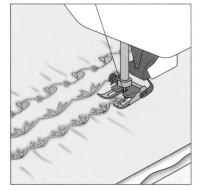

Read Machine Embroidery on pages 220–221. Attach a walking foot. Test the machine's programmed decorative stitches on a sample layered quilt sandwich. Change width or length; stitch gentle curves. Avoid quilting over thick seams to prevent needle breakage.

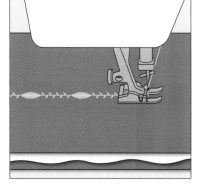

Combine programmed decorative stitches by changing designs manually while stitching (raise needle when changing designs to prevent breakage). Or design and save stitch combinations directly on the screen of computerized sewing machines.

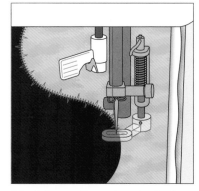

Attach free-motion or hopping/spring foot, or release pressure on the foot (if your machine can do this); do not drop feed dogs. Choose a programmed decorative stitch to outline a shape, and stitch, moving the fabric slowly and evenly beneath the foot as you work.

SINGLE MOTIFS

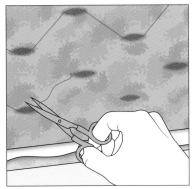

Set machine to stitch one embroidered motif at a time, such as small oval, star, or triangle. Lift needle and presser foot after sewing single motif; gently move to next area to be stitched. Sew another motif. When done, cut off all connecting threads on quilt front and back.

DROPPING THE FEED DOGS

Free-motion machine embroidered with metallic thread by Sheena Norquay.

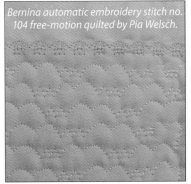

Bernina automatic embroidery stitch no. 104 free-motion quilted by Pia Welsch.

For intricate embroidery, layer quilt top and batting only. Drop or cover feed dogs; attach free-motion foot. Use a straight stitch and specialty threads to free-motion embroider. Add quilt back when embroidery is finished; machine quilt to hold all 3 layers together.

When feed dogs are dropped, or covered, most programmed stitches will not work. However, some motifs will elongate and create repetitive patterns, depending on the speed with which fabric is moved under the foot. Test stitches to find which work best.

TWIN NEEDLES

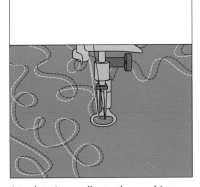

Attach twin needles to the machine. Drop or cover feed dogs, and free-motion quilt using a regular straight stitch to create ribbon-like designs. Try using different color threads. To prevent needle breakage, move fabric slowly and deliberately while stitching.

COMPUTER-GENERATED EMBROIDERY

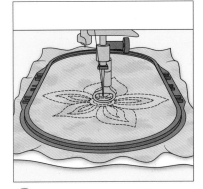

1 See page 221 for how to do computer-generated embroidery designs on the sewing machine. It's best to quilt computerized patterns on a quilt top layered only with batting, so that any knots or other imperfections can be covered later by the quilt back.

2 Hoop quilt top and batting in appropriate sized hoop for motif being quilted, ensuring that both layers are taut and evenly spread in the hoop. Attach hoop to embroidery module and stitch design. When done, add quilt back and machine quilt to secure layers.

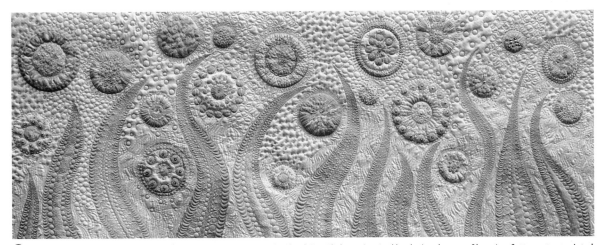

Twenty Circles, Twelve Flames—©Sheena Norquay, Inverness, Scotland. Detail above. Inspired by the London 2012 Olympics. Cotton sateen printed and stenciled with gold fabric paint, layered with batting, machine embroidered with metallic thread. Batting trimmed close to embroidery, work layered with wool batting and a backing; background free-motion quilted. Embellished with beads and sequins. 54½ x 23"/138 x 58cm. 2013.

Pay the Ferry Man—©Annette Morgan, Thetford, Norfolk, UK. Photo by Kevin Mead. Collection of Vivien Finch. This piece is based on images taken at Felixstowe Ferry Boatyard in Suffolk, England. The artist transferred the image in the middle panel to fabric using T-Shirt Transfer Paper printed on an inkjet printer. The boat images in the top and bottom panels were Thermofax screen printed onto dyed fabric; the work was then machine quilted and painted with emulsion paint. Cotton fabric, paper, scrim, foils, emulsion paint. Image printed on inkjet printer and heat transferred, Thermofax screen printed, free-motion machine quilted, painted. 24 x 60"/61 x 152cm. 2010.

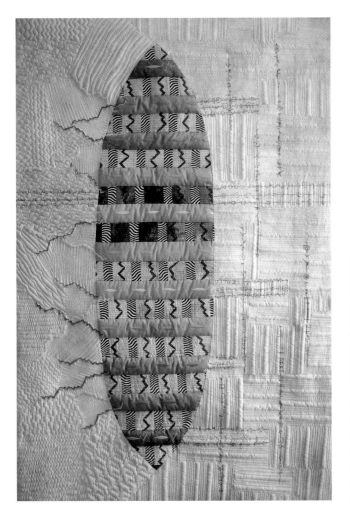

DAX—©Pia Welsch, Homburg, Germany. Hand-dyed fabric by Heide Stoll-Weber and the artist. Collection of Ellen Moschitz-Finger. DAX is the term for the German Stock Index; this quilt gives an impression of the curves and complications that can happen in the stock market. Hand-dyed and commercial cotton fabrics, polyester thread. Machine embroidered with decorative stitches (some using a twin needle), free-motion machine quilted, designs drawn on quilted surface with textile marker. 30 x 47"/77 x 120cm. 2009.

Tideline: After the Storm—©Margaret Ramsay, Brentford, Middlesex, UK. The morning after a spring storm in Paralio Astros, Greece, with intricate interlaced lines of seaweed and detritus deposited on the beach. Hand-dyed and African print cotton fabrics, cotton quilting and embroidery threads, acrylic paints. Machine pieced, free-motion machine quilted, hand stitched, painted after quilting. 33 x 33"/85 x 85 cm. 2008.

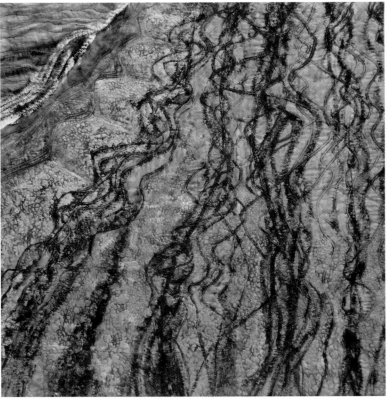

Some art quilters choose to apply color to surfaces that have already been quilted, leading to sensational and surprising effects. Color can be added with fibers, paints or dyes; see pages 200–201 for some examples. Refer to Chapter 3 for instructions on working with paints and dyes; pages 47 and 60–61 go into detail on the various dyes, auxiliaries, textile colors and mediums that can be used. In addition, try water-based emulsion paint, gesso or artists' acrylic paint for denser coverage.

The quilted foundation can be a solid color or busy print. For all methods, the foundation should be well quilted, although small areas can be left unquilted for contrast. If dyeing the work (see opposite page), construct the foundation using a variety of fabrics to produce entirely unforeseen results.

Colorful wool roving fibers can be placed strategically on the surface of a quilt to compliment a design or provide a focus. The fibers can then be needle felted in place and free-motion machine quilted for added texture.

Painting a quilted surface will emphasize the indentations created by the quilting stitches as the paint will pick up and accentuate only the raised areas. In addition, any thick threads or embroidery stitches that sit on top of the surface will be highlighted. Use a paintbrush, roller or palette knife to apply textile or emulsion paint, or use paintstiks. Create well-defined edges using masking tape. Stamps can also be dipped in paint or ink and pressed on a quilted surface for a fragmented effect.

Another way to add color is by precision coloring. This method is dictated by the quilt design and follows the same rules as when coloring in a coloring book: work neatly and stay within the lines. It's best if the quilting designs feature enclosed areas. The advantage of this approach is that the resulting work can look as if it has been appliquéd. Color is filled in with ordinary colored pencils and then made permanent by painting with a textile medium. Unquilted areas can also be colored with metallic or textile paints.

A daring way to add color is to dip an entire finished quilt in a dye bath, or apply dye directly to the surface. The richly colored results can be quite unexpected, particularly if a variety of different fabrics were used in the quilt.

These techniques are not for those with a nervous disposition, because once color is applied to a quilted surface, there is no going back. These instructions assume that the reader is using a layered quilt that has been well quilted. It's imperative to make and test identically quilted samples before committing a large piece of work to a brush or dye bath.

FIBERS

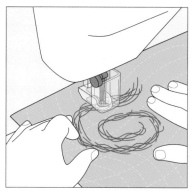

To add wool roving to a quilted surface, gently pull fibers into small pieces; shape into flat spirals, circles, ovals, or curved shapes. Arrange on quilted surface. Needle felt in place (see pages 28–29). Free-motion machine quilt over fibers to add texture.

PAINTS

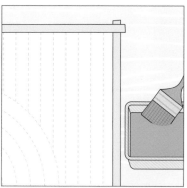

1 For best results, use a densely quilted piece, leaving some areas unquilted for contrast if desired. Stretch quilt in a frame or tape all edges to protected surface until taut. Pour textile or emulsion paint in tray. Coat brush or roller evenly to prevent drips.

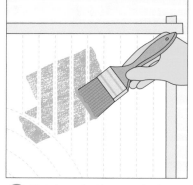

2 Lightly apply thin coat of paint to quilted surface by rolling gently with the foam roller or dragging bristles of the brush across the quilt's surface. Paint will just pick up raised areas. Allow to dry, then apply an additional thin coat if desired.

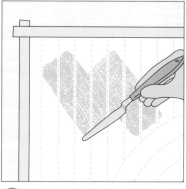

3 Alternatively, load a palette knife with thickened paint; scrape it along the quilt's surface to spread paint on raised areas. If a paint blob forms, scrape gently with palette knife. Work quickly so paint does not seep into indentations formed by quilting.

PAINTSTIKS

See page 79 for instructions on using paintstiks. Remove paintstik film, then drag paintstik lightly across the quilted surface to pick up only the raised areas between the stitches as in this example. *Paintstiks applied to quilt by Laura Kemshall.*

Alternatively, load stencil brush with color from a paintstik. Rub brush on fabric to transfer color, reloading brush frequently. Blend colors together to create depth, or apply a variety of colors as shown here. *Paintstiks applied to quilt by Pia Welsch.*

STAMPS

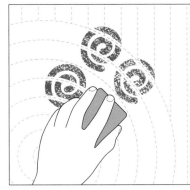

Use stamps to create a repeated design that will look fragmented over the areas with quilting stitches. See page 63 for instructions on applying color to a stamp. Press stamp gently onto quilted surface so color does not seep into indentations.

MASKING

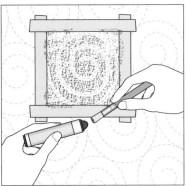

For sharp delineations and greater accuracy when working with paints or paintstiks, mask off areas with tape. Press firmly on edges of tape so no color bleeds underneath. Apply color to unmasked area. Pull off tape promptly after color has been applied.

PRECISION PAINTING

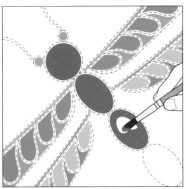

You can use textile, acrylic or metallic paint to color quilted designs. Shake or stir paint well. Load tip of brush, tap off excess and smoothly apply thin layer of color on fabric, staying within quilted outlines. Use delicate brush for tiny areas.

PRECISION COLORING WITH PENCILS

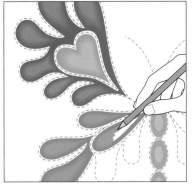

1 Stretch quilted fabric in frame or tape to work surface as in *Paints*, step 1. Using colored pencils, outline and fill in enclosed areas of quilted design. Color neatly within the stitching lines. Vary pencil pressure, making color darker around edges and lighter in the middle.

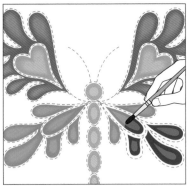

2 When design has been fully colored, dip paintbrush in colorless textile medium or extender. Paint lightly over pencil marks. Air dry thoroughly. Follow manufacturer's directions to fix textile medium or extender. If heat setting, hover iron just above surface.

IMMERSION DYEING

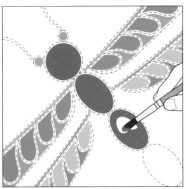

Prepare immersion dye bath in a container large enough to hold quilt; see page 48. Pre-wash quilt; immerse damp quilt in dye and soak, stirring regularly. Add soda ash after ½ hour; stir well. Soak at least one hour. Batch, wash and rinse; see page 46.

DIRECT APPLICATION DYEING

1 Prepare dye solutions for direct application dyeing as directed on page 50; use generous amount of dye for deep color. Keep soda ash solution separate. Pre-wash quilt; arrange flat on plastic covered surface. *Quilt dyed by C June Barnes using direct application.*

2 Pour dyes on quilt, working from light to dark colors. With gloved hands, rub and blend dye into the quilt until fully saturated. Allow dye to soak at least one hour. Pour soda ash solution over quilt; soak one hour. Batch, wash and rinse as directed on page 46.

DRYING

Allow all painted or dyed quilts to thoroughly air dry, flat and undisturbed on a protected surface. If drying out of doors, ensure that piece is not in direct sun. *Quilt by Margaret Ramsay; see page 201 for full image and detail.*

7 EMBELLISHMENTS & 3D

buttons
beads bobbin work
found objects
silk fibers metal
thread painting
machine embroidery
couching
Angelina

7

7

EMBELLISHMENTS & 3D

Although every aspect of quilt making is enjoyable, some find embellishing to be the most pleasurable. In addition to adding sparkle, texture or decorative ornamentation to a quilt, embellishments can enhance a quilt's story or simply make a piece more eye-catching. The choices are vast and the scope for creative interpretation is huge. This chapter covers just some of the possibilities.

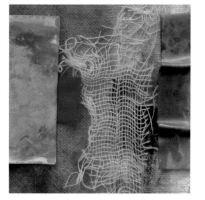

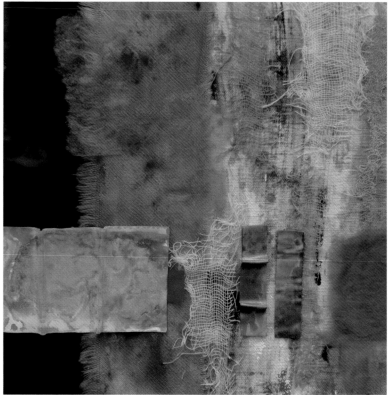

⬆ Markings—©Fenella Davies, Bath, UK. Collection of Mirjam Pet Jacobs. Inspiration was taken from a wall in Venice, Italy—the marks of lives present and past. Cotton, scrim, lead flashing. Hand-dyed and painted fabric, hand sewn, collaged. 8 x 8"/20 x 20cm. 2009.

Mikey of Mallory—©Marie Bergstedt, San Francisco, California. This piece was inspired by the artist's brother, Mikey, who lived as a street musician in Key West, Florida, for eleven years. In 2012 they reunited while she was a resident artist at The Studios of Key West, having not seen each other for 35 years. Needlepoint canvas, cotton threads, buttons, beads, polyester suede and manufactured wool/rayon felt backing. Hand stitched, crocheted, knitted. 24 x 48"/61 x 122cm. 2012.

Traversing the Land— © Dijanne Cevaal, Geelong, Australia. Photo by Kaye Haerland. Inspired by the early Australian explorers who traversed the Great Southern Land in search of rivers and knowledge—yet they rarely sought the knowledge of the indigenous people who knew the land intimately. Hand-spun and woven cotton khadi cloth, hand-dyed with a loose shibori technique. Entirely hand stitched and embroidered. 20 x 49"/50 x 125 cm. 2012.

⬆ Moonlight—©Jane Burch Cochran, Rabbit Hash, Kentucky. Photo by Pam Monfort. The artist wants her quilts to be interesting from a distance with a strong narrative image, and then draw the viewer in closer. She does this by heavily embellishing her work using beads, buttons and recycled fabric items such as gloves and doilies. The background is painted canvas to which she appliquéd the patchwork figure, moon and other pieces using beads. Various fabrics, including cotton, painted canvas, recycled fabric items, beads, buttons. Machine pieced, machine appliquéd, hand appliquéd using beads, hand embellished with beads and buttons, hand quilted and tied with embroidery thread. 61 x 77"/155 x 196cm. 2007.

Art quilters who enjoy embellishing find potential in such disparate items as seashells, keys, twigs, clock parts, gloves, old jewelry and feathers, as well as everyday items such as buttons and beads. The use of machine embroidery, couched threads, and alternative fibers such as Angelina further adds to the huge catalog of possibilities for turning a quilt into a magnum opus.

A natural progression from adding dimension to a flat surface is to construct a 3D object—arguably the most unique and individual type of quilt art, and very difficult to replicate. For this reason, pages 211–213 feature just a small sample of what can be done when quilting is taken to another dimension. Refer to the Bibliography for several excellent books on how to create your own 3D quilt art.

⬆ Poppy Field at Sunset—©Linda Seward, London, UK. Collection of Emily Seward. Strip-pieced patchwork landscape made in the stitch and flip method. Conceived in a workshop with Ineke Berlyn; the design is based on a painting by Ton Schulten, a modern Dutch artist, and featured here with his permission. Machine pieced, machine quilted, embellished with beads. 28½ x 22½"/72 x 57cm. 2009.

➡ Ghosts of Autumn—©Colleen Harris, Johannesburg, South Africa. Photo by Dion Cuyler. The artist was inspired to create this original design by the book *Paper, Metal & Stitch* by Maggie Grey and Jane Wild. She scrunched brown paper, painted it with burnt umber and coated the result with gel medium before adding appliqués and embellishments. Brown paper, paint, gel medium, hand-dyed cotton, stretch lace, paper bark, string, thread waste, beads. Machine appliquéd leaves made from stretch lace and paper bark, machine couched threads and string, embroidered, free-motion machine quilted, beaded. 17 x 24"/44.5 x 62cm. 2011.

⬇ Circuit Board—©Dwayne Wanner, Burlington, Ontario, Canada. Photo by Eric Song. As president of a robotics integration company, the artist decorates his offices with his abstract quilts, but made this representational one so it could be fully appreciated by the engineers. The artist strip-pieced small colored squares into dark blue fabric to make blocks. He programmed an Ellissimo machine with the circuit lines and cathode shapes that were embroidered onto hooped blocks. Cotton fabric, polyester threads. Machine pieced, machine quilted, panels sewn together by hand. 72 x 52"/183 x 132cm. 2011.

The Heritage Sites of Kromdraai, Swartkrans and Sterkfontein—©Jenny Hearn, Johannesburg, South Africa. Photo by Dion Cuyler. Created in appliquéd layers to denote journeying into the depths of a cave. The "rock faces" at the sides were constructed from commercial cotton fabric, faced, embroidered and satin-stitched to replicate watermarks on stone and stalactites. The needlepoint areas represent irregular geological formations within a cave. Commercial cottons, hand-dyed silk and cotton fabrics, variegated cotton and silk threads and yarns. Bargello and half-cross stitch on needlepoint canvas, machine embroidered, machine pieced, free-motion embroidered and quilted. 19 x 19½"/50 x 50cm. 2011.

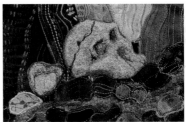

Inner Glow—©C June Barnes, Hastings, East Sussex. Inspired by images of seeds and pollen in the publications by Rob Kesseler and Madeline Harley. The artist made a papier-mâché structure using an exercise ball foundation. A large hole was cut into the surface and hundreds of rosette shapes made out of white viscose and satin fabrics were glued inside. LED lights were attached to the outside of the orb with a glue gun. Metal zippers were stitched to one edge of fabric strips layered with wool/viscose felt; the strips were then free-motion machine quilted and washed—the zipper edges resisted shrinkage, resulting in curved strips. After being space-dyed, the strips were attached to the outside of the orb with a glue gun. Cotton, silk and viscose fabrics, metal zippers, LED lights, wool/viscose felt. 30"/76cm diameter. 2012.

➜ Forever Yours —©Susan Else, Santa Cruz, California. Photo by Marty McGillivray. The artist likes to make work that conflates contradictory ideas and impulses: fear/ tenderness, death/eternity, bone white/vibrant color, and so on. This work is the second in a series of cloth-covered skeletons in benign attitudes. Commercial and hand-treated cloth. Machine collaged, machine quilted, hand sewn over an armature of commercial plastic skeletons. 26 x 13 x 14"/66 x 33 x 36cm. 2010.

⬆ Portal—©Philippa K Lack, Cheyenne, Wyoming. Photo by The Image Maker, Denver, Colorado. This work was inspired by the artist's love of recycling (she used a discarded vent hose pipe) and the concept grew from there. Hand painted silk satin, nylon mesh, beads. Hand-dyed silk, nylon mesh embellishment wrapped with hand painted silk, beaded. Polished ash base: 30 x 9"/76 x 23cm; 12"/30cm high. 2012.

⬆ Round Meadow—©Elizabeth Brimelow, Cheshire, UK. Photo by Michael Wicks. Inspired by an area called "Round Meadow" in the artist's village. The knotting is representative of crops, growth and the surface of the land. Silk fabric, some hand-dyed, card and fabric labels. Hand and machine stitched, hand knotted. 36"/92cm diameter x 3"/8cm high x 814"/2068cm long. 2013.

ANGELINA

To add luminescent embellishments to art quilts, try Angelina—heat-fusible fibers that literally glow and sparkle with color. When melted, these soft, tactile fibers form a shimmering web that can be used as a fabric, cut into appliqués or fused to other textiles. Sheets of fusible film made by the same manufacturer have similar qualities.

Angelina is available in a range of colors that can be altered by mixing the fibers, varying the heat or increasing the melting time. To begin, set iron to very low heat and experiment. High heat will produce a stiff result. If heat is applied long enough, the irridescence can disappear, producing a matte effect.

Angelina will not bond to anything but itself, but can be attached to fabric with bonding powder, fusible web or stitching. Inclusions (below) can be fused into the web to great effect.

EQUIPMENT

Angelina fibers or fusible film, iron, 2 layers baking parchment (or fiberglass pressing sheet), items for inclusions: see list below, textured items: stamp, leaf, doily etc., heat settable inks or paints, paint brush, fusible web, bonding powder, heat gun, heat-proof surface.

FUSING TECHNIQUE

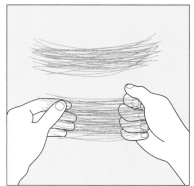

1 Gently pull Angelina fibers and arrange on baking parchment. Work with small amounts at a time. Apply in fine layers, criss-crossing fibers for stronger result. Cover with second sheet of parchment.

STRAIGHTEN EDGES

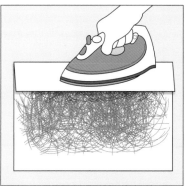

Edges of fused Angelina are wispy. To create straight edges, place fused Angelina on sheet of paper. Fold edge of paper over fibers, catching wispy edges in fold. Press briefly with iron to fuse folded fibers to main piece, making a straight edge; repeat on other edges.

2 Heat iron to silk or very low setting. Pass iron smoothly and evenly over parchment for 3 seconds or until the slight crunching sound is no longer heard. If fibers form a thick layer, or inclusions have been added, turn over and iron briefly on reverse side.

3 Allow to cool for a few seconds. Remove top sheet of baking parchment to reveal fused sheet of Angelina. Gently peel fused sheet off the bottom piece of parchment.

MIX COLORS

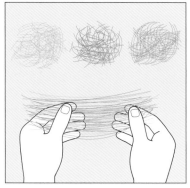

To create unique colors or tweedy effects, mix two or more colors of fibers. Hold fibers together in one bunch, then pull them apart again and again, until the fibers mix and blend to create the desired finished effect. Fuse as described above.

INCLUSIONS

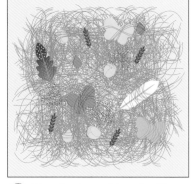

1 Place fine layer of Angelina fibers on parchment. Arrange dried flowers, skeleton leaves, punched paper shapes, feathers, glitter, snips of fabric, yarn, threads, or any other non-fusible materials on top. Top with fine layer of fibers. Cover with parchment; press.

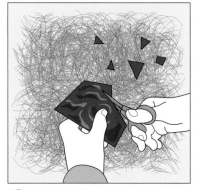

2 Alternatively, place Angelina fibers (unfused or already fused) on parchment. Snip small shreds of different color Angelina fibers or fusible film on top. Cover with parchment; press briefly on both sides to fuse all layers together.

MOLD A DESIGN

1 You can mold a dimensional image on Angelina using a stamp or textured item such as lace, a veiny leaf, a paper doily, etc. Place stamp or item on parchment, textured side up; cover with Angelina. Place parchment on top; press hard with iron for 3 seconds.

2 Allow to cool, then carefully peel Angelina off stamp or textured item. Trim around edges of molded design using scissors to create an appliqué. Alternatively, leave the edges wispy for a more irregular effect as shown.

COLORED IMAGE

To transfer a colored dimensional image to Angelina, color raised or ridged areas of stamp or textured item with heat-settable paint or ink, using a brush. Cover with Angelina fibers. Place parchment on top; press hard with iron for 3 seconds. Peel off when cool.

FUSE TO FABRIC

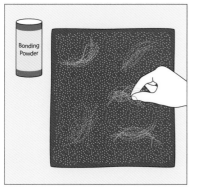

Place fabric, right side up on baking parchment. Shake bonding powder evenly all over fabric. Arrange fine wisps of Angelina on fabric. Cover with parchment and press to fuse. Carefully peel off parchment when cool to reveal an iridescent sparkle on fabric.

APPLIQUÉ

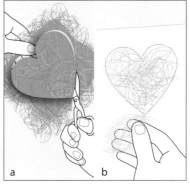

Cut fused Angelina into shapes with scissors (a), a punch paper cutter or rotary cutter; stitch or fuse to fabric. Or place fibers on rough side of fusible web (b). Cover with parchment; press to bond fibers and web. Cut out appliqué; peel off backing paper. Fuse to fabric.

3D SHAPES

You can mold Angelina to make 3D appliqués. First, cut out a shape such as a petal, leaf or wing. Sandwich it between parchment; press until just malleable but not too hot. Pick up and shape by pinching or molding with fingers. Allow to cool in 3D shape.

WEAVING

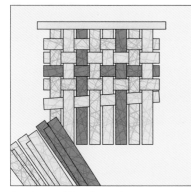

Cut sheet of fused Angelina into strips; place on baking parchment. Tape ends of several long Angelina strips to baking parchment. Weave strips of different colors, over and under the taped strips. Cover with another layer of parchment and fuse together.

FUSIBLE FILM IDEAS

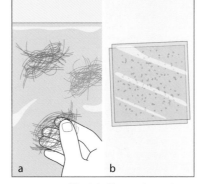

Cut pieces of fusible film to desired size. Lay on parchment. Arrange shreds of Angelina fibers or snips of film in different colors on top (a). Or sandwich non-fusible items between layers of film (b). Cover with parchment; press briefly on each side to fuse.

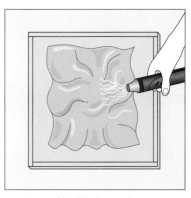

Lay sheet of fusible film on heat-proof surface such as protected glass or a tile. Apply heat with a heat gun until piece moves and changes into desired shape or texture. Stitch or fuse to another fabric. Or, decorate with more Angelina fibers/film; heat to fuse.

BEADS, BUTTONS & FOUND OBJECTS

Embellishing a quilt with beads, buttons and found ojects is a compelling process. Finding exactly the right items to accentuate a design can be absorbing and very satisfactory. Enjoy the search, or make your own bead and button embellishments.

When sewing objects to a quilt, add color by using variegated sewing thread or bright embroidery thread. Alternatively, employ invisible thread so the stitches don't show. Needle choice will depend on the size of the object being attached and the thickness of the thread. Bugle and seed beads will require fine, thin beading needles, while buttons, twigs or feathers call for sturdier needles.

Embellished work needs to be well stablized or weighted at the bottom to prevent unwanted sagging; see Hanging & Framing on pages 240–241.

EQUIPMENT

To make a beading mat, glue velvet inside a plastic tray with raised sides (to prevent losing beads). Use a bead scoop to gather beads. Tweezers help with placement. Thread needle with double strand of mercerized thread in neutral color, or color to match beads.

SEWING BEADS

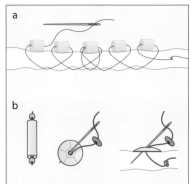

Knot thread; bury inside quilt. To quilt and bead at the same time, stitch bead on with backstitch, going through all layers of quilt sandwich, making an extra anchoring stitch regularly (a). Add seed beads to protect rough edges of bugle beads and secure sequins (b).

FABRIC/PAPER BEADS

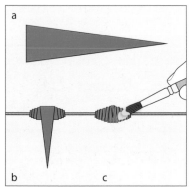

Cut elongated triangle of fabric or paper so base is desired width of bead (a). Roll around wooden skewer (b); apply fabric or glitter glue to secure. Wrap or tie fancy threads (or wire) around bead; glue thread ends. Apply paint or varnish (c); allow to dry.

SYNTHETIC BEADS

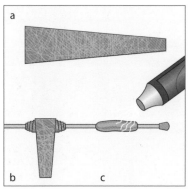

Cut elongated triangle or rectangle of synthetic material such as Tyvek, fused Angelina or Angelina film to desired width of bead (a). Roll around metal knitting needle (b). Wrap with fine wire. Use heat gun to melt fibers so they fuse to each other (c). Allow to cool.

FELT BEADS

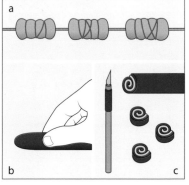

Cut small narrow rectangle of felt. Roll around skewer; wrap with thread (a). Or, layer 2–3 colors of wool roving; felt or needlefelt together (pages 25–28), then roll into a sausage shape (b). Slice into rounds using a craft knife (c).

BUTTONS

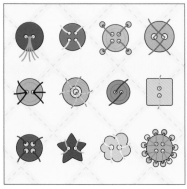

Be creative when choosing and sewing on button embellishments. Use sewing/embroidery thread in various weights and colors. Knot on top, leaving tassels. Add beads on top/sides. Stack buttons over one another. Stitch toward outside of button. Use a variety of shapes.

SHANK BUTTONS

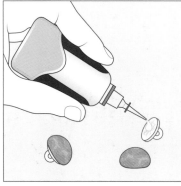

Plastic buttons with small shanks can be used for gluing on objects that are too tricky to stitch, or too rigid to pierce. Sand smooth flat top of button. Apply strong glue to object and top of button; hold together firmly for recommended time. Sew shank to quilt.

POLYMER CLAY

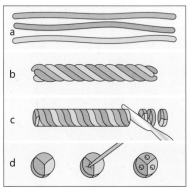

Make colorful beads and buttons from polymer clay; follow manufacturer's instructions for conditioning and baking clay. For swirl effect, roll 3 colors into thin snakes (a); twine together (b). Roll into cylinder; slice (c). Roll into ball or flatten; make holes with skewer (d).

SEASHELLS

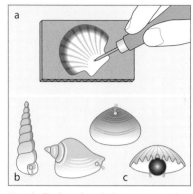

Use shells that already have a natural hole, or use an awl to carefully make a hole well away from edge, to prevent breaking the shell (a). Stitch shell firmly to quilt with invisible thread (b). If using a clam or scallop shell, add a small pearl underneath as a surprise (c).

NATURAL OBJECTS

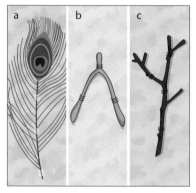

Colorful feathers, bones and twigs can be sewn to a quilt to make a bold statement. Bones should be boiled, thoroughly dried and varnished. Sew feathers with delicate invisible stitches (a). Use matching or contrasting rough threads for bones and twigs (b, c).

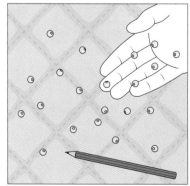

⬆ Beach Landscape—©Linda Seward, London, UK. Based on a detail of a painting by Donald Hamilton Fraser (Landscape No. 1, October 1971). Cotton fabric, cheesecloth, organza, beads, seashells. Machine pieced, raw-edge fused appliqués, free-motion machine embroidered organza for sand, machine embroidered cheesecloth for foam, free-motion machine quilted, embellished with beads and seashells. 18 x 22"/46 x 56cm. 2011.

FOUND TEXTILES

Stitch gloves, doilies, baby clothes, or parts of clothes such as pockets, collars or plackets to a quilt to tell a story. Use embroidery floss and buttonhole stitch to make a feature of such items. or sew them on by machine. *Patch Pocket Night and Day by Jane Burch Cochran.*

SMALL OBJECTS

Work with small objects that will not project much beyond the quilt surface. Some plastic charms have loops that can be used for stitching. Others will have areas suitable for placement of anchoring stitches. See page 219 for other ways to attach small objects.

PLACEMENT

To create a spontaneous look, scatter a handful of beads, buttons or shells randomly on quilt surface. Mark each spot with a pencil dot before removing the items, then stitch one over each marked dot. Position heavier items near bottom of the quilt for level hanging.

METAL

Adding metal embellishments to a quilt can turn a prosaic piece into a stunning composition. The twinning of hard unyielding metal with the soft fibers of a quilt makes an unorthodox, but fascinating combination. Opening your mind to the possibilities of metal use will add an entirely new dimension to the way you embellish art quilts. As most quilters find it difficult to throw things away—add interesting bits of lightweight metal to the items you collect, and watch the stockpile grow quickly. To ease into the concept of using metal in your work, utilize the sewing implements you already have on hand, such as zippers, safety pins, needles and snaps.

As with many styles of art quilts, try to start with a theme—either the kind of metal that is used or its shape or application. It's best to add metal pieces judiciously; covering a quilt with all kinds of metal objects will just end up looking like a junkyard, which is obviously undesirable. You must also consider the weight of the metal on your quilt. If adding a lot of metal embellishments, you might need extra support to prevent the fabrics from pulling and sagging.

Basic stitching techniques such as straight stitch, cross stitch and couching will enable you to add most types of metal to your quilts. Adding grommets and eyelets will enable the attachment of other metal objects or rings that can connect sections together. Many metal objects already have openings ready-made for stitching. However, some metal items will require drilled holes to accommodate the fastening thread. Always wear gloves and protective glasses when cutting metal. Cut edges will be extremely sharp; use a metal file and steel wool to dull sharp edges.

⬆ Prehistoric Mammoth Tooth (detail)—©Linda Seward, UK. Photo by Nigel Bird. African hand-woven and tie-dyed fabrics. Machine pieced, machine quilted, hand embroidered, embellished with Swarovski crystals and Chinese coins. 28 x 30½"/ 71 x 76 cm. 2011.

ALUMINUM FOIL

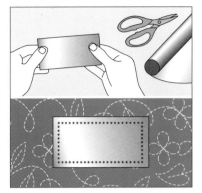

Cut aluminum foil with craft scissors to desired shape. Stitch to quilt by hand or sewing machine. If using machine, slowly stitch foil to quilt using slightly longer stitch length than usual. Decrease pressure on foot, as heavy pressure will score the foil.

BRADS

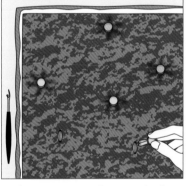

Brads come in many shapes and colors. To hide prongs in quilt sandwich, attach brads before layering. Or, use brads to hold quilt layers together in same way as ties; allow prongs to show on back. Pierce hole in fabric first using a seam ripper.

METAL CLOTH

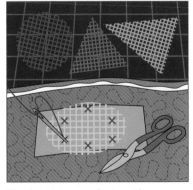

Metal cloth is manufactured from copper, stainless steel, brass, silver and gold. Cut fine mesh screens into shapes using scissors and appliqué to quilt with straight or cross stitches. Use hardware cloth, which has a more open weave, to make a bold statement.

FOUND OBJECTS

Use light, thin metal objects to embellish quilts. Collect coins, keys, old jewelry, sewing fasteners (as mentioned left), hardware such as nuts, bolts, washers and screws, lightweight tools, grommets, eyelets, paper clips, parts from watches or clocks, buckles, hooks, etc.

WIRE

Hand-stitch or couch wire to quilts. Use needle-nose pliers to bend wire into interesting shapes and swirls. If desired, flatten wire with a hammer and anvil once it's been shaped. Alternatively, wrap wire around an item such as a twig or bone, then attach to quilt.

SHEET METAL

Cut lightweight, pliable metal sheets into shapes with metal sheet cutters; be careful as cut edges will be very sharp—smooth with metal file and steel wool. Use an awl or metal hole puncher to make holes along edges for stitching.

ATTACHING METAL

1 Fasten metal to fabric with strong waxed thread, embroidery floss or string in a large-eyed sewing needle. Make a single stitch through each hole or at intervals through opening. Ensure threads do not touch sharp edges which can cause abrasion and breakage.

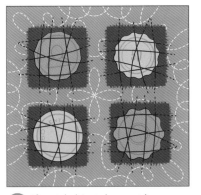

2 If metal object does not have a hole, secure it to the quilt surface with a web of stitches that run over the piece and through the batting. Hide knots beneath the metal.

3 Place a small flat metal object beneath a sheer fabric, clear plastic or metal screen. Stitch in place on quilt close to the metal object, using decorative or colored thread to make a feature of the stitches.

4 Use grommets and metal rings to hold parts of a quilt together or to add an edging. With seam ripper, slit small hole where each grommet should go. Separate grommet parts; place back section under hole. Use grommet setter to secure top section in place.

Heavy Metal— ©Jamie Fingal, Orange, California. Collection of Gregory Maguire. A complex self-portrait of the maker—part punk rock with dark fabrics and metal, part colorful with a tweak of bright fabrics. Commercial and hand-dyed fabrics, rickrack, netting, tulle, beads, household metal screen, metal ring trim, springs, flanges, washers. Raw-edge appliqué, free-motion machine quilted. 20½" x 29½"/52 x 75cm. 2006.

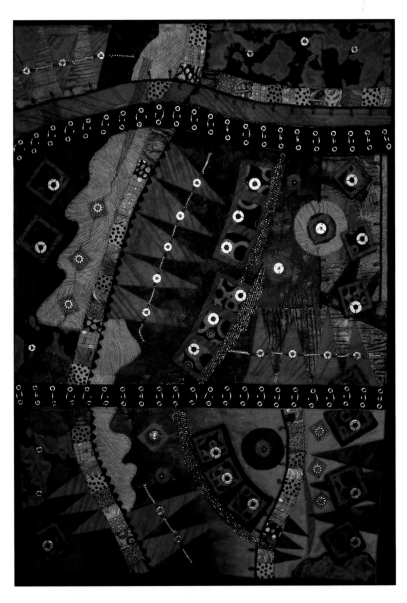

MACHINE EMBROIDERY

Embellish an art quilt with machine embroidery, either with programmed designs that are built into the machine, or with a computer-generated pattern using an embroidery module. This section touches on some of the many options for doing machine embroidery; see the Bibliography for books that provide more detailed instructions. For free-motion embroidery, see Thread Painting (page 222). To use embroidery for quilting, see pages 198–199.

While machine embroidery is not difficult, its success is influenced by the needle, thread, the foot and the correct tension. Using a stabilizer is essential; stabilizers can be permanent or temporary, but must be substantial enough to prevent the fabric from distorting as it is stitched. Use water-soluble stabilizers to create lacy fabrics and shaped edges; see page 239.

NEEDLE & THREAD

70/10 topstitch needles work best for machine embroidery threads. Replace the needle after 5–6 hours of stitching. Experiment with a variety of threads to create different effects: shiny, metallic and variegated threads add interest and depth to an embroidered design.

FEET

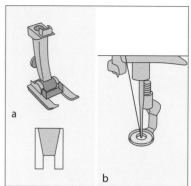

To make decorative stitches using a standard machine, attach an open-toe embroidery foot with a channel in the bottom to accommodate thick stitches (a). If using an embroidery module, attach the foot recommended by the manufacturer (b) or a free-motion foot.

TENSION

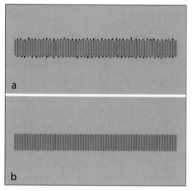

Test tension before beginning using satin stitch. Thread machine with different colors in top and bobbin; use correct foot on hooped, stabilized fabric. Bobbin thread should not show on top of fabric (a). If it does, lower top tension and decrease sewing speed (b).

STABILIZERS: PERMANENT & TEMPORARY

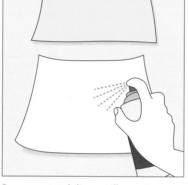

Permanent stabilizers will remain after embroidering, and must be fixed smoothly to wrong side of fabric to keep embroidery from puckering when stitched. Iron on a fusible stabilizer, or spray one side of a non-fusible with fabric adhesive.

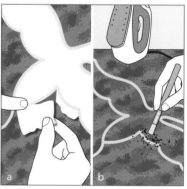

Temporary stabilizers can be fixed to either side of fabric. After embroidery, tear off (a), cut away with scissors or dissolve with water (see below). Use a heat-away stabilizer on non-synthetic fabric: iron after stitching to melt stabilizer into pellets; brush away (b).

WATER-SOLUBLE STABILIZERS

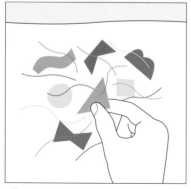

1 Water-soluble stabilizers dissolve in water after stitching. To create a lacy design, place stabilizer on work surface. Arrange thread, fabric scraps and other stitchable items on top as shown. When design is complete, top with another layer of the stabilizer.

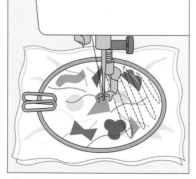

2 Hoop layered stabilizers in a clip frame. Place frame under machine needle. Drop feed dogs; use free-motion foot. Free-motion machine stitch all over stabilizer. Criss-cross stitches so that threads and scraps are interconnected, forming a lacy grid.

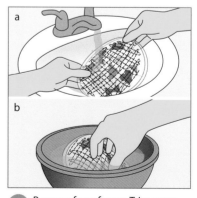

3 Remove from frame. Trim away any excess stabilizer. Place under warm to hot running water. Rinse until stabilizer dissolves and no residue remains (a). Or, soak in warm soapy water, changing water frequently until water is clear (b). Allow to dry on flat surface.

LIQUID STABILIZER

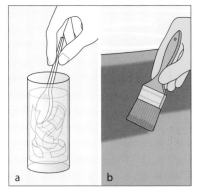

To make liquid stabilizer, melt water-soluble stablizer in warm water (a): a good way to use up scraps. Flatten fabric on plastic-covered surface; paint stabilizer on with brush or roller (b). Fabric will stiffen as stabilizer dries. Wash out when embroidery is done.

PROGRAMMED DECORATIVE STITCHES

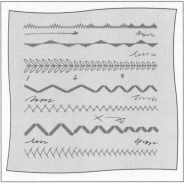

Experiment with the programmed decorative stitches built into your machine, using different threads and stabilizers. Start each stitching line using the machine's default setting; change width/length while stitching to observe changes. Make notes on fabric.

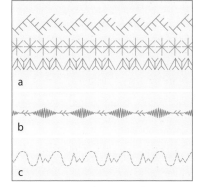

Try combining different stitches to create unique designs either side by side (a) or in a continuous line (b). Drop the feed dogs and free-motion stitch to create unusual effects (c). Note that not all programmed stitches will work with the feed dogs dropped.

COMPUTER-GENERATED MACHINE EMBROIDERY

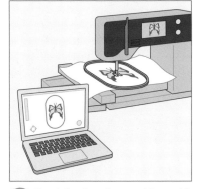

1 Specialized sewing machines with embroidery modules can be programmed with images designed on a computer. The image is automatically stitched on hooped fabric attached to the module, although threads must be manually changed for each color.

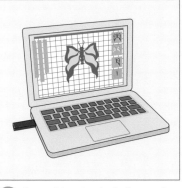

2 Start with a simple design on the computer. Using embroidery software and following manufacturer's instructions, convert a graphic image into a digitized stitch file, choosing stitch types to fill each section of the design. Save design on memory stick.

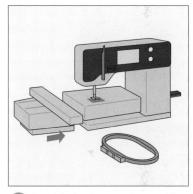

3 Load design into sewing machine from memory stick. Prepare machine for embroidery: use single hole throat plate, drop feed dogs, attach embroidery needle and foot, thread machine. Attach embroidery module following manufacturer's instructions.

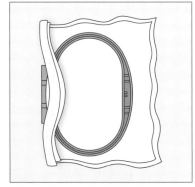

4 Affix stabilizer to wrong side of fabric in one of the ways shown on page 220. Choose correct size hoop for design being stitched. Place fabric and stabilizer in hoop so all layers are taut. Clip hoop onto the embroidery module as directed by manufacturer.

5 Begin sewing design with first color thread; after a few stitches, clip off thread ends. Continue sewing until all areas in that color thread are completed—sewing machine will do this automatically. Change threads for each new color area.

6 When design is finished, unclip hoop from module; remove fabric from hoop. Remove excess stabilizer. Steam-press embroidery face down on a thick towel. *Design created with Bernina computer software and embroidered on a Bernina 780 by Hannah Blackbourne.*

THREAD PAINTING

Art quilters often compare their fabrics to an artist's palette of paints. The same can be said for those who have discovered thread painting, although in this case, the threads are like crayons or colored pencils and the fabric is the paper. Thread painting is a method of densely covering fabric with machine stitches—either on a home sewing machine or a longarm machine. These directions are for those using a home sewing machine.

The technique is very similar to free-motion machine quilting, where the feed dogs on the sewing machine are lowered or covered, and hands move the fabric around freely to create the design. An alternative is thread sketching, which simply highlights certain areas of a design with free-motion stitches, a less time consuming prospect as the stitching is not so dense. Both processes are thoroughly enjoyable and mesmerizing, justifiably making a quilter feel like an artist.

To thread paint (or sketch), trace, draw or print a design on fabric or follow an already printed image on a commercial fabric—an excellent way to practice. Or, trace a design onto water-soluble stabilizer, place on fabric and stitch over that, removing the stabilizer when done.

Work on a smooth, medium-weight stabilized fabric, hooping the stabilized fabric for the best results. Use an open free-motion foot and an 80/12 sharp needle. Select polyester, rayon, cotton or silk threads; variegated threads are a good choice. For greater coverage, thread the needle with two threads, adjusting the thread tension as needed (see page 37). Select a size 60 bobbin thread that blends with the top thread; slightly lower the top tension so the bobbin threads don't show.

PREPARATION

Press two layers of fusible interfacing on wrong side of fabric to stabilize it. Transfer design to right side of fabric, or center design that is marked on water-soluble stabilizer on right side. Insert all layers in clip frame until taut; ensure there are no puckers on top or bottom.

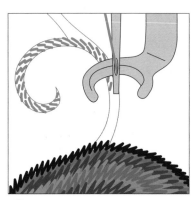

② Outline area to be stitched with zigzag stitch, working slowly. Always position design so stitching line is horizontal, then move work from side to side as you stitch, turning work continually in curved areas. Program needle to stop in the down position.

④ Change back to zigzag stitch to fill in design, following natural direction and curves of the design. Stitch slowly and carefully, thoroughly filling in any gaps that form. Needle may make a knocking sound as it stitches through thick threads; this is normal.

TECHNIQUE

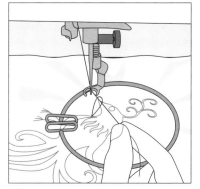

① Set stitch length to zero and drop or cover feed dogs of sewing machine. Place hooped design under free-motion foot. Choose starting point. Lower and raise needle to pull bobbin thread up. Make a few stitches; cut off threads close to fabric surface.

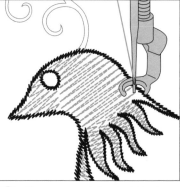

③ Change to straight stitch (and different thread color if desired). Make a series of stitches across the design, to imprecisely cover the area to be filled in. These stitches do not have to be perfect as they form a base padding and will be hidden.

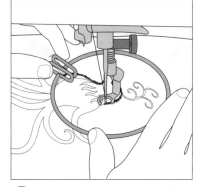

⑤ Add highlights with different color threads if desired. Try to vary length and position of highlight stitches to create a natural, random appearance. Cover any finely detailed areas with tiny straight stitches. If design is larger than hoop, rehoop as required.

FINISHING

Remove water-soluble stabilizer (if using) as directed on page 220; allow to dry flat. Place thread painted fabric, face down, on thick towel. Steam-press lightly with iron using a press cloth. Any puckered areas can be adjusted when work is layered and quilted.

⬆ Odd Pods—©Gwen Lowery, Shaw Island, Washington. Photo by Eric Hawley. Inspired by the artist's survey of the American Arts and Crafts Movement, when so many of the designs from that time portrayed simplified plant forms. Unprimed cotton artist canvas, silk dyes, rayon and cotton thread. Design transferred to canvas, painted with silk dyes, and thread painted using a longarm machine. 69 x 84"/175 x 213cm. 2012.

COUCHING

Sometimes art quilters wish to embellish work with cord, yarn or decorative threads that are too thick to fit in the sewing machine needle, and that are inappropriate for bobbin work. Couching, where strands are zigzag-stitched on the fabric's surface, provides the perfect solution. Couching can be done on stabilized fabric before it's quilted or as part of the quilting process—the method is the same.

Art quilters can experiment when couching, using a variety of weights and textures for the strands, assorted threads in the needle, and a range of decorative stitches. Ribbon, rickrack, metallic threads, pearl cotton and yarn can be couched, as long as the strand fits beneath the presser foot. Use couching to outline important areas, to create texture, or to highlight a focal point on a quilt.

FOOT

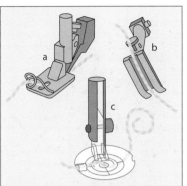

Use a special couching/cording foot that will automatically guide the strand(s) as you stitch (a). Or, use an embroidery foot with a bottom groove to accommodate strands (b)—cord will need to be guided by hand. Or, buy a free-motion couching foot (c).

STRANDS

See main text for some ideas on what can be couched on fabric. Choose from silken cords, novelty or variegated yarns, embroidery and metallic threads, etc. Once a strand has been chosen, use matching, contrasting or monofilament thread for machine needle and bobbin.

TECHNIQUE

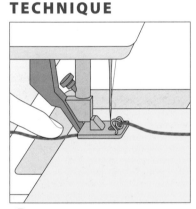

1 If couching unquilted work, stabilize fabric; see page 220. Attach couching/cording foot. Lay strand(s) to be couched on fabric or insert in foot as directed by manufacturer. Hold 6"/15cm tail behind foot. Lower foot. Stitch forward and back to lockstitch.

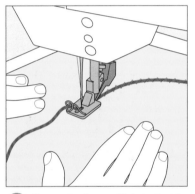

2 Change to zigzag stitch, just wide enough to fit over strand(s). Stitch smoothly forward, slowly moving fabric rather than strand(s), as couching foot will automatically guide strand(s) into correct position. At end, lockstitch and cut strand(s) leaving 6"/15cm tail.

EMBROIDERY

Couching by Jane Glennie.

To enhance couched strands, set machine to a decorative embroidery stitch and embroider over or into the strands. Use matching, contrasting or metallic thread. Experiment on sample pieces to determine the best embroidery stitches to use.

FREE-MOTION COUCHING

1 Attach a special free-motion couching foot and drop/cover feed dogs. Insert strand through foot using wire threader as directed by manu-facturer. Thread machine with thread to match strand. Set machine on straight stitch with needle in center position.

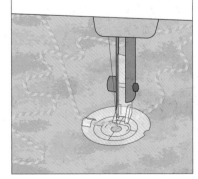

2 Lower foot at starting point, leaving 6"/15cm tail behind foot. Set machine to needle down position. Lockstitch, then stitch slowly in gentle curves as if free-motion quilting (pages 176–182). Machine thread will invisibly couch strand in place.

FINISHING

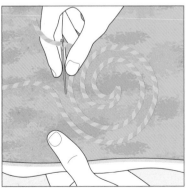

Extend ends of strands into seam allowances for easiest finish. To finish an end in the middle of a piece, thread end of strand in large-eyed sharp embroidery needle and pull to wrong side. Tie off on back with the bobbin thread.

BOBBIN WORK

To embellish with strands that can't fit through the eye of a needle, stitch upside-down—a technique known as bobbin work. In this approach, a decorative strand is wound onto a bobbin; see *Strands* on page 224 for a list of what can be used. The filled bobbin is inserted in the machine or a case with a loosened tension (page 37 and right). Stitching is done on the wrong side of the fabric or quilt, while the strands are automatically couched on the right side. Bobbin work can be done with programmed or straight stitches, with free-motion work or by using an embroidery module with a computer generated design. The thrill comes when the piece is turned over and the bobbin work is revealed. However, to prevent that excitement from turning sour, stitch a test piece to ensure that the tension is correct.

WINDING

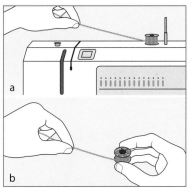

To wind by machine, wrap end of strand around bobbin a few times, then wind slowly, guiding strand as bobbin fills. For thick strands, bypass tension disc; squeeze strand between fingers as it winds to control tension (a). By hand, wind strand with steady tension (b).

BOBBIN CASE

If your machine uses a bobbin case, buy a dedicated case for bobbin work; mark with nail polish to avoid a mix-up. Loosen bobbin case tension by turning the screw to the left, and test until tension is perfect (page 37). Adjust upper tension if needed.

MARK A DESIGN

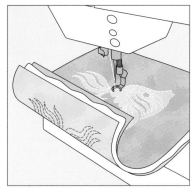

Work on layered quilt sandwich or stabilize wrong side of fabric (page 220). Mark design on quilt back or stabilizer. Or stitch design from right side with invisible thread as shown; use contrasting bobbin thread so stitches show up well on wrong side/back.

STITCHING

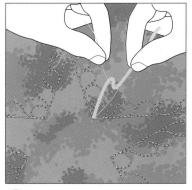

1 Thread machine with invisible thread or color to coordinate with bobbin strand. Attach suitable foot. Place work on machine, wrong side up. At starting point, lower and raise needle to pull bobbin strand up; hold threads out of the way. Stitch on marked lines.

2 Stitch slowly. Turn fabric gently at curves; pivot sharply at points. At end, raise foot; cut threads, leaving 6"/15cm tails. Remove stabilizer if using. Pull bobbin thread up; knot with top thread as shown. Insert tails in needle; run through batting or stitches on back.

FREE MOTION

Bobbin work by the author.

Drop or cover feed dogs; attach free-motion foot. Place stabilized fabric or layered quilt wrong side up on sewing machine; hoop if desired. Free-motion stitch a random design as shown here, or follow a pattern drawn or stitched on the stabilizer or quilt back.

PROGRAMMED

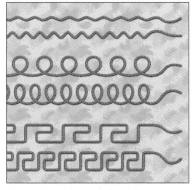

Use embroidery or walking foot to do bobbin work with programmed decorative stitches. Select simple open stitches for best results. Try lengthening or enlarging stitches. Refrain from using satin stitch or intricate designs as bobbin strand may jam machine.

EMBROIDERY

Load simple computer generated design into machine. Hoop stabilized fabric or layered quilt sandwich with wrong side facing up. Attach hoop to embroidery module and stitch at a slow pace, allowing bobbin strand to create design underneath (right side, as shown here).

8 FINISHING

basting
zipper bindings
irregular shapes
blocking
hanging framing
jagged edges
labels raw edge
beaded fringe

8

8

FINISHING

Finishing is a key component of an art quilt. Edging, hanging and even the label should be integral elements. It is important that you take time to block your work and give serious consideration to the finishing of the piece because no matter how fabulous the colors, design and quilting, a slack appearance or an unintentionally wavy edge will detract from the total effect. Consider framing or hanging your quilts in unusual ways to enhance their appeal.

⬆ Kate's Book of Un-Common Prayer— © Kate Crossley, Oxford, UK. Photo by Keith Barnes. Inspired by the artist's seemingly endless collection of fabric, paper, artifacts (both found and made), thoughts, books and sleepless nights. Recycled silk and cotton fabric, beads, arrowheads, bottles. Hand and machine embroidered, images photo transferred using Bubble Jet Set treated fabric and inkjet printer, acid etched, painted with walnut ink and Pebo Setasilk. 59 x 45"/150 x 115cm. 2011.

Finishing a quilt with a traditional binding is no longer the only option. Take a look at the quilts featured throughout this book and in the art and contemporary sections of any quilt show, and you will find unlimited ways to finish an edge. This chapter covers visible and invisible edge finishes that can be combined or customized to create hundreds more possibilities.

Your first task is to choose a finish that is in harmony with the central design of your quilt. Unstructured effects such as raw fabric edges or exposed batting can be very effective for some quilts, while others will be better served by more structured techniques.

The quilts pictured in this section will provide you with a glimpse of the variety of shapes, finishes and hanging methods that are being used by art quilters today.

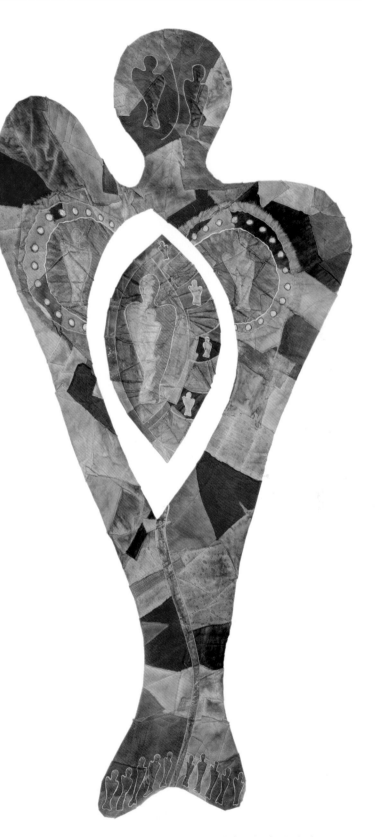

⬆ Unsung Muses (detail)—©Gillian Cooper, Balfron, Scotland. Photo by Alan McCredie. Part of a series based on the forgotten goddesses of our ancestors. The figure is hung using monofilament attached to three points. The middle section is also attached by monofilament and can rotate freely. There is no formal binding; the fabrics were pinned on one side and wrapped around the edge onto the other. Cotton fabric, oil paint. Hand-dyed, painted, stenciled, machine quilted. 31 x 59"/80 x 150cm. 2011.

⬆ Destructive Beauty 2—©Tilly de Harde, Johannesburg, South Africa. Photo by Amy. Collection of Mrs. Bridget Ferguson. The artist has always been fascinated by the beauty of a raging fire, especially at night. Cotton fabric, felt, organza, soluble film, rayon embroidery threads. Background silhouette was digitized by the artist and sewn on an embroidery machine, quilt was tied, felt/organza frame was heat distressed with a soldering iron. 26 x 16"/65 x 40cm. 2012.

⬅ Tide—©Susan Hotchkis, Guernsey, UK. Photo by Dave Bennett. This piece evolved from a collection of images taken in Iceland, mainly of an old fishing boat and some of the landscape. Silk, felt, cotton, velvet, synthetic voile fabrics. Free-motion machine stitched and quilted, screen printed with pigment and expandable paint, reverse appliquéd, heat distressed, edges cut, melted, stitched and left raw in parts. 27 x 35"/70 x 88cm. 2009.

Walk in the Woods: April 5, 2013—©Linda Seward, London, UK. Inspired by forest materials collected during a walk in misty woods. A backdrop of trees was painted on handmade paper "fabric", machine quilted, then layered with organza stitched in squares. Feathers, wood, pine cones, etc. were inserted in the squares. Organza was heat distressed with a heat gun and a soldering iron to expose the inclusons and parts of the backdrop. Edges were heat soldered. Cotton fabric, tissue paper, fabric glue, textile paint, thread, organza, forest materials. Painted, free-motion machine quilted, heat distressed, hung from branch with rope. 31 x 45"/80 x 114cm. 2013.

Stranger Among His Own—©Aina Muze, Riga, Latvia. Photo by Gints Lusis-Grinbergs. Inspired by the exclusion of certain people from society because they look, think or behave differently. The artist combined traditional techniques with modern media to reflect the romantic against the rough not only in the form and content of the work, but also in the use of materials. 100 year old linen, polyester dress fabric, felt, stabilizers for embroidery. Raw edge appliquéd, machine embroidered, machine quilted, outer edges left raw. 81 x 65"/205 x 165cm. 2011.

⬆ Morning Train—©Jayne Bentley Gaskins, Amelia Island, Florida. The artist spent a morning sitting and watching people in Grand Central Station, New York City. Most carried briefcases, backpacks or satchels and she wondered about this common element connecting people who pass each other every day. Cotton broadcloth, threads. Digitally manipulated photography printed on fabric with inkjet printer, appliquéd, trapunto, free-motion machine quilted and embroidered, mounted on stretcher frame and gallery wrapped. 16 x 20"/41 x 51cm. 2011.

➡ Trees—©Katrina Parris, Great Wakering, Essex, UK. Photo by Gareth Parris. This piece was inspired by the early morning light viewed through the trees. The woodland floor created interesting colors and textures as mud, leaves and other vegetation built up in layers. The irregular edging in the foreground leads the eye into the picture. Muslin, scrim, cotton fabrics in variety of textures. Hand painted, cut and torn fabric collage, raw edge appliquéd, free-motion machine quilted, sides folded under and stitched, bottom edges frayed. 18 x 24"/45 x 60cm. 2012.

Las Tusas: Ponderosa Pine—©Martha Wolfe, Davis, California. From a photograph by Ellen Bulger. Inspired by the pine trees that grow in the mountains of New Mexico, where the artist spent time as a teenager; the smell of the pine needles baking in the sun conjures warm memories of youth and adventure. Polyester organza, stabilizer, fusible web. Raw edge appliquéd, machine embroidered and quilted, faced edge. 37 x 46"/94 x 117cm. 2011.

Tornado— © Brigitte Morgenroth, Kassel, Germany. Photo by Albrecht Morgenroth. This wall hanging was inspired by the fabrics that came from a sample book of decorative materials. Cotton fabrics. Patchwork hand sewn over papers, machine quilted, pillowcase finished. 29 x 42"/73 x 106cm. 2009.

Floating Spiral— © Irene MacWilliam, Belfast, Northern Ireland, UK. For 14 years this artist has been playing with black and white stripes to produce illusory pieces. Cotton fabrics. Raw edge appliquéd, machine quilted, pillowcase finished. 12"/30cm diameter. 2012.

BASTING & SIGNING

Art quilters creating a quilt sandwich (top, batting and back) must hold those layers together to prevent them from shifting when quilting. Quilts are traditionally basted by hand, or secured with safety pins or a basting tack gun. These methods work well, but are slow. Spray basting is a quick, easy alternative, and the adhesive will wash out when the quilt is blocked (page 235).

When layering a quilt sandwich, cut batting and back 3"/8cm larger than the quilt top on each side. Wear a mask when spraying, and work in a well-ventilated area on a protected surface; this can also be done vertically on a protected design wall. Spray baste a small piece as a test before beginning.

Signing an art quilt is an important but sometimes overlooked element. Provide basic information on a label and attach it securely to the quilt.

SPRAY BASTING

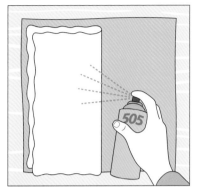

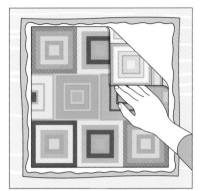

1 Spread a protective covering on a flat surface. Smooth quilt back, wrong side up, on covering. Center batting on back. Fold half of the batting over as shown. Spray batting lightly and evenly with temporary fabric adhesive, holding can about 12"/30cm away.

2 Fold sprayed batting onto quilt back; pat in place to adhere. Repeat for other half of batting. Center quilt top on batting, right side up. Fold back each half of quilt top as in step 1, left; spray exposed batting with adhesive and replace top in same manner.

SECURING EDGES

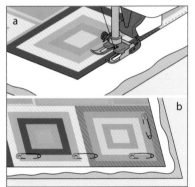

Secure quilt edges so they don't separate when quilting. Machine baste edges of quilt using a walking foot and water-soluble thread (a), which will wash out (along with the basting spray) when quilt is blocked (page 235). Or safety pin edges together (b).

MAKING LABELS

Sign an art quilt with a label Include quilt title, maker's name, where quilt was made, and year it was finished; add recipient's name or occasion if desired (a). Include care instructions if relevant. Alternatively, stitch maker's name and date in the quilting (b).

Inkjet print Use heat transfer sheets to print text and/or photos for a label; see Image Transfers (pages 96–98). Reverse text before printing as it will transfer to fabric in mirror image. Lighten a small area of a photo to feature text as shown here. See another idea on page 98.

[Permanent fabric markers]

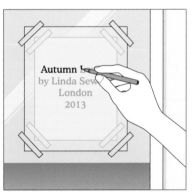

Permanent fabric markers Iron freezer paper onto wrong side of label fabric (page 130). Print label text on paper. Tape paper and fabric to light source; trace text. Or hand write text (page 131) on stabilized fabric. Remove freezer paper; use hot iron to heat set text.

SECURING LABEL

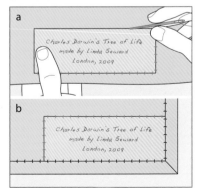

Trim label to correct size, leaving allowances for turning edges under if desired. Hand sew to quilt back so stitches do not penetrate to front (a). Or position label in corner; sew binding over two edges (b—stitches shown in black); hand sew remaining edges.

Embroidery Trace or write label text on right side of fabric with pencil or water-soluble pen. Hoop fabric; hand embroider letters (a). Embroider additional design elements if desired. Or create computer generated design (b) and machine embroider (page 221).

BLOCKING

Blocking imparts a professional finish to an art quilt by ensuring that it hangs straight and true. It will remove water-soluble marking lines and the fabric adhesive from spray basting. Blocking will also dissolve water-soluble threads from machine trapunto (pages 196–197). Blocking will work only on natural fibers, such as cotton and wool.

Because blocking entails wetting the quilt, always test whether the fabrics are colorfast. If any bleeding occurs, do not block the quilt. Even if fabrics are colorfast, use Color Catchers as an added precaution when washing the quilt. Quilts that are distorted may require pinning to keep their shape when drying; in this case use a carpet or other pinnable surface for blocking. These instructions are for a square or rectangular piece; block shaped quilts in the same way, omitting steps 3 and 4.

COLORFAST TEST

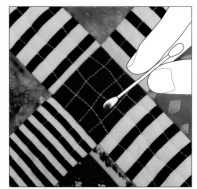

To test whether a fabric on a finished quilt is colorfast, moisten tip of a cotton swab/bud; rub over questionable fabric. If any color transfers to to swab/bud, do not risk blocking the quilt. See page 240 for suggestions on how to encourage a wavy edge to hang straight.

EQUIPMENT

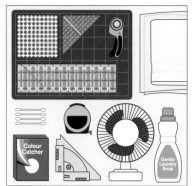

Cotton swab/bud, washing machine, gentle laundry soap, Color Catchers, large cotton towel, flat waterproof blocking surface such as plastic table-cloth, measuring tape, rotary cutter, rulers, squares & triangles, cutting mat, fan. Optional: laser level square.

BLOCKING TECHNIQUE

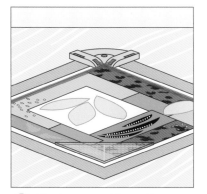

1 Test fabrics for colorfastness; see above. If colorfast, wash quilt in machine on gentle cycle with warm water, 1 tbl gentle laundry soap and 4–6 Color Catchers, depending on quilt size. Spin to remove excess water. Gently lift quilt from machine directly onto towel.

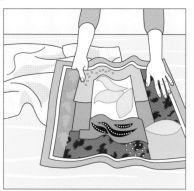

2 Carry quilt in towel to blocking area. Carefully arrange on flat surface, so wet fibers are not pulled or stretched. Flatten quilt, working from middle outward, patting any rippled areas until smooth. Manipulate edges/corners so they are straight and square.

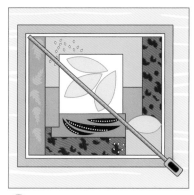

3 When quilt looks flat and even visually, use tape measure to check diagonal measurements. If not the same, manipulate damp quilt until they are equal. Check length/width measurements on opposite sides of quilt; adjust until they are identical.

4 Check corners, sides and inner design lines using rulers, squares, triangles or laser level (laser level shines straight red lines). Check repeatedly, as moving one area may change another. Pat and smooth any crooked areas until edges and seamlines are in alignment.

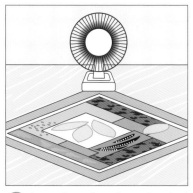

5 Leave the quilt to dry undisturbed on the flat blocking surface for 24–48 hours, or until totally dry. An electric fan, positioned to blow gently over the quilt, will aid in the drying process; move fan around sides of quilt regularly.

TRIM EDGES

When quilt is thoroughly dry, do not move it. Slide a cutting mat under an edge. Use rotary cutter and ruler to trim off excess fabric and batting; leave a ¼"/6mm seam allowance for binding if required. Move mat along after each cut until entire quilt is trimmed.

EDGE FINISHES: INVISIBLE

Some art quilters prefer their work to have a plain edge without a border or binding. This means that the quilt design is displayed without constraints, which can be a useful artistic strategy. This invisible edge finish is achieved by the use of a facing, a technique that will be familiar to dressmakers.

Make the facing in the same fabric as the back of the quilt so it will blend in readily. Ensure that the seamline along the edge of the quilt always rolls to the quilt back so that it is not visible on the front. If the seamline is visible from the front, manipulate it with your fingers so it rolls to the back, pin and slipstitch the edges in place with matching thread. For a decorative touch, insert piping, lace, zippers or prairie points (see page 104) between the quilt and facing. When the facing is turned over, the additions will protrude outwards from the edge of the quilt.

FACING BASICS

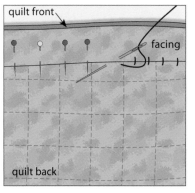

Use a walking foot for all stitching. Trim finished quilt to size, adding ¼"/6mm seam allowance. Topstitch ⅛"/ 3mm from edges to stabilize. Stitch facing to quilt with right sides together. Roll facing to quilt back so seam is not visible on front; pin. Slipstitch facing in place.

TRIMMING/CLIPPING

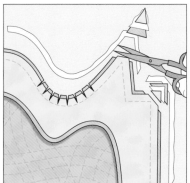

Batting can add bulk to a faced edge, so trim it away from within seam allowances, close to stitching, using small sharp scissors. Clip into seam allowances at concave angles or curves; convex curves do not require clipping. Trim off points and corners at an angle.

STRAIGHT FACINGS

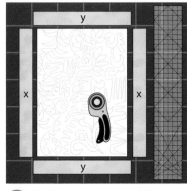

1 Cut facing strips on straight grain, each 2½"/6cm wide. Measure edges of quilt. Cut 2 strips to match longest edges (x). For remaining edges, cut 2 facings, adding 1"/2.5cm to measurement (y). Press one long edge of each facing strip ¼"/6mm to wrong side.

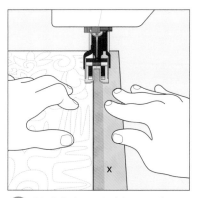

2 Stitch facing strip (x) to one long edge of quilt; see *Facing Basics*. Open facing and flatten on top of seam allowance; stretch fabrics apart to open seam fully. Topstitch facing close to seam with matching thread, so stitching goes through seam allowance.

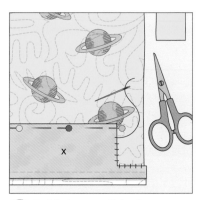

3 Roll facing to quilt back so seam is not visible on front (topstitches will help facing to roll over easily). Pin pressed edge of facing to quilt back. Trim 1"/2.5cm of facing from each side edge. Slipstitch facing to quilt back. Repeat for opposite edge.

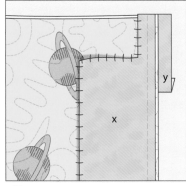

4 For remaining edges, repeat steps 2 and 3 using (y) facing strips (but do not trim fabric at edges). Center first (y) strip on quilt, with right sides together, matching raw edges. Allow ½"/12mm of facing to extend beyond each side edge of quilt as shown. Stitch.

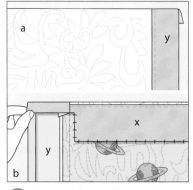

5 Open out facing. Short ends will project beyond edge of quilt, so fold those ends ½"/12mm to wrong side so fold is even with quilt edge (a). Finger press fold in place on wrong side (b). Topstitch facing in place as for step 2.

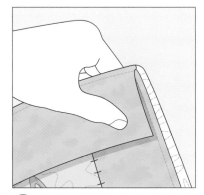

6 Roll facing over to quilt back. At each corner, manipulate folded end of facing strip so it is even with edge of quilt but doesn't show on front. Pin, then slipstitch facing to quilt. Repeat for the other side of quilt with last (y) facing strip.

OFFSET FACINGS

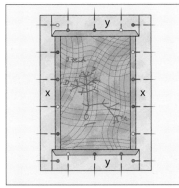

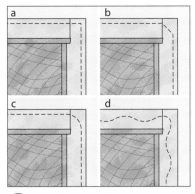

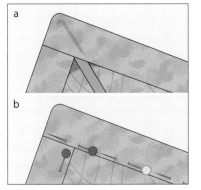

1 Cut facing strips, each 2½"/6cm wide. Measure quilt edges. Cut 2 strips to match long edges (x). For remaining edges, cut 2 facings, 2"/5cm shorter than measurement (y). Press one long edge of each strip ¼"/6mm to wrong side. Pin to quilt front as shown.

2 Machine-stitch facings to quilt using walking foot and making a ¼"/6mm seam. Shape of corner can be varied with this method. Try making sharp corner (a), angled corner (b), curved corner (c) or even a sinuous curving edge (d).

3 Trim batting and seam allowances, and clip curves; see *Trimming/Clipping*. Turn facings over to quilt back, using a wooden chopstick to help smooth and poke out fabric in corners (a). Adjust and pin facings to quilt back (b); slipstitch in place.

TRIMMED WHOLECLOTH FACING

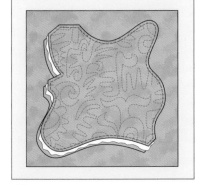

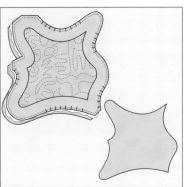

1 Use fabric for facing that matches quilt back; cut slightly larger than quilt. Pin quilt front to fabric with right sides together; stitch together as in *Facing Basics*. Trim facing fabric same size as quilt. Clip corners and curves; trim batting.

2 Use pencil to draw a line on facing fabric 2"/5cm away from stitching line within quilt. Pinch facing fabric on marked line; pull away from quilt. Make small hole, then cut fabric along marked line, taking care not to cut quilt top. Remove cut fabric.

3 Roll facing to back; pin so seam is not visible on front. Fold raw edges of facing under, clipping curves; slipstitch to quilt back. **To make a faced border on quilt front,** as shown here, stitch facing to quilt back with right sides together; complete following steps 1–3.

PILLOWCASE FINISH

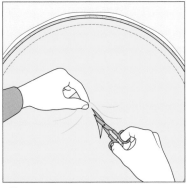

1 With this method, the back of the quilt is hidden; do not use for competitions that require inspection of quilt back. Follow *Trimmed Wholecloth Facing* step 1 to prepare and stitch facing fabric to quilt front. Illustration shows exaggerated position of layers.

2 Lift middle of facing away from quilt; cut opening in facing. Turn quilt right side out through opening; push out points/corners with a wooden chopstick. Overlap edges of opening and baste together; cover with a label. Tack facing to quilt so it doesn't sag.

CURVED FACING

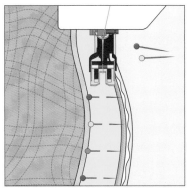

Cut 2½"/6cm bias strips (page 122); piece to the required length. Prepare quilt and facing; see *Facing Basics*. Pin facing to quilt before stitching; manipulate fabric to follow curves smoothly. Sew facing to quilt as in steps 2 and 3, *Straight Facings*. Slipstitch in place.

EDGE FINISHES: VISIBLE

A quilt edge can be finished in hundreds of different ways. The traditional method of a single-fold or double-fold mitered binding is well covered in other books, so won't be included here. Pages 236–237 describe edge finishes that do not show on the front. These pages show a variety of visible contemporary finishes that can be copied or altered to create a unique edge on an art quilt.

It's important to keep quilt edges from distorting, so consider stabilizing the edges using a tear-away, heat-away or water-soluble stabilizer, particularly if doing embroidery; see page 220.

For couched edges, use a plain cotton cord and colorful or variegated thread to fully cover it. Alternatively, use a decorative strand (see Couching on page 224) and secure it to the quilt edge with invisible thread.

MACHINE STITCH

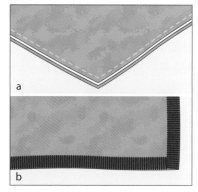

Straight stitch the edges together by machine, using a walking foot; trim neatly (a) and leave raw edges exposed. Or, for a rich satin stitch finish, straight stitch close to edges, cover with narrow zigzag stitch, then finish edges with a wide zigzag satin stitch (b).

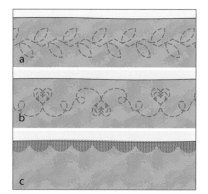

Tear narrow strip of binding fabric; wrap and pin over quilt edge. Embellish with programmed decorative stitches (a) or free-motion machine embroidery (b). Alternatively, embroider raw quilt edge with a programmed decorative stitch that has one straight edge (c).

OVERCAST

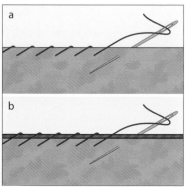

Hand stitching an edge adds a folk art quality to a quilt. Embroider the edges of a quilt with a simple blanket stitch (page 149), or an overcast stitch such as a whip-stitch (a). Work stitches over a cord for extra dimension (b).

BEADS/SHELLS

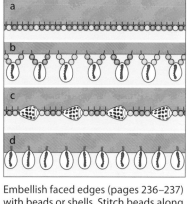

Embellish faced edges (pages 236–237) with beads or shells. Stitch beads along edge (a). String beads and/or shells on strong thread; stitch to make scalloped edge (b). Decorate an edge with a mixture of beads and shells (c), or attach dangling shells to edge (d).

FRINGE

Beaded fringe by Angela Maves.

Buy beaded fringe by the yard/meter; stitch to bottom edge of quilt. Or make fringe using strong thread and beading needle. Stitch through quilt edge; string beads on thread. Insert needle back up through beads except for bottom bead. Secure fringe to quilt and repeat.

COUCH

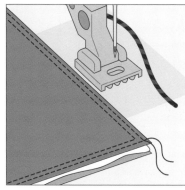

1 Stitch 2 lines of small stitches close to edge of quilt. To help guide fabric when turning corners, sew doubled thread to each corner. Use pintuck foot (see Couching, page 224), and choose strand that fits into groove of foot.

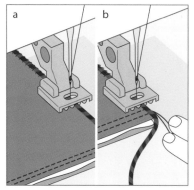

2 Set machine to zigzag just wide enough to cover strand; loosen top tension. Position strand over stitches at edge under central groove of foot. Stitch so right edge of zigzag goes over edge, and left edge encloses strand (a). Hold threads taut at corners (b).

Three cotton cords couched on quilt edge by Pauline Barnes.

3 Couch second strand next to first, moving first strand into next groove of foot. Repeat for another strand if desired. **Tip**: Before stitching, color strand with fabric marker to match thread. Or, use invisible thread to couch decorative strands.

RAW EDGES

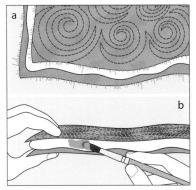

Raw edges should look deliberately unfinished rather than sloppy. Tear fabric for quilt edges rather than cutting, and tease out threads and/or batting to make a rough fringe (a). Paint edges of exposed batting, using fabric paint and flat brush if desired (b).

HEAT DISTRESS

On sturdy synthetic material such as Lutradur or recycled felt, machine embroider a design with elements that project outward. Use a soldering iron to melt off excess material around edges of stitches as shown; see *Soldering Iron* on page 101.

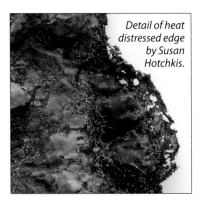

Detail of heat distressed edge by Susan Hotchkis.

To introduce holes and shaped or ragged edges, use recycled felt or Lutradur. First layer and stitch, then cut and shape edges with scissors. Heat distress last, as fibers become hard and difficult to sew through when melted. See Heat Distressing on pages 100–101.

PRAIRIE POINTS

Detail of prairie point edge by the author.

Make prairie points as directed on page 104; use them to decorate a simple bound edge as shown here. Alternatively, insert raw edges of prairie points between quilt and facing (pages 236–237) so the points project outward when facing is turned to right side.

JAGGED EDGES

Detail of jagged edges by Katrina Parris.

Jagged edges make a bold impact. Stabilize edges with fusible web so they don't fray, or cut edges in a jagged design and allow to fray. Alternatively, finish edges with any of the techniques shown here or employ a faced or pillowcase finish (pages 236–237).

BEYOND THE EDGE

To draw the eye outward, allow design elements to extend beyond the edge. Stabilize any elements that project outward from top or sides so they maintain their shape and do not flop over (page 240). Use a visible edge finish, or apply facing (pages 236–237).

ZIPPERS

Detail of zipper edge by Sandy Snowden.

Zippers can be used effectively as an edge treatment; stitch to quilt edge using a zipper foot and matching thread. Position zipper with the teeth facing inward as shown here, or with the teeth facing outward as shown on page 211.

HEAT-AWAY & WATER-SOLUBLE STABILIZERS

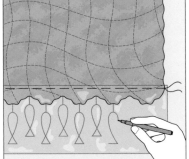

1 Create a lacy or irregular bottom edge by using heat-away or water-soluble stabilizers (page 220). Baste stabilizer to quilt so it extends beyond bottom edge. Mark a design on the stabilizer. Hoop fabric and stabilizer. Machine embroider design.

2 Before removing stabilizer, ensure that any dangling elements are securely connected to the main body of the quilt with sturdy stitches (a). Remove heat-away or water-soluble stabilizers as directed by the manufacturer (b).

The way an art quilt is displayed is just as important as the way it was made.

A hanging sleeve is often required by quilt shows and exhibitions, usually with a minimum width of 4"/10cm. A sleeve can also be used to help prevent shaped quilts from sagging, or correct a wavy edge. Use a fabric to match the quilt back so the sleeve is unobtrusive.

Some art quilters employ unusual hanging devices as a vital component of their work. In this case, use hanging loops so that the apparatus is visible.

Mounting a finished piece is another popular display method; use sturdy interfacing or foam board, covered with complementary fabric.

Small art quilts often benefit by being professionally framed under glass (not shown here); ensure that the framer adds spacers so the fabric does not come in contact with the glass.

SLEEVE

1 Cut fabric strip for sleeve 9½"/24cm wide and as long as the width of the quilt. Fold each short end ¼"/6mm to wrong side twice; press and topstitch in place. With wrong sides facing, stitch long edges of strip together, making a ½"/12mm seam.

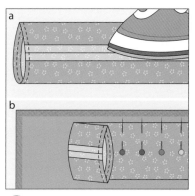

2 Center seam on one side of tube. Press seam allowance open, at the same time pressing one long edge for top of sleeve (a). Position seamed side of sleeve on quilt back, with pressed edge ½"/12mm below top edge. Allow sleeve bottom to hang freely (b).

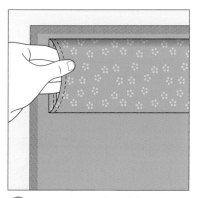

3 Slipstitch top edge of sleeve to quilt, sewing into batting every few stitches for added strength. Next, insert hand into opening at each end of sleeve as shown, and slide sleeve up until top edge is just below top of quilt. Pin top of sleeve in place.

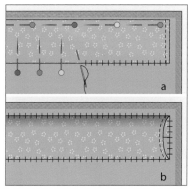

4 Smooth sleeve fabric flat and pin bottom edge to quilt back; sleeve will be flat against quilt. Slipstitch bottom edge to quilt (a). Unpin top edge of sleeve and stitch short side ends (b). Sleeve will bulge outward slightly so it can accommodate hanging device.

SPLIT SLEEVE

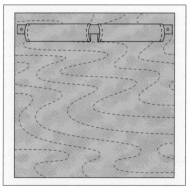

For wide quilts that need support in the middle, or to hang a quilt from the midpoint, make sleeve as described here, but cut in half. Trim off 1"/2.5cm from each piece; fold and stitch ends under. Stitch to quilt back in two sections, leaving opening in middle.

SHAPED QUILTS

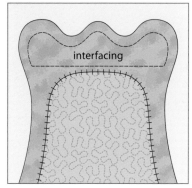

If top or side edges of quilt are shaped, stiffen with sturdy interfacing such as Timtex/Vilene (shown as dotted area). Cut interfacing to fit within seam allowance; baste to quilt back. Add a trimmed wholecloth facing (page 237); facing should fully cover interfacing.

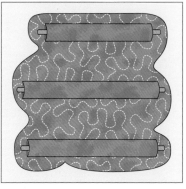

Shaped quilts need support to prevent sides and edges from drooping when hung. Make one or more sleeves to fit shape at strategic points; sew to quilt back as described above. Cut lightweight wooden slats or dowels to size, sand edges and insert in sleeves.

WAVY EDGES

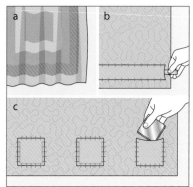

If bottom edge of quilt is wavy when hung (a), make a sleeve and attach to bottom edge. Insert flat metal strip cut to size into sleeve (b)—treat metal with rust-proof paint and protect sharp edges. Or stitch small pockets to bottom edge of quilt; slip a curtain weight in each (c).

HANGING LOOPS

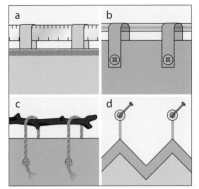

Loops should complement quilt and hanging device. Here are some ideas: plain fabric loops hung from a ruler (a); embellished fabric loops attached with buttons (b); rope loops hung from a branch (c); shaped edge hung from metal rings with twisted cord (d).

INTERFACING MOUNT

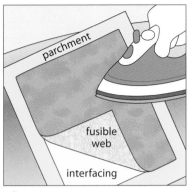

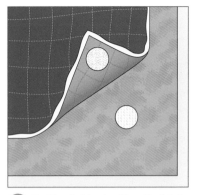

1 For mount, cut sturdy interfacing (Timtex/Vilene) 3–4"/8–10cm larger than quilt. Cut two pieces of fabric same size, in a color to complement quilt; apply fusible web to wrong side of each piece (page 148). Fuse fabric to each side of interfacing.

2 Position finished quilt on the fabric-covered interfacing mount. Secure at strategic points with invisible thread, or use strong Velcro strips or dots. Straighten or shape edges of mount with rotary cutter; use decorative blade (page 121) if desired for wavy edge.

GALLERY WRAP

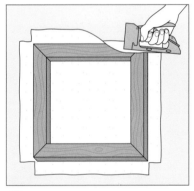

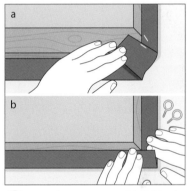

1 Buy stretcher bars same size or larger than finished quilt. Assemble frame. Lay frame over batting; wrap and staple batting to frame, trimming away excess at corners. Measure and cut tightly woven fabric to complement quilt 4"/8cm larger all around than frame.

2 Center and pin quilt on right side of fabric; secure at strategic points with invisible stitches. Position work over frame; wrap fabric to back; tape to frame. Turn over to check that quilt is straight; when satisfied, staple edges to frame, gently pulling fabric so it is taut.

3 At each corner, smoothly fold right side edge of fabric up at an angle over the frame; staple (a). Neatly fold up bottom edge of fabric to cover angled fabric, so there are no visible pleats or creases (b); staple in place. Attach screw eyes inside frame for hanging wire.

CANVAS MOUNT

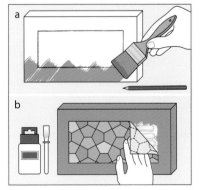

Buy stretched artist canvas same size or larger than quilt. Mark quilt position on canvas. Paint outer edges and sides (a). When dry, apply gel medium within marked area. Press wrong side of quilt into medium (b). Allow to dry. Or sew quilt to canvas with invisible thread.

FOAM BOARD

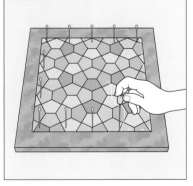

Cut foam board to size with ruler and craft knife. Cut fabric 3"/8cm larger than board. Glue fabric to board with fabric spray adhesive; wrap and glue excess to back. Position and pin finished quilt to foam board. Sew to board using sturdy needle, invisible thread and thimble.

PLASTIC MOUNT

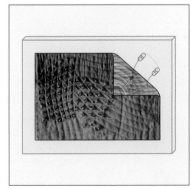

Quilt will appear to float on a plastic mount. Buy ¼"/6mm Plexiglas cut to size and flamed (edges melted with blowtorch). Mark the center and corner positions of quilt on plastic. Using tiny drill bit, drill 2 holes in each marked area. Sew quilt to plastic through holes.

SCHOOL & COMMUNITY PROJECTS

Making a quilt is a creative and rewarding experience that many enjoy in contented isolation, but sharing quilt making techniques with schools or community groups can take that gratification to another level. Whether a project is organized to expose others to new methods and possibilities, as a process of art therapy or a team function, or to raise money for charity, much enjoyment and fulfillment can be derived by everyone involved.

Although many of the art quilts featured in this book are quite complex, the techniques used to create them have been broken down into simple steps. Teachers and group leaders can interpret and adapt many of these methods for the age or experience level of their audience, and the outcome does not necessarily have to be a "quilt." With the huge range of techniques featured in this book, there is something for everyone to explore and try.

Through these creative activities, participants learn new skills that can build their confidence and and develop their potential. Cultural and even language barriers can also be broken down through shared artistic experiences. Making a project to raise money for charity, or to celebrate a local event, brings people together for a common purpose and can build camaraderie through enterprise. Collective work can be an excellent way to explore and express issues that are of concern to a community. School and community group projects really can make a difference in people's lives.

While sewing or patchwork might not be to everyone's taste, cutting fabric shapes to make a picture or create a fabric mosaic may encourage participation by people who have never considered attempting these methods before. Just as the recent emphasis on modern quilting is introducing traditional quilting to a new generation, art quilt techniques can draw people into the creative textile art experience and provide traditional quilters with new ways of approaching their work.

Featured in this section are projects organized by artists whose work appears in this book. Some projects were structured to introduce techniques to beginners, several to simply produce a shared piece of work, and others were made to raise money for charity.

⬆ Natural History— a commission by Cas Holmes for the Kaleidoscope Museum, Library & Art Gallery in Sevenoaks, Kent, UK. It is made from found materials donated by local people and incorporates images, photos and text developed in response to "Meet the Artist" sessions. 2008.

⬆ Helping Hands—made by a wide range of patients and staff, under the guidance of Karina Thompson, for University Hospitals NHS Foundation Trust Birmingham. 2007.

⬅ Classic Literature Quilt—made by 14 year old students in Bronwyn Stephanz's English class, James Monroe Middle School, Albuquerque, New Mexico, with the help of Cheryl FitzGerald. Featured blocks by Adam Parker, Danielle Wrasman and Leah Cody, done with raw edge appliqué. The quilt hangs in the school library. 2008.

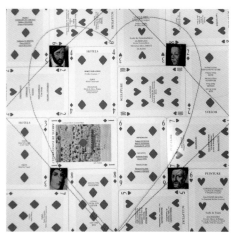

Patriotic House Quilt—made by Jamie Fingal for The House Quilt Project. Established in 2010, this organization makes wall hangings that are donated to Furnishing Hope, a charity that works with designers to improve living spaces for those in crisis. 2013.

Paper Patchwork—made by Joe Page, age 13, with Becky Knight at an Art Factor Masterclass, Oriel Davies Gallery, Newtown, Powys, Wales. Used playing cards, machine sewn. 2013.

Formosa Taijiang—made by members of the TAQS (Taiwan Art Quilt Society), organized by Lin Hsin-Chen for an exhibition of quilts highlighting Taiwanese ecology and the environment. Photo by Wu Chung-Yen. 2013.

⊙ Tent of Emotions—made by 10–11 year old pupils at St. Mary's School, Henley-on-Thames, UK, with Kate Findlay. Children drew around themselves; their body shapes were outlined in wax, then the fabric was painted with dyes to depict an emotion. Part of the Henley Youth Festival. 2010.

⬆ Mosaic Bunting—made by 3–4 year old children at South Ascot & Cheapside Preschool, Ascot, UK, with Jane Glennie. Mosaic "tiles" prepared with fusible web were arranged on flags by the children, then pressed. Finished flags were free-motion machine stitched with invisible thread. 2012.

⬅ A Year in Tuscany—made by students of Pauline Barnes. Each strip was stitched by a different quilter to represent the seasons: (from left to right) Heather Cocker, Diane Prentice, Ule Nicholls, Liz Bowers, Sybil Goer, Ruth Dobbins, Jackie Kearsey, Jeanette Jones, Philippa Wilson, Gill Raven. 2009.

PRODUCTS, CONTACTS, WEBSITES

Most of the products listed in this book are available from local or online vendors of art, craft, fabric, quilting, and sewing supplies. Look up items online to learn more about them and to find a convenient local or mail-order supplier. Many websites also provide tutorials on how to use their products.

CUTTING TOOLS

Fiskars
www.fiskars.com

Olfa Corporation
www.olfa.com

DYES, DISCHARGE, AUXILIARIES

Art Van Go
+44 (0)1438 814946
www.artvango.co.uk

Colourcraft Ltd
+44 (0)1142 421431
www.colourcraftltd.com

Dharma Trading Co.
+1 (800) 542-5227 (toll-free USA & Canada) +1 (707) 283-0390
www.dharmatrading.com

Jacquard Products
+1 (800) 442 0455 (toll-free USA & Canada) +1 (707) 433 9577
www.jacquardproducts.com

Kemtex Educational Supplies
+44 (0) 1257 230220
www.kemtex.co.uk

Mulberry Silks
UK Distributor of deColourant
www.mulberrysilks.co.uk

Pro Chemical & Dye
Technical Support: +1 (508) 676 3838
www.prochemicalanddye.com

George Weil & Sons Ltd
+44 (0)1483 565800
www.georgeweil.com

FABRICS

Jo-Ann Fabric and Craft Stores
www.joann.com

P&B Textiles
www.pbtex.com

Robert Kaufman Co., Inc.
www.robertkaufman.com

The African Fabric Shop
www.africanfabric.co.uk

The City Quilter
www.cityquilter.com

Whaleys (Bradford) Ltd.
www.whaleys-bradford.ltd.uk

LONGARM QUILTING MACHINES

Handi Quilter, Inc.
+1 (866) 697 8458
+1 (801) 292 7988
www.handiquilter.com

SEWING MACHINES

Bernina International +41 52 762 1111
www.bernina.com

Bernina UK Bogod & Company Ltd
+44 (0)20 7549 7849
www.bernina.co.uk

SURFACE DESIGN & EMBELLISHMENTS

Angelina:
Meadowbrook Inventions Inc.
+1 (908) 766 0606
www.meadowbrookglitter.com

Bonding Powder, Pressing Sheets:
Bo-Nash (North America) Inc.
+1 (800) 527 8811   www.bonash.com

Cyanotype Pretreated Fabrics:
Blueprints on Fabric
www.blueprintsonfabric.com

Inktense pencils/blocks:
The Cumberland Pencil Company
www.pencils.co.uk

Gelli printing plates, foiling, rubbing, paintstiks, stencils:
Laura Murray Designs
lauramurraydesigns.com

Image transfers:
C. Jenkins Co.
www.cjenkinscompany.com

Color Plus Fabrics
www.colorplusfabrics.com

Crafty Computer Paper
+44 (0)116 2744 755
www.craftycomputerpaper.co.uk

Marbling:
Galen Berry's MarbleArt
www.marbleart.us

Marking tools, notions:
Clotilde www.anniescatalog.com/index-clotilde

Shibori:
World Shibori Network: www.shibori.org

Aizenkobo Indigo Workshop:
www.aizenkobo.jp

Indigo-Dyed Shibori notes:
Hydrotherm DD (Hydros): sodium hydrosulphite or sodium dithionite is a strong reducing agent and color remover. Indigo Vat 60% grains are synthetic indigo granules.

Stabilizers & Synthetic Textiles:
Sulky
www.sulky.com

Nid Noi www.nid-noi.com

Pellon +1 (800) 223 5275
www.pellonprojects.com

Threads:
Superior Threads +1 (800) 499 1777
www.superiorthreads.com

Web of Thread +1 (800) 955 8185
www.caron-net.com

WEBSITES

Claire Benn and Leslie Morgan
www.committedtocloth.com

Paula Burch "All About Hand Dyeing"
www.pburch.net/dyeing

Jane Dunnewold
www.artclothstudios.com

Caryl Bryer Fallert
www.bryerpatch.com

Quilting Arts
www.quiltingarts.com

The Sixty Two Group of Textile Artists
www.62group.org.uk

QUILT SHOWS

AQS QuiltWeek Paducah
www.aqsshows.com

International Quilt Festivals
www.quilts.com/home/shows

Festival of Quilts UK
www.thefestivalofquilts.co.uk

Grosvenor Quilt Shows UK
www.grosvenorshows.co.uk

ORGANIZATIONS

American Quilter's Society
www.americanquilter.com

London Quilters
www.londonquilters.org.uk

Modern Quilt Guild
www.themodernquiltguild.com

Quilters' Guild of the British Isles
www.quiltersguild.org.uk

SAQA (Studio Art Quilt Associates)
www.saqa.com

Surface Design Association
www.surfacedesign.org

QUILT TV

Justhands-on TV
www.justhands-on.tv

QNN TV
www.qnntv.com

Quilting Arts TV
www.quiltingdaily.com

The Quilt Show
www.thequiltshow.com

GALLERY

Galerie Ton Schulten
Chez-Moi Ton Schulten Galerie International, Marktstraat 4-6, 7631 CB Ootmarsum, Nederland
www.tonschulten.nl

MUSEUM

Victoria & Albert Museum
www.vam.ac.uk/page/q/quilting-and-patchwork

THE BASICS

Guerrier, Katherine. *Quilting Masterclass*. London, UK: Quarto Publishing, 2000.

Seward, Linda. *The Complete Book of Patchwork, Quilting & Appliqué*. London, UK: Mitchell Beazley Publishers, 1987, 1996, 2009, 2010.

Sixth&Spring Books. *Vogue Sewing*. New York, NY: Sixth&Spring Books, 2006.

Zimmerman, Darlene. *The Quilter's Edge: Borders, Bindings and Finishing Touches*. Iola, WI: KP Books, 2005.

ART QUILTS & INSPIRATION

Benn, Claire, Leslie Morgan and Jane Dunnewold. *Finding Your Own Visual Language*. Surrey, UK: Committed to Cloth, 2007.

Berlyn, Ineke. *Collections*. Bromsgrove, UK: Ineke Berlyn, 2013.

Bornemisza, Eszter. *Eszter Bornemisza: Bornemisza 2010* (catalog). Budapest, Hungary: Grafium, 2010.

Bresenhan, Karey (introduction). *500 Art Quilts*. Asheville, NC: Lark Books, 2010.

Contemporary Quilt Group. *Breakthrough*. Yorkshire, UK: The Quilters' Guild of the British Isles, 2010.

Contemporary Quilt Group. *CQ @ 10: A Decade of Making Art Through the Medium of the Quilt*. Yorkshire, UK: The Quilters' Guild of the British Isles, 2012.

Crow, Nancy. *Nancy Crow: Quilts and Influences*. Paducah, KY: American Quilter's Society, 1989.

Davila, Jane and Elin Waterston. *Art Quilt Workbook*. Lafayette, CA: C&T Publishing, 2007.

European Art Quilt Foundation. *European Art Quilts I through VII*. Molenschot, NL: European Art Quilt Foundation, 1999–2012.

Gillespie, Spike. *Quilts Around the World: The Story of Quilting from Alabama to Zimbabwe*. Minneapolis, MN: Voyageur Press, 2010.

Impey, Sara. *Text in Textile Art*. London, UK: B T Batsford, 2013.

Kerr, Mary W. *Cutting-Edge Art Quilts*. Atglen, PA: Schiffer Publishing, 2013.

Johnston, Ann. *The Quilter's Book of Design*. Lake Oswego, OR: Ann Johnston, 2008.

Johnston, Ann and Jeannette Meyer. *Speaking in Cloth: Six Quilters, Six Voices*. Lake Oswego, OR: Ann Johnston, 2006.

Loughman, Gloria. *Quilted Symphony*. Lafayette, CA: C&T Publishing, 2010.

Meech, Sandra. *Creative Quilts: Inspiration, Texture & Stitch*. London, UK: B T Batsford, 2006 and 2013.

Meech, Sandra. *Connecting Design to Stitch*. London, UK: B T Batsford, 2012.

Meech, Sandra. *Connecting Art to Stitch*. London, UK: B T Batsford, 2009.

Midgelow-Marsden, Alysn. *The Continuous Thread of Revelation: An Evolution of Work*. Nottingham, UK: Artfully Bound, 2006.

Parrot, Helen. *Mark Making in Textile Art*. London, UK: B T Batsford, 2013.

Sielman, Martha. *The Natural World: Art Quilt Portfolio*. New York, NY: Sterling Publishing Co., 2012.

Sielman, Martha. *Masters: Art Quilts: Major Works by Leading Artists*. Asheville, NC: Lark Books, 2008.

Seward, Linda (foreward). *The Art Quilt Collection*. New York, NY: Sixth&Spring Books, 2010.

Shaw, Robert (introduction). *Art Quilts: A Celebration*. New York, NY: Sterling Publishing Co., 2005.

Triston, Julia and Rachel Lombard. *How to Be Creative in Textile Art*. London, UK: B T Batsford, 2011.

Wells, Jean. *Intuitive Color and Design: Adventures in Art Quilting*. Lafayette, CA: C&T Publishing, 2009.

Yde, Charlotte (editor). *Quilt Art Voices*. Colchester, UK: Quilt Art, 2011.

Yde, Charlotte (editor), *Quilt Art at 25*. Caerphilly, Wales: Quilt Art, 2010.

Yde, Charlotte (editor), *Quilt Art—Under Construction*. Caerphilly, Wales: Quilt Art, 2007.

ACID ETCHING

Lee, Iris. *Fabric Etching: Creating Surface Texture and Design Using Fiber Etch*. Worthington, OH: Dragon Threads, 2001.

APPLIQUÉ WITH FUSIBLE WEB

Ash, Bethan. *Instinctive Quilt Art: Fusing Techniques and Design*. London, UK: B T Batsford, 2011.

Ash, Bethan. *Vibrant Quilt Collage: A Spontaneous Approach to Fused Art Quilts*. Loveland, CO: Interweave Press, 2012.

BATIK

Gaffney, Diane. *Batik Transitions: From Classic to Contemporary*. UK: The Batik Guild, 2006.

Ehling, Katalin. *Waxing Life*. CreateSpace Independent Publishing Platform, 2011.

⬆ Hatching—©Margaret Cooter, London, UK. In response to a theme of "Breakthrough," the artist showed ideas breaking out of their shells and into the wide world. Cotton and silk fabrics, velvet, fabric paint. Fabric stamped, fused appliqué, machine quilted. 24 x 24"/60 x 60cm. 2009.

COLLAGE

Carlson, Susan. *Serendipity Quilts: Cutting Loose Fabric Collage*. Lafayette, CA: C&T Publishing, 2010.

de la Melena Cox, Alma. *Collage Fusion: Vibrant Wood and Fabric Art Using Telamadera Techniques*. Cincinnati, OH: North Light Books, 2009.

Meier, Rebekah. *More Fabric Art Collage*. Lafayette, CA: C&T Publishing, 2012.

Meier, Rebekah. *Fabric Art Collage*. Lafayette, CA: C&T Publishing, 2009.

COLOR & DYEING

Barnes, C June. *Stitching to Dye in Quilt Art: Colour, Texture and Distortion*. London, UK: B T Batsford, 2008.

Benn, Claire and Leslie Morgan. *Tray Dyeing*. Surrey, UK: Committed to Cloth, 2006.

Buffington, Adriene. *Hand-Dyed Fabric Made Easy*. Bothell, WA: That Patchwork Place, 1996.

Curtis, Bailey. *Dyeing To Colour: Microwave Dyeing and Other Quick and Easy Methods of Colouring Fabric with Dye*. Gloucestershire, UK: Bailey Curtis, 2001.

Deighan, Helen. *Dyeing in Plastic Bags*. Surrey UK: Crossways Patch, 2001.

Dunnewold, Jane. *Complex Cloth*. Bothell, WA: Martingale & Co., 2000.

Johnston, Ann. *Color by Accident: Exploring Low-Water Immersion Dyeing* (DVD). Lake Oswego, OR: Ann Johnston, 2013.

Johnston, Ann. *Color By Design: Paint and Print with Dye*. Lake Oswego, OR: Ann Johnston, 2001.

Issett, Ruth. *A Passion for Colour*. Kent, UK: Search Press, 2013.

Mori, Joyce and Cynthia Myerberg. *Dyeing to Quilt*. Chicago, IL: The Quilt Digest Press, 1997.

Twinn, Janet. *Colour in Art Quilts*. London, UK: B T Batsford, 2011.

Well, Kate. *Fabric Dyeing & Printing*. London, UK: Conran Octopus, 2000.

Wilcox, Michael. *Blue and Yellow Don't Make Green*. Kent, UK: Search Press, 1987.

CYANOTYPE

Brown, Ruth. *Cyanotypes on Fabric*. East Yorkshire, UK: SC Publications, 2006.

Hewitt, Barbara. *Blueprints on Fabric—Innovative Uses for Cyanotype*. Loveland, CO: Interweave Press, 1995.

Ware, Mike. *Cyanotype: the History, Science and Art of Photographic Printing in Prussian Blue*. London, UK: Science Museum and National Museum of Photography, Film & Television, 1999.

EMBELLISHMENTS & BEADING

Cox, Shelley. *Bead Embroidery*. Kent, UK: Search Press, 2013.

CRK Design and Yasuko Endo. *Bead Embroidery Stitch Samples*. Loveland, CO: Interweave Press, 2012.

Chandler, Ruth and Liz Kettle. *Fabric Embellishing: The Basics & Beyond*. Urbandale, IA: Landauer Publishing, 2009.

Fingal, Jamie. *The Whimsical House Quilt* (DVD). Loveland, CO: Quilting Arts/Interweave, 2008.

Fingal, Jamie. *Embellished Mini Quilts*. Asheville, NC: Lark Books, 2007.

Kettle, Liz. *First Time Beading on Fabric* Urbandale, IA: Landauer Publishing, 2013.

Lawrence, Sarah. *Stitch, Cloth, Shimmer & Shine*. Kent, UK: Search Press, 2012.

Midgelow-Marsden, Alysn and Viv Arthur. *Between the Sheets with Angelina*. Evesham, UK: Word4Word, 2003.

Morgan, Annette. *Glitzy Quilts* (CD). Exeter, UK: Vivebooks, 2007.

Morgan, Annette. *Creative Fabric Techniques for Quilters, Embroiderers and Textile Artists* (CD). Exeter, UK: Vivebooks, 2010.

Morgan, Annette. *A Creative Textile Journey, Sticks and Stones*. Kent, UK: Teamwork Craft Books, 2013.

Trentini, Cécile. *Daily Beauty—365 Ways to Play with Everyday Quilt Embellishments*. Concord, CA: C&T Publishing, 2013.

Van Horn, Larkin Jean. *Beading on Fabric: Encyclopedia of Bead Stitch Techniques*. Loveland, CO: Interweave Press, 2006.

EMBROIDERY

Albin, Patty. *Machine Embroidery Makes the Quilt*. Lafayette, CA: C&T Publishing, 2004.

Beaney, Jan and Jean Littlejohn. *A Complete Guide to Creative Embroidery*. London, UK: B T Batsford, 1997.

Brown, Christen. *Embroidered & Embellished*. Lafayette, CA: C&T Publishing, 2013.

Grey, Maggie. *Raising the Surface with Machine Embroidery*. London, UK: B T Batsford, 2006.

Hedley, Gwen. *Surfaces for Stitch*. London, UK: B T Batsford, 2000.

Holmes, Val. *The Encyclopedia of Machine Embroidery*. London, UK: B T Batsford, 2003.

Linduska, Karen. *Your Machine's Decorative Stitches*. Paducah, KY: American Quilter's Society, 2011.

Tinkler, Nikki. *The Quilter's Stitch Bible: The Essential Illustrated Reference to Over 200 Stitches with Easy to Follow Diagrams*. UK: Chartwell Books, 2013.

Twigg, Jeanine. *Embroidery Machine Essentials: How to Stabilize, Hoop and Stitch Decorative Designs*. Iola, WI: Krause Publications, 2001.

Twigg, Jeanine. *More Embroidery Machine Essentials: How to Customize, Edit, and Create Decorative Designs*. Iola, WI: Krause Publications, 2003.

Waugh, Carol Ann. *Stupendous Stitching: How to Make Fun and Fabulous Fiber Art*. Denver, CO: Xcellent Press, 2012.

Zieman, Nancy. *Machine Embroidery with Confidence: A Beginner's Guide*. Iola, WI: kp books, 2005.

FABRIC, PAPER, SYNTHETIC MATERIALS

Sixth&Spring Books. *Simplicity Fabric Guide: The Ultimate Fiber Resource*. New York, NY: Sixth&Spring Books, 2011.

Cotterill, Wendy. *Spunbonded Textile & Stitch: Lutradur, Evolon and Other Distressables*. London, UK: B T Batsford, 2011.

Lawrence, Sarah. *Silk Paper for Textile Artists*. London, UK: A & C Black Publishers, 2008.

Riley, Lesley. *Fabulous Fabric Art with Lutradur*. Lafayette, CA: C&T Publishing, 2009.

Wiebe, Carol. *Turn A Series Of Small Paper Quilts Into an Art Book* (ebook). Kitchener, ON: Carol Wiebe, 2010.

HEAT DISTRESSING

Beal, Margaret. *New Ideas in Fusing Fabric: Creative Cutting, Bonding and Mark-Making with the Soldering Iron*. London, UK: Anova Books, 2013.

Beal, Margaret. *Fusing Fabric*. London, UK: B T Batsford, 2007.

Maxwell, Faye. *Burning and Slashing*. Hampshire, UK: Fay Maxwell, 2003.

Thittichai, Kim. *Layered Textiles: New Surfaces with Heat Tools, Machine and Hand Stitch*. London, UK: B T Batsford, 2011.

Thittichai, Kim. *Hot Textiles: Inspiration and Techniques with Heat Tools*. London, UK: B T Batsford, 2007.

IMAGE TRANSFERS

Knapp, Susan Brubaker. *Point, Click, Quilt! Turn Your Photos Into Fabulous Fabric Art*. Lafayette, CA: C&T Publishing, 2011.

Grey, Maggie. *From Image to Stitch*. London, UK: B T Batsford, 2008.

Hansen, Gloria. *Digital Essentials: The Quilt Maker's Must-Have Guide to Files, Images, and More*. Bowling Green, OH: The Electric Quilt Company, 2008.

Heim, Judy and Gloria Hansen. *The Quilter's Companion*. San Francisco, CA: No Starch Press, 1998.

Laury, Jean Ray. *The Photo Transfer Handbook: Snap It, Print It, Stitch It*. Lafayette, CA: C&T Publishing, 2011.

Laury, Jean Ray. *Imagery on Fabric*. Lafayette, CA: C&T Publishing, 1997.

McElroy, Darlene Olivia and Sandra Duran Wilson. *Image Transfer Workshop*. Cincinnati, OH: North Light Books, 2000.

Rymer, Cyndy Lyle with Lynn Koolish. *Innovative Fabric Imagery for Quilts*. Lafayette, CA: C&T Publishing, 2007.

Stein, Susan. *The Complete Photo Guide to Textile Art*. Minneapolis, MN: Creative Publishing International, 2010.

Tuttle, Susan. *Digital Expressions: Creating Digital Art wtih Adobe Photoshop Elements*.Cincinnati, OH: North Light Books, 2010.

Ziebarth, Charlotte. *Artistic Photo Quilts*. Lafayette, CA: C&T Publishing, 2009.

LANDSCAPES

Becker, Joyce R. *Quick Little Landscape Quilts*. Lafayette, CA: C&T Publishing, 2011.

Berlyn, Ineke. *Landscape in Contemporary Quilts*. London, UK: B T Batsford, 2006.

Endo, Noriko. *Confetti Naturescapes: Quilting Impressionist Landscapes*. Worthington, OH: Dragon Threads, 2010.

Holt, Alison. *Machine Embroidered Seascapes*. Kent, UK: Search Press, 2012.

Loughman, Gloria. *Radiant Landscapes*. Lafayette, CA: C&T Publishing, 2013.

Loughman, Gloria. *Luminous Landscapes*. Lafayette, CA: C&T Publishing, 2007.

Malaney, Jeanine Rvard. *Painting with Fabric: Creating Art with Fabric Collage and Landscape Quilting*. CreateSpace Independent Publishing Platform, 2012.

Matthews, Kathleen. *Stitched Textiles: Landscapes*. Kent, UK: Search Press, 2013.

MARBLING

Chambers, Anne. *Marbling on Fabric*. Kent, UK: Search Press, 1995.

Schmidt-Troschke, Ursula. *Stoff Marmorier Kunst*. Stuttgart, Germany: Frech-Verlag, 1989.

METAL

Benn, Claire, Jane Dunnewold and Leslie Morgan. *Paper & Metal Leaf Lamination*. Betchworth, Surrey, UK: Committed to Cloth & Art Cloth Studios, 2008.

Fingal, Jamie. *Rebel Quilting: Thinking Outside the Block* (DVD). Loveland, CO: Quilting Arts/Interweave, 2010.

Midgelow-Marsden, Alysn. *Stitch, Fibres, Metal & Mixed Media*. Tunbridge Wells, UK: Search Press, 2014.

Midgelow-Marsden, Alysn and Viv Arthur. *This Lustr'ed Cloth: a Fibre Artists' Workbook of Metals*. Nottingham, UK: Artfully Bound, 2007.

MODERN QUILTS

Gering, Jacquie and Katie Pedersen. *Quilting Modern*. Loveland, CO: Interweave Press, 2012.

Martingale & Company. *Modern Quilts from the Blogging Universe*. Seattle, WA: Martingale & Company, 2013.

NATURAL DYEING

Buchanan, Rita. *A Dyer's Garden*. Loveland, CO: Interweave Press, 1995.

Dean, Jenny. *The Craft of Natural Dyeing*. Kent, UK: Search Press, 1994.

Flint, India. *Eco Colour: Botanical Dyes for Beautiful Textiles*. Sydney, Australia: Murdoch Books, 2008.

Goodwin, Jill. *A Dyer's Manual, 2nd edition*. East Yorkshire UK: Ashmans Publications, 2003.

POJAGI

Chung, Jiyoung and Chunghie Lee (editors). *2012 Korea Bojagi Forum— From Rich Tradition to Contemporary Art*. Providence, RI: Beyond & Above, 2012.

Dong-hwa, Huh. *The Wonder Cloth: Traditional Korean Wrapping Cloths*. Seoul, Korea: The Museum of Korean Embroidery, 1988.

Lee, Chunghie. *Bojagi & Beyond*. Providence, RI: Beyond & Above, 2010.

QUILTING

Barry, Patricia C. *ABCs of Longarm Quilting*. Iola, WI: Krause Publications. 2007.

Day, Leah. *365 Free Motion Quilting Designs*. Earl, NC: Day Style Designs, 2012.

Day, Leah. *Free Motion Quilting From Feathers to Flames*. Earl, NC: Day Style Designs, 2011.

Day, Leah. *Free Motion Quilting From Daisy to Paisley*. Earl, NC: Day Style Designs, 2010.

Fritz, Laura Lee. *250 More Continuous-Line Quilting Designs for Hand, Machine and Longarm Quilts,* Lafayette, CA: C&T Publishing, 2002.

Gaudynski, Diane. *Quilt Savvy: Gaudynski's Machine Quilting Guidebook*. Paducah, KY: American Quilter's Society, 2006.

Naylor, Philippa. *Quilting in the Limelight*. Worthington, OH: Dragon Threads, 2008.

Shackelford, Anita. *A Modern Mix: Machine & Hand Quilting*. Paducah, KY: American Quilter's Society, 2007.

Taylor, Linda V. *The Ultimate Guide to Longarm Machine Quilting*. Lafayette, CA: C&T Publishing. 2002.

Thelen, Carol A. *Long-Arm Machine Quilting*. Seattle, WA: Martingale, That Patchwork Place, 2002.

Walters, Angela. *Free-Motion Quilting with Angela Walters*. Lafayette, CA: Stash Books, 2012.

Woodworth, Judy. *Freemotion Quilting*. Paducah, KY: American Quilter's Society, 2010.

QUILTS IN THE COMMUNITY

Holmes, Cas. *Connected Cloth: Creating Collaborative Textile Projects*. London, UK: B T Batsford, 2013.

Line, Joanne Larsen and Nancy Loving Tubesing. *Quilts from the Quiltmaker's Gift*. New York, NY: Scholastic, 2000.

Morris III, Charles E. *Remembering the AIDS Quilt*. East Lansing, MI: Michigan State University Press, 2011.

RESISTS & SHIBORI

Kerpoe, Lisa. *Visual Texture on Fabric: Create Stunning Art Cloth with Water-Based Resists*. Lafayette, CA: C&T Publishing, 2012.

Gunner, Janice. *Shibori for Textile Artists*. London, UK: B T Batsford, 2006.

Wada, Yoshiko Iwamoto, Mary Kellogg Rice and Jane Barton. *Shibori: The Inventive Art of Japanese Shaped Resist Dyeing*. Tokyo: Kodansha International, 1983, 1999.

SURFACE DESIGN: PAINTING, PRINTING & DISCHARGE

(books that cover Discharge marked with D*)*

Benn, Claire and Leslie Morgan. *Making Your Mark*. Betchworth, Surrey, UK: Committed to Cloth, 2011. D

Benn, Claire and Leslie Morgan. *Thermofax Printing*. Betchworth, Surrey, UK: Committed to Cloth, 2010. D

Benn, Claire and Leslie Morgan. *Screen Printing*. Betchworth, Surrey, UK: Committed to Cloth, 2009. D

Benn, Claire and Leslie Morgan. *Breakdown Printing*. Betchworth, Surrey, UK: Committed to Cloth, 2005. D

Berlyn, Ineke. *Journal Quilts, Dye and Print*. Bromsgrove, UK: Ineke Berlyn, 2011.

Blair, Pat. *Painted Quilt Art Step By Step* (DVD). Fort Collins, CO: Jukebox Quilts, 2005.

Brackmann, Holly. *The Surface Designer's Handbook: Dyeing, Printing, Painting and Creating Resists on Fabric*. Loveland, CO: Interweave Press, 2006. D

Britnell, Bobby. *Stitched Textiles: Flowers*. Kent, UK: Search Press, 2013.

Corwin, Lena. *Printing by Hand*. New York, NY: STC Craft, 2008.

Dunnewold, Jane. *Art Cloth: A Guide to Surface Design for Fabric*. Loveland, CO: Interweave Press, 2010. D

Edmonds, Janet. *From Print to Stitch*. Kent, UK: Search Press, 2010.

Gillman, Rayna. *Create your own Hand-printed Cloth*. Lafayette, CA: C&T Publishing, 2008. D

Green, Jean Drysdale. *Arteffects*. New York, NY: Watson Guptill Publications, 1993.

Hedley, Gwen. *Drawn to Stitch*. London, UK: B T Batsford, 2010.

Issett, Ruth. *Colour on Cloth*. London, UK: B T Batsford, 2004. D

Issett, Ruth. *Print, Pattern & Colour*. London, UK: B T Batsford, 2007.

Johnson, Vicki L. *Paint and Patches: Painting on Fabrics with Pigment*. Paducah, KY: American Quilter's Society, 1995.

Kahn, Sherrill. *Mixed-Media Master Class*. Lafayette, CA: C&T Publishing, 2013.

Kemshall, Linda & Laura Kemshall. *The Painted Quilt*. Cincinnati, OH: David & Charles. 2007. D

Laury, Jean Ray. *Imagery on Fabric*. Lafayette, CA: C&T Publishing, 1997. D

McElroy, Darlene Olivia and Sandra Duran Wilson. *Surface Design Workshop*. Cincinnatti, OH: North Light Books, 2011.

Meech, Sandra. *Design, Surface & Stitch*. London, UK: B T Batsford, 2003.

Mundwiler, Judith and Gabi Mett. *Siebdruck auf Stoff mit Recyclingmaterial, Schaum und Farb* (screenprinting). Sissach, CH: Atelier M+M, 2013. (www.atelier-mm.ch)

Stokes, Shelly. *Paintstiks on Fabric*. Alexandria, MN: Cedar Canyon Textiles, 2005.

Wells, Kate. *Fabric Dyeing & Printing*. London, UK: Conran Octopus, 2000. D

Wisbrun, Laurie. *Mastering the Art of Fabric Printing and Design*. San Francisco, CA: Chronicle Books, 2011.

Wisbrun, Laurie. *Embellish Me: How to Print, Dye, and Decorate Your Fabric*. Loveland, CO: Interweave Press, 2012. D

TEXTURE

Davis, Jodie. *Three-Dimensional Pieced Quilts*. Iola, WI: Krause Publications, 1995.

Kim, Rami. *Folded Fabric Elegance*. Paducah, KY: American Quilter's Society, 2007.

Rayment, Jenny. *Creative Tucks and Textures*. Hampshire, UK: J. R. Publications, 2004.

Reid, Alison. *Stitch Magic*. New York, NY: Stewart, Tabori and Chang, 2011.

Singer, Ruth. *Fabric Manipulation*. London, UK: David & Charles, 2013.

Wolff, Colette. *The Art of Manipulating Fabric*. Iola, WI: Krause Publications, 1996.

THREAD PAINTING

Bates, Debbie & Liz Kettle. *Threads: The Basics & Beyond*. Urbandale, IA: Landauer Publishing, 2010.

Blair, Pat. *Simple Thread Painting* (DVD) . Fort Collins, CO: Jukebox Quilts, 2006.

Knapp, Susan Brubaker. *Thread Sketching 101* (ebook). Lafayette, CA: C&T Publishing, 2013.

Smith, Sarah Ann. *Threadwork Unraveled*. Paducah, KY: American Quilters' Society, 2009.

Weiner, Leni Levenson. *Thread Painting*. Iola, WI: Krause Publications. 2007.

UPCYCLING

Holmes, Cas. *The Found Object in Textile Art*. London, UK: B T Batsford, 2010.

Holmes, Val. *Creative Recycling in Embroidery*. London, UK: B T Batsford, 2010.

McDonough, William and Michael Braungart. *Cradle to Cradle: Remaking the Way We Make Things*. New York, NY: North Point Press, 2002.

Morgan, Annette. *Creative Fabric Techniques for Quilters, Embroiderers and Textile Artists* (CD). Thetford, UK: Rainbow Disks, 2010.

Williamson, Jean. *The Uncommon Quilter: Small Art Quilts Created with Paper, Plastic, Fiber, and Surface Design*. New York, NY: Potter Craft, 2007.

WET FELTING & NEEDLE FELTING

Hunter, Andrea. *Creating Felt Pictures*. Marlborough, Wiltshire, UK: The Crowood Press, 2012.

Lane, Ruth. *The Complete Photo Guide to Felting*. Minneapolis, MN: Creative Publishing International, 2012.

Mackay, Moy. *Art in Felt and Stitch: Creating Beautiful Works of Art Using Fleece, Fibres and Threads*. Kent, UK: Search Press, 2012.

Smith, Sheila. *Felt Fabric Designs*. London, UK: B T Batsford, 2013.

Smith, Sheila. *Embellish, Stitch, Felt Using the Embellisher Machine and Needle-Punch Techniques*. London, UK: B T Batsford, 2008.

Smith, Sheila. *Felt to Stitch: Creative Felting for Textile Artists*. London, UK: B T Batsford, 2006.

3D QUILT ART

Barnes, C June. *Exploring Dimension in Quilt Art*. London, UK: B T Batsford, 2012.

Barnes, C June. *Stitching to Dye in Quilt Art: Colour, Texture and Distortion*. London, UK: B T Batsford, 2008.

Berlyn, Ineke. *The Quilted Object*. London, UK: Anova Books, 2009.

Deighan, Helen. *Textile Coil Pots and Baskets: Easy Ways with Fabric and Cord*. Hindhead, Surrey, UK: Crossways Patch, 2004.

Draper, Jean. *Stitch and Structure: Design and Technique in Two- And Three-Dimensional Textiles*. London, UK: B T Batsford. 2013.

Edmonds, Janet. *Three-dimensional Embroidery*. London, UK: B T Batsford, 2005.

Lee, Ruth. *Three-Dimensional Textiles with Coils, Loops, Knots and Nets*. London: B T Batsford, 2010.

Sider, Sandra. *The Studio Quilt, No. 8: Quilted Sculpture*. CreateSpace Independent Publishing Platform, 2012.

QUILT ARTISTS

I am so grateful to the following artists, listed in alphabetical order, who have contributed to this book. Please contact them if you wish to commission an art quilt. Numbers in parenthesis following each name indicate pages where the artist's work can be found; credits for chapter opener details are on page 255. Please note that all photographs of quilts in this book were taken by the artist unless a photographer is credited in the caption.

BJ Adams (6, 11)
bjfiber@aol.com
www.bjadamsart.com

Natalya Aikens (161)
natalya@artbynatalya.com
www.artbynatalya.com

Margaret Applin (43, 73)
www.margaretapplin.com
margaretapplinartdesign.com/
  margaretapplindesigns/

Penny Armitage (92)
penny_armitage@hotmail.com

Maria Lúcia Ázara (82)
www.quiltarte.com.br

David Paul Bacharach (18)
mail@bacharachmetals.com
www.bacharachmetals.com

Khurshid Bamboat (6)
khurshid@bamboat.co.uk

C June Barnes (203, 211)
june@cjunebarnes.co.uk
www.cjunebarnes.co.uk

Pauline Barnes (226, 238, 244)
paulinebarnesquilts@yahoo.co.uk
www.paulinebarnesquilts.co.uk

Linda Beach (110, 114)
linda@lindabeachartquilts.com
www.lindabeachartquilts.com

Marie Bergstedt (207)
www.mariebergstedtartist.com

Ineke Berlyn (20, 25)
ine@inekeberlyn.com
www.inekeberlyn.com

Hannah Blackbourne (221)
info@bernina.co.uk
www.bernina.co.uk

Patt Blair (45, 166)
patt@pattsart.com
www.pattsart.com
www.pattsart.blogspot.com

Eszter Bornemisza (14, 20)
eszter@bornemisza.com
www.bornemisza.com

Jenny Bowker (140, 145)
jenny.bowker@gmail.com
www.jennybowker.com

Hildegard Braatz (40, 89)
h.braatz@quiltware.de

Ann Brauer (110, 118)
ann@annbrauer.com
www.annbrauer.com

Laura Breitman (160)
breitman@optonline.net
www.laurabreitman.com

Elizabeth Brimelow (204, 213)
ebrimelow@hotmail.com
www.quiltart.eu

Jane Brunning (81)
jm.brunning@tiscali.co.uk

Jo Budd (40, 90, 91)
jo.budd1@virgin.net
www.jobudd.com

Lucinda Carlstrom (19)
lucindacarlstrom@yahoo.com
lucindacarlstrom.com

Cher Cartwright (119)
www.chercartwright.com

Leonie Castelino (110, 139)
leoniecastelino@gmail.com
www.leoniecastelino.com

Dijanne Cevaal (207)
dcevaal@gmail.com
www.origidij.blogspot.com

Kyoung Ae Cho (110, 117)
www.kyoungaecho.com

Jane Burch Cochran (204, 208, 217)
www.janeburchcochran.com
www.artofthequilt.com

Marlene Cohen (69, 140, 159)
mrlncohen@gmail.com
www.mcquiltart.co.uk

Gillian Cooper (229)
info@gilliancooper.co.uk
www.gilliancooper.co.uk

Margaret Cooter (226, 246)
www.margaretcooter.co.uk

Cathy Corbishley Michel (95)
www.quiltersguild.org.uk/members/
  page/catherine-corbishley

Kate Crossley (85, 228)
www.katecrossley.com

Ros Crouch (6)
roscro@me.com

Bailey Curtis (226)
www.baileycurtis.com

Fenella Davies (206)
fenelladavies@btinternet.com
www.fenelladavies.com

Leah Day (183)
support@daystyledesigns.com
www.leahday.com
www.freemotionproject.com

Angela Daymond (45)
angela@fenlandtextilestudio.co.uk
www.fenlandtextilestudio.co.uk

Tilly de Harde (101, 230)
tilly@psti.co.za

Alma de la Melena Cox (6, 11)
almaartcompany@aol.com
www.almaart.com

Katalin Ehling (40, 82)
www.katalinehling.com
www.katalinehlingbatiks.blogspot.com

Susan Else (212)
www.susanelse.com

Kate Findlay (8, 114, 244)
kate@findlays.net
art.findlays.net

Jamie Fingal (219, 243)
jamie.fingal@gmail.com
www.jamiefingaldesigns.com
jamiefingaldesigns.blogspot.com

Dianne Firth (140, 146)
dianne.firth@canberra.edu.au
www.craftact.org.au
www.tactilequilts.net

Cheryl FitzGerald (147, 242)
cherylf@swcp.com
cherylfquilts.com

Carol L Fletcher (140, 170)
fletchcl@icloud.com
fireandfiberart.com

Laura Fogg (140, 161)
fogg.laura@gmail.com
www.fogwomancreations.com

Sheila Frampton-Cooper (52)
www.zoombaby.com

Cynthia D Friedman (6, 15)
cindy@cindyfriedman.com
www.cindyfriedman.com

Jayne Bentley Gaskins (20, 232)
jaynegaskins@comcast.net
www.jaynegaskins.com

Lynne Gefre (58)
lynnegefre@msn.com

Jane Glennie (20, 24, 32, 140, 204, 244)
jane@janeglennie.co.uk
www.janeglennie.co.uk

Hilary Gooding (40, 53)
www.hilarygooding.weebly.com

Janice Gunner (32, 58, 166)
janice@janicegunner.co.uk
www.janicegunner.co.uk

Judith Hammersla (140)
judysewforth@hammersla.net

Gloria Hansen (99)
gloria@gloderworks.com
www.gloriahansen.com
www.gloriahansen.com/weblog

Colleen Harris (210)
ccharris@yebo.co.za

Merete Hawkins (40)
hwkns_merete@yahoo.co.uk

Jenny Hearn (211)
kabewhy@iafrica.com

Gudrun Heinz (17)
info@quiltsundmehr.de
www.quiltsundmehr.de
www.berninablog.com

Anna Hergert (172, 204)
anna@annahergert.com
www.annahergert.com
annahergert.wordpress.com

Pam Holland (13)
pamholland3@mac.com
www.pamhollanddesigns
  andproductions.com

Cas Holmes (20, 83, 242)
casholmestextiles.co.uk

Susan Hotchkis (226, 230, 239)
susanhotchkis@yahoo.co.uk
www.suehotchkis.com

Lin Hsin-Chen (147, 243)
jenny.quilt@msa.hinet.net
www.linhsinchen.idv.tw

Inge Hueber (110, 137)
inge.hueber@netcologne.de
www.ingehueber.de

Sara Impey (166, 169)
sara.impey@gmail.com
www.quiltart.eu

Terry Jarrard-Dimond (23)
tjarrard-dimond@att.net

Anne Jolly (20, 32)
anne.jolly@xtra.co.nz

Marianne Jørgensen (16)
joergensen.marianne@gmail.com
www.marianneart.dk

Yoshiko Katagiri (140, 142)
quiltyoshiko@yahoo.co.jp

Laura Kemshall (77, 171, 202)
laurakemshall@gmail.com
www.fingerprintfabric.com
www.laurakemshall.blogspot.com

Linda Kemshall (40, 42, 166)
linda@lindakemshall.com
www.lindakemshall.com
www.lindakemshall.blogspot.co.uk

Lisa Kijak (140, 143)
lisakijak@yahoo.com
www.lisakijak.com
lisakijak.blogspot.com

Becky Knight (110, 116, 243)
www.beckyknight.co.uk

Phillippa K. Lack (204, 213)
www.pkldesigns.com

Aryana B. Londir (59)
aryana@aryanalondir.com
www.aryanalondir.com

Kathy Loomis (115)
artwithaneedle@gmail.com
www.kathleenloomis.com

Gwen Lowery (223)
gwen@gwenlowery.com
www.gwenlowery.com

Irene MacWilliam (140, 233)
irenemacwilliam@hotmail.com
www.macwilliam.f9.co.uk

Angela Maves (226, 238)
www.angelamaves.ca

Fay Maxwell (6, 40)
fay@fayandkay.co.uk

Erilyn McMillan (151)
create.stitch.quilt@gmail.com

Sandra Meech (98)
sandrameech@gmail.com
www.sandrameech.com
www.sandrameech-art.blogspot.com

Alicia Merrett (98, 110, 133)
alicia@aliciamerrett.co.uk
www.aliciamerrett.co.uk

Alysn Midgelow-Marsden (6, 19, 20)
alysnmm@gmail.com
alysnsburntofferings@blogspot.com

Beth Miller (146)
bethmiller1505@gmail.com
www.bethmillerquilts.com

Kim Misik (110, 115)
kmisik@naver.com
blog.naver.com/kmisik

Dean and Linda Moran (89)
deanm@marbledfab.com
www.marbledfab.com

Annette Morgan (6, 83, 200)
annette@annettemorgan.co.uk
www.annettemorgan.co.uk

Leslie Morgan (40, 73)
lm@committedtocloth.com
committedtocloth.com

Brigitte Morgenroth (233)
abmorgenroth@t-online.de
www.morgenroth-quilts.de

Patti Morris (144)
www.morrisfabricartdesigns.com

Aina Muze (204, 231)
ainamuze@inbox.lv
www.ainamuze.lv

Philippa Naylor (166, 173, 179)
www.philippanaylor.com

Roxanne Nelson (20, 22)
stargazer_designs@shaw.ca

Sheena Norquay (199)
sites.google.com/site/sheenajnorquay

Jenny O'Neill (226)
jenny16o@yahoo.co.uk

Wil Opio Oguta (93)
wilopiooguta@hotmail.com
www.wilopiooguta.com

Arunas Oslapas (6, 18)
arunas.oslapas@wwu.edu

Mary B Pal (12, 140)
marybpal@gmail.com
www.marypaldesigns.com

Katrina Parris (226, 232, 239)
www.katrinaparris.com

Tracey Pereira (195)
www.quiltmehappy.co.uk
www.quiltmehappy.co.uk/tutorials.html

Tom Phillips (117)
www.tomphillips.co.uk

Annabel Rainbow (166, 170)
www.annabelrainbow.co.uk

Margaret Ramsay (166, 201, 203)
www.magsramsay.co.uk
magsramsay.blogspot.com/

Lisa White Reber (76, 77, 92)
lisa@dippydyes.com
www.dippydyes.com

Chloe Redfern (226)
www.slightlytriangle.co.uk

Martine Rendle (6)
tibushker@hotmail.com

Christine Restall (40, 71, 72, 110, 113)
restallc@btinternet.com
www.christinerestall.co.uk

Latifah Saafir (16, 166)
latifah@thequiltengineer.com
thequiltengineer.com

Rute Sato (104)
rutesato@gmail.com
rutesato.blogspot.com.br

Ursula Schmidt-Troschke (87)
chaosprint@arcor.de

Kim Schoenberger (14, 226)
info@kimschoenberger.com
www.kimschoenberger.com

Deborah Schwartzman (166, 168)
deb.schwartzman@gmail.com
www.debschwartzman.com

Marina Shkolnik (20, 29)
shkolnik.mari@gmail.com
www.feltedpleasure.com

Fraser Smith (12)
fraser@gofraser.com
www.gofraser.com

Sandy Snowden (204, 226, 239)
snsnowden@harmonyinformation.com
sandysnowden.blogspot.co.uk

Kati Spencer (166, 173)
fromthebluechair@gmail.com
www.fromthebluechair.com

Janet Steadman (110, 112)
jandon@whidbey.com
www2.whidbey.net/jandon

Kate Stiassni (53)
katestiassni.com

Averil Stuart-Head (20, 33)
avehead@gmail.com
www.averilstuarthead.com

Karina Thompson (107, 242)
karina@karinathompson.co.uk
www.karinathompson.co.uk
www.karinathompsontextiles.
  blogspot.com

Odette Tolksdorf (6, 10)
odettet@iafrica.com
www.odettetolksdorf.co.za

Ben Venom (17)
ben@benvenom.com
www.benvenom.com
benvenom.blogspot.com

Dwayne F Wanner (210)
dwanner@sympatico.ca
www.dfwannerquilts.com

Kitty M Watt (88)
kittyandalan@waitrose.com

Carol Ann Waugh (109)
www.carolannwaugh.com

Barbara Weeks (152)
www.barbaraweeks.com

Pia Welsch (166, 201, 203)
hello.pia@gmx.de
www.pias-quilt-werkstatt.de

Carol Wiebe (13)
www.carolwiebe.com

Jayne Willoughby (40, 44)
jaynew100@gmail.com

Vivian Wilm Pinto (172)
vivian.wp@globo.com

Martha Wolfe (6, 233)
mwfiberart@me.com
www.marthawolfe.com

Alice Wood (117)
www.alicewood.co.uk

Anne Woringer (44)
anne.woringer@wanadoo.fr
anneworinger.com

Sally Gould Wright (179)
www.sallywrightquilts.com
www.sallygouldwright.blogspot.com

Sandra Wyman (40, 48, 49, 51)
djangorodney@aol.com

Charlotte Yde (9)
charlotte@yde.dk
www.yde.dk
www.ydesign.dk

AUTHOR'S DETAILS

Linda Seward (5, 170, 231, 256)
www.lindaseward.com

DETAILS FOR CHAPTER OPENERS:

Chapter 1 (page 6)—
1st row: Martine Rendle, Cindy Friedman, Alma de la Melina Cox.
2nd row: Odette Tolksdorf, Ros Crouch, Alysn Midgelow-Marsden.
3rd row: Fay Maxwell, Arunas Oslapas, Martha Wolfe.
4th row: Annette Morgan, Khurshid Bamboat, B J Adams.

Chapter 2 (page 20)—
1st row: Jane Glennie, Ineke Berlyn, Roxanne Nelson.
2nd row: Alysn Midgelow-Marsden, Cas Holmes, Linda Seward.
3rd row: Linda Seward, Jayne Gaskins, Averil Stuart-Head.
4th row: Anne Jolly, Marina Shkolnik, Eszter Bornemisza.

Chapter 3 (page 40)—
1st row: Hilary Gooding, Linda Seward, Jo Budd.
2nd row: Merete Hawkins, Jayne Willoughby, Christine Restall.
3rd row: Linda Kemshall, Leslie Morgan, Katalin Ehling.
4th row: Hildegard Braatz, Sandra Wyman, Fay Maxwell.

Chapter 4 (page 110)—
1st row: Leonie Castellino, Linda Beach, Linda Seward.
2nd row: Ann Brauer, Alicia Merrett, Inge Hueber.
3rd row: Linda Seward, Becky Knight, Kim Misik.
4th row: Kyoung Ae Cho, Janet Steadman, Christine Restall.

Chapter 5 (page 140)—
1st row: Carol Fletcher, Laura Fogg, Yoshiko Katagiri.
2nd row: Marlene Cohen, Judith Hammersla, Jane Glennie.
3rd row: Lisa Kijak, Irene MacWilliam, Mary Pal.
4th row: Dianne Firth, Jenny Bowker, Jane Glennie.

Chapter 6 (page 166)—
1st row: Linda Seward, Deborah Schwartzman, Janice Gunner.
2nd row: Philippa Naylor, Sara Impey, Kati Spencer.
3rd row: Linda Kemshall, Latifah Saafir, Pia Welsch.
4th row: Annabel Rainbow, Margaret Ramsay, Patt Blair.

Chapter 7 (page 204)—
1st row: Linda Seward x3.
2nd row: Elizabeth Brimelow, Jane Glennie, Jane Burch Cochran.
3rd row: Aina Muze, Linda Seward, Sandy Snowden.
4th row: Linda Seward, Phillippa K Lack, Anna Hergert.

Chapter 8 (page 226)—
1st row: Sandy Snowden, Susan Hotchkis, Jenny O'Neill.
2nd row: Bailey Curtis, Chloe Redfern, Linda Seward.
3rd row: Katrina Parris, Margaret Cooter, Linda Seward.
4th row: Kim Schoenberger, Angela Maves, Pauline Barnes.

ACKNOWLEDGEMENTS

This book has been work of many hands, and I would like to thank everyone who has been involved since its inception.

The first person I must mention is Charles Nurnberg, who believed in me and this book. Charlie, there were times when thanking you wasn't on my mind, but now that it's done I'll admit that I'm glad you talked me into it.

At Sixth&Spring, Trisha Malcolm has been an enthusiastic proponent of this book from the beginning. Joy Aquilino provided excellent suggestions and has been very supportive. Beth Baumgartel did a great job editing the book, and Lisa Silverman pulled it all together. I am grateful to you all.

This book wouldn't be what it is without the work of two very important people: the illustrator, Tom Messenger, and the book designer, Jane Glennie. This project was much more complex than any of us imagined when we started, and I can't thank Tom and Jane enough for helping me to create exactly the book that I envisaged, and with such care and finesse.

The patience and good humor displayed by Tom was utterly commendable, particularly after my umpteenth correction, which then needed changing just one more time. His illustrations brought my photographs and stick-figure drawings to life, and I'm sure will be greatly appreciated by the readers of this book.

Jane created a layout that is easy to follow and lovely to peruse, and her attention to detail was unsurpassed. She was also very patient with all the changes that had to be made, and was of huge help in compiling the Upcycling, Wet Felting and School & Community Projects sections.

A big thank you goes to Margaret Cooter for giving the book a critical examination before the handover to the publishers, and for her editorial advice.

Lynne Gefre gets a special mention for reading and editing the chapter introductions, for her invaluable suggestions and common sense, and for her uncanny ability to keep me calm and make me laugh.

Much appreciation goes to all the quilt artists who have provided photos of their work, and who have been so amenable and supportive to me. One of the great joys of writing this book has been getting to know these generous and inspirational quilters from all over the world. See pages 254–255 for the contact details of these talented individuals. If you like their work, get in touch and commission your own piece of quilt art.

I'd like to convey my gratitude to the quilters who instructed me in their particular areas of expertise, and then checked my text and illustrations to see if they had taught me properly: Marlene Cohen, Kate Crossley, Jane Glennie, Janice Gunner, Philippa Naylor, Tracey Pereira, and Christine Restall. Thanks also to Paula Burch, Laura Murray, Sylvie Brabant from Fiskars, Beryl Emberson-Nash from Bo-Nash, Nancy Rodrigues from Pro Chemical & Dye, Roberta Ruschmann from Meadowbrook Inventions, Stuart Smethurst from Kemtex, Hannah Blackbourne and Rebecca Lutchman from Bernina, and Mark D Hyland and Brenda Groelz from Handi Quilter for their help and advice (contact details on page 245).

Special thanks to Tracey Pereira, who taught me how to longarm quilt, and who tested and perfected all the quilting patterns in this book. I am so appreciative of the time and effort she put into teaching me this wonderful skill and making the designs just right for quilters.

I am indebted to the textile artists and art quilters who generously gave up their time to provide advice, read the text, and/or check the finished spreads. I hugely appreciate their input and guidance. Thank you to: C June Barnes, Pauline Barnes, Ineke Berlyn, Jenny Bowker, Hildegarde Braatz, Jane Brunning, Jo Budd, Leonie Castelino, Cathy Corbishley Michel, Kate Crossley, Angela Daymond, Katalin Ehling, Jamie Fingal, Janice Gunner, Gloria Hansen, Inge Hueber, Laura Kemshall, Lisa Kijak, Erilyn McMillan, Sandra Meech, Alicia Merrett, Annette Morgan, Leslie Morgan, Philippa Naylor, Sheena Norquay, Margaret Ramsay, Lisa Reber, Christine Restall, Karina Thompson, Ursula Schmidt-Troschke, Kitty Watt, Carol Ann Waugh, Barbara Weeks, Pia Welsch, Carol Wiebe, and Brenda Wroe. Special thanks to Sandra Wyman, who went above and beyond…

Members of the Contemporary Quilt discussion group have answered queries, given advice, and provided much needed support throughout the writing of this book. Contemporary Quilt is a specialist group of The Quilters' Guild of the British Isles.

Thanks to Galerie Ton Schulten for giving me permission to feature a quilt based on a painting by Ton Schulten (see page 209); details for contacting the gallery are on page 245. Thank you to Judith Fraser who permitted me to feature a quilt based on a painting by her late husband Donald Hamilton Fraser (see page 217).

Profuse thanks to Michael Fitzgerald, who kept me going in body (and often, mind) during our weekly workouts, and who helped immeasurably to keep my life in perspective.

I would like to commemorate two quilting friends who started this book's journey with me, but didn't live to see it come to fruition: Monica Millner and Em Dahlgren. I know they would have been so proud to hold this book in their hands.

I am grateful to my children, Alysson, Emily, and Keith, and to my family, in particular my parents, Robert and Evelyn Macho, and my sister Danae Maxwell, for putting up with me and the stresses and strains of writing this book. They often asked me, "Why did you ever take this on?" I honestly didn't know what to say, so blamed it on Charlie (see second paragraph). They are so glad I'm done.

But the biggest credit must go to my husband Robert, who has been there for me from day one. He started out as my contract lawyer, then became my photographer—he became quite adept at taking photos of my hands from just the right angle for Tom's art references. He also assumed the role of health advisor, ensuring that I took breaks to walk our dog, Jack, every day. Finally, he surprised me with his excellent editorial advice. Thank you for everything, Robert—I could never have done this without your love and support.